Perma-bound 1969

The African Assertion

THE
AFRICAN
ASSERTION

A Critical Anthology of
African Literature

EDITED BY
AUSTIN J. SHELTON
State University College
New Paltz, N.Y.

The Odyssey Press : New York

ACKNOWLEDGMENTS

I wish to express my gratitude to the persons and publishers listed below for their kind permission to use the works mentioned:

Mr. Chinua Achebe for his story "The Sacrificial Egg."

Dr. Agostinho Neto for his poem "Aspiration."

M. Flavien Ranaivo for his poem "Chanson de jeune femme."

Mr. Colin Legum for Ali Abdullah Gureh's poem "To Arms!"

Mr. Emile Ologoudou for his poem "La Flambée."

Mr. Richard Rive for his story "The Bench."

Dr. R. Pankhurst of Haile Selassie I University, for Tsegaye Gabre Medhen's poems "Ours," "Bad Days," and "Home-Coming Son."

The Western Nigeria Ministry of Education for "Oriki for Lagunju" from *A Short History of Édé* by Chief Olunlade.

The editors of *Afrique* for Abdoul Kéré's poem "Pays natal" and Tshakatumba's poems "Message" and "Prière sans écho."

The editors of *Poésie Vivante* (11 rue Hoffmann, Geneva, Switzerland) for Assoi Adiko's poem "Le danseur" and Bernard Dadié's poems "Hommes de tous les continents" and "Aux poètes."

The editors of *Africa Report* and Jean Contini for Scek Gabiou's poem "Prophecy."

The editors of *Black Orpheus* and Longmans of Nigeria for L. Peters' poems "Parachute," from p. 20 of *Black Orpheus* No. 14 (1964), and "Homecoming," from p. 64 of *Black Orpheus* No. 11 (1962); for G. Okara's poem "Piano and Drums," from p. 33 of *Black Orpheus* No. 6 (1959).

The editors of *Transition* for Mbelle Dipoko's poem "To Pre-colonial Africa."

African Universities Press, Ltd., Lagos, for Mabel Segun's poem "Conflict," from *Reflections* by Frances Ademola.

The Clarendon Press, Oxford, for extracts from *Swahili Poetry* by L. Harries; for Faarah Nuur's poems "The Limits of Submission" and "On the Partitioning of Somalia" and Mahamad Hasan's poem "The Death of Richard Corfield," from *Somali Poetry* by B. Andrzejewski and I. Lewis.

The editors of *Ibadan* for Imoukhuede's poem "One Wife for One Man."

Editions Pierre Jean Oswald, for the following: Tchicaya U Tam'Si, "Au sommaire d'une passion," Epitomé, collection "L'aube dissout les monstres," Editions Pierre Jean Oswald, 1962.

The Ghana Broadcasting Corporation for Efua Sutherland's story "New Life at Kyerefaso" and Frank Parkes' poem "Africa Heaven."

Heinemann Educational Books, Ltd., for D. Rubadiri's poem "Stanley Meets Mutesa"; for T. Chacha's story "Road to Mara" from D. Cook's *Origin East Africa;* and for J. Ngugi's story "The Martyr" from *Modern African Prose* by R. Rive.

Présence Africaine for the following: D. Diop's poems "Afrique" and "A une danseuse noire"; B. Dadié's story "Le pagne noir"; S. Ousmane's poem "Nostalgie"; Yambo's poem "1901."

Presses Universitaires de France for D. Diop's poem "Défi à la force"; "Nuit de Sinê" by L. S. Senghor; and J. J. Rabéarivelo's poems "Flûtistes" and No. 3 "Traduit" from *Traduit de la nuit.*

The editor has made every possible effort to trace all persons having rights in material used in this anthology and to obtain permission from them to reprint the materials. The unsettled conditions in Africa today, and the great mobility of many educated Africans, create difficulties for the earnest researcher. No copyright or other right to the materials of this anthology has been intentionally violated, and the editor asks indulgence if any right may inadvertently have been infringed.

CONTENTS

INTRODUCTION   1

African Literature: Preliminaries

Africa: Yesterday and Today   3

     The "Old" Life   4
     Change   7
     Slavery   8
     Colonialism   11
     Missionary Activity   12
     The Middle Passage   14
     The Nationalist Reaction   17

ONE   **TRADITIONS**   19

[*Swahili*]   Utendi wa Liyongo Fumo / The Epic of
     Liyongo, the Spear-Lord   22
[*Yoruba*]   Oriki (Praise Names) for Lagunju of Ede   36
BERNARD DADIÉ   *The Black Loincloth*   40
CHINUA ACHEBE   *The Sacrificial Egg*   44
     CRITICAL EXERCISE I   50

T W O   **IMAGES OF AFRICA**   53

ABIOSEH NICOL   The Continent That Lies Within Us   55
ABDOUL KADER KÉRÉ   Pays Natal / Native Land   60
JEAN-JOSEPH RABÉARIVELO   Flûtistes / Flute Players   62
                          Traduit No. 3 / Translation
                             No. 3: Sacrifice and Rebirth   66
LÉOPOLD SÉDAR SENGHOR   Nuit de Sinê / Night of Sinê   68
                        Le Totem / The Totem   72
BERNARD DADIÉ   Hommes de tous les continents / Men of
   All Continents   74
DAVID DIOP   Afrique, à ma Mère / Africa (To My Mother)   76
             A une danseuse noire / To a Black Dancer   78
ASSOI ADIKO   Le danseur / The Dancer   82
J. P. CLARK   Night Rain   84
              Girl Bathing   87
TSHAKATUMBA   Message à Mputu Antoinette, fille de la
   brousse, amie de mon enfance / Message to Mputu
   Antoinette, Girl of the Bush, Friend of My Childhood   88
TSEGAYE GABRE MEDHEN   Ours   90
                       Bad Days   94
FLAVIEN RANAIVO   Chanson de jeune femme / Song of a
   Young Woman   96
MABEL DOVE-DANQUAH   *Anticipation*   100

T H R E E   **MIDDLE PASSAGE**   105

DAVID RUBADIRI   Stanley Meets Mutesa   107
        C R I T I C A L   E X E R C I S E   I I   111
MBELLE SONNE DIPOKO   To Pre-Colonial Africa   113
LENRIE PETERS   Parachute   113
                Homecoming   115
ÉMILE OLOGOUDOU   La flambée / The Blaze   116
KWESI BREW   A Plea for Mercy   118

Contents ix

GABRIEL OKARA   Piano and Drums   *119*
CHRISTOPHER OKIGBO   Lustra, Part IV of *Heavensgate*   *120*
EFUA SUTHERLAND   *New Life at Kyerefaso*   *123*
ABIOSEH NICOL   *The Devil at Yolahun Bridge*   *131*
              C R I T I C A L E X E R C I S E I I I   *148*
ADELAIDE CASELY-HAYFORD   *Mista Courifer*   *153*
TOM CHACHA   *Road to Mara*   *163*

F O U R   **REACTIONS**   **171**

TSHAKATUMBA   Prière sans écho / Prayer Without Echo   *174*
TCHICAYA U TAM'SI   *from* Au sommaire d'une passion / from
    Toward an Abstract of a Passion   *178*
BERNARD DADIÉ   Aux poètes / To the Poets   *180*
GEORGE AWOONOR-WILLIAMS   The Years Behind   *182*
SEMBÈNE OUSMANE   Nostalgie / Nostalgia   *184*
OUOLOGUEM YAMBO   1901 / 1901   *188*
AGOSTINHO NETO   Aspiration / Aspiration   *192*
LÉOPOLD SÉDAR SENGHOR   Prière aux masques / **Prayer to**
    the Masks   *196*
TSEGAYE GABRE MEDHEN   Home-Coming Son   *198*
FRANCIS E. K. PARKES   African Heaven   *200*
FRANK AIG-IMOUKHUEDE   One Wife for One Man   *204*
DAVID DIOP   Défi à la force / Defiance Against Force   *206*
FAARAH NUUR   The Limits of Submission   *207*
                On the Partitioning of Somalia by the
                    Europeans   *208*
SCEK AHMAD GABIOU   Prophecy   *209*
MAHAMMAD 'ABDILLE HASAN   The Death of Richard Corfield   *209*
ALI ABDULLAH GUREH   To Arms!   *211*
JAMES T. NGUGI   *The Martyr*   *213*
RICHARD RIVE   *The Bench*   *223*

READINGS, TOPICS, AND QUESTIONS FOR FURTHER STUDY   *231*

SUGGESTED READINGS   *255*

NOTES   261

INDEX OF AUTHORS   271

INDEX OF TITLES   273

The African Assertion

INTRODUCTION

African Literature: Preliminaries

The literature with which this anthology is concerned is sub-saharan African, including selected writings by Africans from Senegal to the Somali Republic and the regions south of this line. It is literature written mainly by Negro Africans of this area, including such variants of "Negro" as Cape Colored, Hova-Imerina, Mestiço, and Shirazi. Although some representative works drawn from oral traditions are included, such as *Utendi wa Liyongo Fumo*, the majority of the selections were written, and almost all of these in a vehicular rather than a vernacular language—that is, in a language which acts as a "vehicle" of communication between groups of people otherwise linguistically separated. To those who might argue that "African literature" must include, if not the writings of Europeans resident in Africa, at least the works of *maghrebin* and Arab writers, one can only reply that there is no more similarity between Negro and Semite than between Negro and European.

This is not to suggest that only race and color are the distinguishing factors in African literature (for most if not all of the "racial" distinctions between Yemeni and Nilote, Nilote and

1

Negro, Southern Arab and Nilote, Negro and "Hamite," are imagined rather than real), but that racial attitudes certainly constitute an important means for identifying a group. If people are brown-skinned but consider themselves to be "white" Sicilians or Moroccans or Arabs, and are so considered even by other brown-skinned peoples who consider themselves, in turn, to be Negroes, then attitudes are probably more important than other realities about "race" or "color."

Two criteria were used in selecting individual works for the present anthology. First, the selection should be short enough to be included in its entirety. An excerpt would never be intended by the author to represent the whole, and its literary value would therefore be limited. Second, each work, in conjunction with the other works, should contribute to a true picture of Negro Africa and the attitudes, content, and styles common to African literature and thought. It was also necessary to consider whether the collection as a whole represented the African area fairly. Indeed, in this anthology Nigeria, Rhodesia, Senegal, and South Africa are under-represented. The best and most important writers of Nigeria, Senegal, and South Africa are—with the exception of Senghor—dramatists and novelists whose works are simply too long for a classroom anthology. Rhodesia is not represented because the English settler government sponsored the development of various indigenous literatures under the aegis of the Rhodesian Literature Bureau, and the productions tend more toward cookbooks and "how-to-do-it" manuals than to artistic literature.

Drawing upon various comments made about it, one might say of African literature:

1. *The most typically African literature is vernacular, that in the tribal languages.*[1] °

2. *Nonvernacular African literature is a result of the contact between African and European.*

° These superscript numbers in the text, as well as numbers enclosed in parentheses in the explanatory notes, refer to specific book and article sources listed in the "Notes" at the end of the book. Purely explanatory notes fall at the foot of the text page and are signalled by a degree symbol [°] at the appropriate point in the text.

Our contact with whites has given birth to a neo-African culture. We can really only speak of neo-African culture to define the content arising from the contact between Western and African cultures. . . .[2]

3. *African literature arises from and mirrors the African community and the historical experiences of Africa.*

African writing is writing based on the living heritage of the African people. It reflects African history as a background to today's events and tomorrow's crises. It is a critique of present-day society and a projection into the future.[3]

4. *African literature is therefore "committed" and is seldom an expression of art for art's sake.*

African writing . . . intimately identifies itself with the people of Africa, their aspirations, failures, hopes, frustrations, their culture, history, and soul.[4]

African literature is important as a reinstatement of the dignity and pride which the black man lost through slavery in the New World and Colonialism in the Old. As more and more countries in Africa gain their political independence there will be a greater desire to re-establish African culture in the modern world.[5]

Africa: Yesterday and Today

The literature of a group of related societies furnishes insights into both their general and their specific cultures, but one should also know something about the societies themselves in order to understand the literature and to avoid provincialism in making judgments about it. Like other artifacts of a culture, the literary work is not an island unto itself, and to study it in isolation can be misleading. Accordingly, this part of the introduction describes broadly what might be called the "old" life of Negro Africa, the traditions of that life, and the changes which occurred because of the contact between African and non-African cultures, especially between those of Africa and Europe.

The "Old" Life

Although Negro African cultures manifest many striking similarities, there are vast differences among them, and there is always danger of inaccuracy in describing the "old" life. Yet if we limit the meaning of the "old life" to the life of the agrarian villager, and admit freely that it varies greatly in detail from place to place, we will be able to gain some broad idea of the African experience.

Culture change is occurring throughout Africa, in the "simple" agrarian village as well as in the bustling cities, but its effects are not everywhere the same. Many children are born of illiterate parents who practice their time-sanctioned customs and who, out of poverty or neglect or disagreement with attempts to alter traditions, will resist or actually block overt change in their children. Of course there are also many parents, particularly in the cities, who have attained certain of the educational and cultural "standards" of their societies, or who realize the powers of having "book" and are "westernized," and who consequently wish to see the advantages of westernization (higher standard of living, political influence, and social prestige) extended to their children. Here, though, we are concerned, as we have suggested, with the farming village, which is the early home of most African children today.

The patterns of family life in the different village or town cultures from which the present generation of African writers have sprung (with the exception, perhaps, of many South Africans) do not vary from one another in essence nearly so much as an outsider might imagine. Although most Africans are monogynous out of economic necessity, polygyny is sanctioned and found almost everywhere. A man will usually have more than one wife if he can afford it, for this eases the work load of his wife, increases his prestige by proving his affluence, and provides him with more opportunity to have a large number of children who will ultimately bring more income to the family and who will revere him as an ancestor.

In due course after a marriage, or in certain cases before, a child "arrives" or is "given" through the mother's womb, the father (and God, usually) having given life to it. The child will live with its mother and learn from her for the first years of its life. At a certain age it will begin to receive further special training from other persons of different age levels, culminating in the child's "coming of age" or initiation into manhood or womanhood. The early close ties with the mother will usually remain and be important throughout life; thus, if a male adult must seek refuge outside the village of his father, he will go to his mother's people.

Early in life the child will be taught respect for others. Through emulation of elders and the semiformal telling of proverbs and tales he will learn the behavior required of a member of his society. By observing and participating in the ceremonies and traditions of his people during his period of growth, and through direct teaching by initiators and parents, the child will develop awareness of his people's religion, even though today the educational influence of Islam and Christianity is strong in many villages. Perhaps more important, the child will grow to understand the range of accepted and acceptable behavior in his society, and will acquire a basic understanding of "right" and "wrong" or, rather, of those attitudes and actions which are sanctioned or rejected.

After a young man's initiation, which often includes circumcision, he thinks more seriously of his responsibilities. The first and most important of these is marriage, accompanied by elaborate bargaining and ceremony fixed by custom but today undergoing great change. Seldom a matter of one young man marrying one young woman, marriage is usually a means of establishing a relationship between two groups of people—lineages or clans or villages, however the larger family unit or kin-group is designated. Exogamy—marriage outside the village or tribal unit—is the more common form of marriage because of widespread prohibitions against incest, so the man and woman are of separate groups. The marriage is sometimes arranged years in advance. Arrangements for betrothal will be made, often quite publicly, with a gathering of elders from the two families as well as some witnesses from outside these groups; the bride wealth° will be arranged through elaborate "palava" (discussion and argument), and thus two hitherto separate peoples will be closely united.

Upon acceptance of the responsibilities of marriage and parenthood, the tribal man becomes more aware of his relationship to his people in his normally communal society. He will usually work seriously to acquire the prestige and status which is so important in African societies. He might take a title, which usually involves the performance of deeds determined by custom, or the outlay of a large sum of money and goods for feasting, or both. Through hard work and perseverance and the accumulation of wealth he will gain the respect of other members of his society, and he will produce offspring who will revere him as he ages. He will usually attempt to develop his personal character or at least his reputation as a trustworthy man in the important village or clan council politics, especially in times of group crisis. Respect for him will increase, and his voice will be heard more and more; as years advance the young men will approach him for advice and help, as he in his own time sought the advice and help of his elders.

Thus as he grows older the villager who conforms to the patterns of behavior in his society will have done good things not merely for himself but for his children. By the time he has become an important member of his village he will probably have risen in status by acquiring more wives, although if his first wife is still alive she will invariably be the more prestigious "Senior Wife"; he will have increased his landholdings or the number of his cattle and other livestock, and he will therefore exemplify opulence and merit further praise. He will have become a member of one or more closed associations or "secret societies" and will have brought himself closer to the customs and spiritual life of his people. In the old days he might have proved his mettle in at least one raid against enemies, who abounded simply because

---

bride wealth: money, goods, and services paid by the husband to the bride's family to ensure his proper treatment of the woman. Payment of bride wealth usually legalizes the marriage.

anyone outside the village limits or the kingdom was suspect. As an elder, the villager will have developed the art of "palava," which has always been important in most societies of Negro Africa.

Now, with death near, this village elder, this judge and legislator and teacher and father and husband, will see his last transformation as a joining with the ancestors from whom he sprang and to whom he has always paid respect, and it will be for him another stage in the continuum of existence. For the village African all is a vast cycle of realities and powers, spiritual and material, not always thoroughly differentiated in his mind.[6]

The "old" life before the white men came was a way of life which is still going on in many Negro African villages.[7] The traditionalistic African has a sense of justice, orderly government, democracy even if applied only to the narrowly defined in-group, love, mercy, honor, charity, cleanliness, and modesty (although not necessarily in European terms); he is intelligent but sometimes unprogressive; he is ambitious but sometimes relatively uninventive, partly because of the strength of traditions and because of the sanctions given to memorized wisdom rather than to the development of new ideas or methods of doing things. Of course, there have always existed the usual gamuts of vices as well as virtues in most African societies: there were and are liars and thieves and adulterers and the cruel and uncharitable and the backbiters. To say, then, that "when the Europeans arrived, they saw an innocent, hospitable and bold people,"[8] is to present a rather romanticized and simplified view of the traditional African. What is more important and should be emphasized is that, as Nkrumah has said, before the white men came to Africa the African was perfectly capable of governing himself. He had governed himself as long as any other group of human beings on the earth.[9]

Change

The "old" life still exists within the African, whether he is "acculturated" or not, or to whatever degree he has been assimilated by European culture. Perhaps it existed in the past more outwardly than at present because the various layers of outside influences had not been spread like so much European paint upon the African's behavior, but certainly it still exists, at least covertly. Yet in the past the white men came, especially from Europe, and Europe-directed assimilation and culture change began. Nothing really fell apart, but things and people began to change: the African began to adapt, however superficially in some instances, to the ways of outsiders different from any outsiders he had ever before known.

Slavery

The first contact of real importance between the white and African cultures centered on the overseas slave trade, which as developed by the Europeans was brutal and degrading and had a shattering effect on the African's culture. As an opponent of slavery, William Balfour Baikie, said, one wonders "why the poor African should have been solely selected as the victim of the cupidity of his brother man"; but the answer is not quite as Léopold Sédar Senghor argued when he said, "It is, precisely, the natural virtues of the African Negro which gave rise to the trade."[10] It was a combination of factors, among which is the fact that slavery was a common practice among the Africans themselves. It was perfectly natural for the first contacted Africans to sell slaves to the interested Europeans, and from that point onward the profits of slavery became more and more clear to the African entrepreneurs.

The process of enslavement was peculiarly designed to be profoundly shocking for the slave. Most of the slaves were taken in wars and surprise raids on villages; and rank, titles, and other status were no guarantee of security because all captives were reduced to the same level. At the wholesale markets the slaves were sorted and branded. Driven like animals, the selected slaves were put aboard ship, chained down, and the long voyage across the seas, the "middle passage," began. Approximately one of every three slaves purchased in Africa survived the slave ships to reach the New World, where the Negroes landed brutalized by suffering and fear. Then, in a strange land, again they were herded and sold like animals. They were split up so that individual purchasers could not accumulate too many of the same linguistic stock, and the slave was thus forced to learn the master's language.

In his 1774 *History of Jamaica,* a Mr. Long (quoted by K. Little[11]) said of the slaves in the West Indies:

We cannot pronounce them *unsusceptible of civilisation since even apes* have been taught to eat, drink, repose and dress *like men.* But of all the human species hitherto discovered, their *natural baseness of mind* seems to afford the least hope of their being . . . so refined as to think as well as act like *men.*

Little argues that this early development of racial prejudice tended to depersonalize human relations in order to exploit men more effectively. The entire phalanx of stereotypes about Negroes was indeed drawn forth to rationalize the system, but in the early nineteenth century some Europeans were beginning to lose faith in the rationalizations, and the trade began to come to an end.

Slave trading was abolished by England in 1807, and in 1833 the slaves in the British colonies were set free. The English set out to patrol the high seas and to take over any slave ship they might encounter, the slaves often being reshipped to Freetown, Sierra Leone. But English decree and attempts at international enforcement did not stop the trade in "black ivory." It went on practically undiminished in Africa; the traders simply had to work a bit more secretively than earlier.

Thomas Fowell Buxton, who had succeeded William Wilberforce as the leader of the British antislavery movement, in *The African Slave Trade and Its Remedy* (1840), argued that the slave trade could best be ended by missionary activity and the development of natural resources, and held that Africa could be regenerated by means of the Bible and the plow. This was not a new idea. The same point had been made earlier and had motivated the Laird and Oldfield expedition of 1832, which was perhaps more commercial than missionary. Some years later, Baikie wrote that the only method of really stopping the trade was to strike

at the root of the supply. . . . It is by doing our utmost to improve the natives, by softening their feelings, and by showing them how much more advantageous it would be for them to retain their countrymen

at home, even as hewers of wood and drawers of water, than to de-
populate the land, that we shall succeed in our efforts.[12]

The ending of the slave trade, together with a realization that
commercial possibilities in Africa had been opened up by the
contacts which the slave traders had already made, now brought
the white men to conquer, to govern, to convert, and to educate.

Much of the natural evolution of African cultures had been fro-
zen in time by the slave trade; some tribal and clan groups were
almost completely destroyed, and whole areas of land which at
one time had been cleared and cultivated reverted to bush. The
African throughout the years of the slave trade was adapting his
own culture to that of the outsiders with whom he had contact,
and among these were many of the most brutal men of Europe
and New England. This is not to suggest that the African was a
peaceful rustic living in a green utopia: he was seldom any better
than the average non-African. Nonetheless, the slave trade
brought out the worst in the white man, and since the white man
impressed the Africans with the profits he brought, what the African adopted was much of his wolfish behavior.

In other ways, too, however, the African was changing. Writing
of his voyages from 1786 to 1800, John Adams said of the people
of Old Calabar (now Calabar, Nigeria):

Many of the natives write English; an art first acquired by some of
the traders' sons, who had visited England, and which they have had
the sagacity to retain up to the present period. They have established
schools and schoolmasters, for the purpose of instructing in this art
the youths belonging to families of consequence.[13]

With the movement of Europeans into the interior, changes
which were occurring among Africans simply because of contact
became more controlled. In penetrating the interior, the Europeans were often entering strange and dangerous areas, so they
required protection and, better yet, means of "pacifying the natives." The stages of controlled culture change were: (1) conquest, which was the demonstration to Africans that the Europeans possessed special powers: (2) colonialization, which in
West Africa appeared as the establishment of colonial administra-

tive structures rather than the settlement of Europeans on the land, although in eastern and southern Africa it was actual colonization; (3) education of Africans to bring about their overt acceptance of the white man's rule. This third objective was effected largely through missionary activity, especially through formal Christian education which included almost everywhere that strange subject called "Character Formation." These three developments, all direct results of the ending of the slave trade, when added to the natural acculturation which had already begun, were to make the most lasting impression upon African societies.

Colonialism

Sékou Touré argued that "the imperialists used cultural, scientific, technical, economic, literary and moral values to justify and maintain their regime of exploitation and oppression."[14] Africans were oppressed militarily unless they cooperated, culturally so that some practices which the Europeans disliked or which constituted hardship or danger for the Europeans would be ended, and economically so that Africans would not compete with Europeans in gathering the larger profits from trade. The behavior the African was urged and in some cases forced to emulate was the behavior which the colonial governments and personnel considered "best" and "proper." Changing to suit the European was the chief means by which the African could gain position and earn a salary, if not personal acceptance. In the various African territories the changes in behavior were very similar, although the French and Portuguese gave a name to their system (*assimilation*) whereas the British and Germans chose to let the process remain nameless, or perhaps referred to it simply as "educating the natives."

For the French, the apparent purpose in assimilation was to integrate Overseas France with Metropolitan France and, through the creation of *évolués* (Portuguese, *assimilados*)—those who had "evolved" into black Europeans through the process of education—to make the Africans of the French territories more or less equal to the Europeans. The attempt failed, in both the French and the Portuguese colonies (despite even the present-day attempts of Portugal to claim Angola, Mozambique, and Portuguese Guinea as provinces of the nation). It is not true that in Overseas France "the Africans in French employment were always treated well; they were considered in no way inferior to the white man," as Easton has argued.[15] For one thing, France entered the scramble for Africa with the same diplomatic and economic purposes which inspired England, Germany, and the other nations. France was in Africa because she believed that France would benefit; the French colonies existed for France and not in their own right. Similarly, French-speaking Africans existed for France rather than for Africa, for their territory or tribe, or for themselves.

Slightly different motives for changing the African prompted the English and Germans in Africa. Whereas the French and Portuguese preferred imitators of the metropolitan culture, and said so, the English wanted to "domesticate" the African but, perhaps in very British fashion, did not philosophize the process. The Englishman tended to prefer (although at a distance) the "simple" bush villager to the "arrogant" élite, perhaps because the "bushiness" of the former assured the Englishman that his presence in Africa was truly necessary. All the colonialists indulged in cultural vanity, and in every case the white man's manifest cultural "superiority" was made quite clear to the Africans. English, French, Germans, and Portuguese wanted Africans to do things precisely as they stipulated, for they considered themselves the superior group.

With colonialism, the Europeans were in Africa to remain, and they were intent upon making conditions (including Africans) as conformable to European desires as possible. Although colonial establishment and administration were important in the change of social groups, what came to be more important was the stress on effecting social and cultural changes in the individual. Alterations in the African's personality, the Europeans naively felt, could be made easily enough and could be made most effectively through missionary activity and education.

Missionary Activity

Christian missionary activity was often less "Christian" than European and thus, unlike Islam, tended to bring widespread overt change to Africa. It began early in western and southern Africa and is still going on; the largest number of schools are still those owned and operated by various Christian mission groups. What did the missionary wish to do?

Most of the changes desired by the missionaries fell into the category of "civilizing the natives," a category which included a number of related changes. By "civilizing," the missionary usually meant to teach the African that it was morally right to obey the law of the Europeans (including the abolition of slavery, human sacrifice, and headhunting), to understand that the presence of the colonialists and missionaries was meant to help the African, and to demonstrate to the African the alleged superiority of European culture. Such "superiority" was impressed upon the African by the teaching of what proselytizers of different faiths chose to call the "The Truth." One taught Christian precepts according to one's particular sect and pointed out the errors inherent in other sects as well as in traditional African religions, which were "uncivilized." Commonly stressed or implied was that God came to the Europeans, but not to the Africans, although the good Europeans were carrying the "white man's burden" as apostles among the "benighted heathens."[16] "The Truth," furthermore, included all the missionary's proscriptions against native customs and, one suspects, anything which the missionary personally believed was unpleasant or evil.

Related to the "civilizing mission" was the missionary intention to develop "decency" and "cleanliness." The missionary commonly fought against nudity, arguing that going about half-dressed created "occasions of sin" (perhaps most often among the Europeans). Polygyny was considered a shocking acceptance of "fornication," the payment of bride wealth was treated as if it were the purchase of women, initiation ceremonies were attacked as "unclean" teaching about sexual matters, and secret societies were called "heathen" and "immoral." African dancing was opposed along with divination and so-called "witchdoctoring," and even the use of African names was discouraged because it was felt that a Christian should have a Christian name.

The missionary, then, tried to "civilize" and to bring what he believed was the truth to Africa. He rarely "went native," although perhaps in some cases he tried to set what he considered to be a good example for his converts to follow and to imitate. He wanted to bring about basic changes of character; he wanted the African convert not merely to adopt the outward forms of his teaching but to develop, within, an automatic Christian response to any situation he might encounter. That is what the missionary wanted to do and tried to do. What did he do in fact?

The missionary brought a new form of education—European education—which within the period of a few generations developed in Africans a broad knowledge about European ways and a new awareness of African history, and consequently an increased desire for freedom from European rule. The most important element in this education was the use of the vehicular language, which enabled the African to communicate very effectively with other peoples not only in Africa but throughout the world. In the schools the African was taught to emulate the European and to adopt European culture, dress, and general conduct. But the missionaries also unwittingly taught the African much about their own European methods of doing things and of effecting social change. This led to the rise of Africanism, a sense of national identity and nationalism, and a pride in race (*négritude*), but it also left the African in many ways confused among cultures, so impressed by conflicting cultural demands that he was at first almost lost until he began to develop the mixed culture which is in part a product of both his pasts, the traditional or "old" and the colonial. Yet in this he often finds himself in a sort of "middle passage" to which it is difficult to adjust.

The Middle Passage

During the "middle passage," the name given that segment of the journey in which they were carried from Africa to America, the slaves, usually chained in the dark hold of the ship, were carried by forces beyond their control, destined for a land they did not know, unsure of their fate, frightened, insecure, at times hopeful for an opportunity to revolt, yet nevertheless upon a great sea which they did not understand and across which they had little chance of returning. Just as the African in the actual middle passage was physically a slave, the African in the middle passage of his personality orientation after the consolidation of the white man's governments in Africa was a "cultural slave." And just as throughout history the physically enslaved have often revolted—at times successfully—so too against this cultural "enslavement" many Africans have revolted. But in either case it is as difficult to find the way back to one's home and traditions as to adjust to the port ahead.

In the traditional African situation the village possessed a fair degree of stability because of the extended family systems, the various members within larger tribal units being politically interdependent. "Governmental" authority arose from hereditary or, more usually, elected leaders—elders, titled men, or rulers chosen by a group of elders or special chief-makers. Although political squabbles and, at times, serious internecine conflicts occurred, such disruptions of the social order fell within the range of traditional experience, and the solutions of the problems came from the people or their leaders rather than from any outside force.

In the course of the cultural middle passage, however, multitudes of new social and political patterns appeared. The older tribal organization remained, but new towns were created by the Europeans who tolerated and even encouraged the large numbers of strangers that helped disrupt tribal bonds. Older traditional authorities remained, but new and alien authorities now appeared who somehow possessed greater powers than the previous leaders. Moreover, new "traditional" authorities were created by the alien powers—such as puppet emirs, warrant chiefs, and favored individuals—and were maintained in their positions so long as they cooperated with the colonialists.

With the partial breakdown of older authority, the African had to learn new methods of coping with new problems. What had been right and good in the past was now wrong and evil; whereas his grandfather had boasted of taking so many heads of enemies, he dare not even get into a fistfight without running the risk of facing a European magistrate and having to pay a fine in unfamiliar European money. It was even worse to face a judge in the European-sponsored "native court" where bribes were often necessary to obtain simple justice. This new justice paid little heed to an individual's position in his village society, and indeed the judge often tried to reduce all to the common level of subjects.

Like the social and political structures, economics and technology in the traditional African societies were validated by custom. Again, this is not to say that there was never any change, but that change did not normally result from totally alien causes. For instance, the introduction of brass-casting from Ife to Benin in southwestern Nigeria meant a change in Benin technology, but this change came from peoples essentially like the Bini and was therefore easily adopted. During the cultural middle passage, diversity and multiplicity began to characterize African economies. Old technologies were maintained, some were lost, and most were supplemented by new technology introduced by the Europeans. Furthermore, the alien technology, combined with European colonialist and missionary activity, brought with it the European money economy which caused some of the most sweeping of all the alterations of African societies. Because of the new money economy the African's means of amassing wealth changed, forcing him to conform to the alien system and to secure a European education in order to gain wealth in pounds, escudos, or francs. The money economy and the growth of European-style towns which became the major centers of employment resulted in further breakup of the African's traditions.

Tribal bonds were broken because young men seeking employment were drawn away from the villages and the traditional social and political controls of the family or tribal group. The dispersion of peoples also helped to weaken traditional societies and age-groups, which further tended to break down village social controls because many of the age-groups and societies had possessed policing functions. Traditional marriage systems and morality controls were weakened because young women were able to secure employment or to become prostitutes. The surplus of unmarried girls who were thus able to go forth resulted partly from the missionary fight against polygyny but as much from the increases in bride wealth because of greed stimulated by the money economy. Traditional religion and ritual were weakened because individuals were separated from the village shrines and thus from the customary worship with the family group. Because the religion was partly ancestral, such weakening led to further deterioration of the family system itself. Finally, traditional village education was rendered invalid because it was not relevant to the new situation: money and prestige were to be gained by learning the European way of doing things.

Naturally, problems of values arose, and the persons most aware of means of ridding themselves of the Europeans—that is, the educated Africans—were those who became most troubled by conflicts of values. Marris argued that

As people respond to the opportunity to improve their wealth and status, they tend to become insecure; their feelings become restricted to the relationships which can adapt to their changing style of life, and the loyalties they have abandoned dog them with a sense of guilt.[17]

The African in the middle passage was compelled to rediscover himself, to make his way in a new world which neither he nor his ancestors had created, and in so doing he learned a new sort of individualism. The negative effect of this individualism was a disobedience of the traditional moral and governmental sanctions of his society. More positive was a new awareness that individuals, regardless of former tribal antagonisms, could cooperate successfully against the colonialists.[18] In the changes which he experienced, the African did not lose what he possessed of the past: the new was layered over what already existed, for his change was additive rather than substitutive.[19] The changes caused some personality disorientation, often making the African a purely pragmatic eclectic who took from either side (traditional or European) whatever suited his purposes at the moment. Old value judgments remained and were applied to the new situations of the cultural middle passage. But new value judgments were acquired for new situations and were often applied to traditional behavior. At the same time, choices among behavioral norms and lines of action were endlessly multiplied.

The Nationalist Reaction

Those Africans who formed the group of modern nationalists in almost every instance studied in France, Great Britain, Portugal,

or the United States. Awareness of their own capabilities and of
the changes that had been forced on Africans aroused in such
men a desire to be their own masters and to rule their own countries. The first stage in their grand expression of the African self
had to be the immediate struggle for and attainment of independence.

Nationalism and independence movements varied according to
the particular colonial governments against which the nationalist
struggled, the tribal and ethnic bases, and the varying ambitions
and personalities of the nationalists themselves. However, there
were several constant factors in the growth of African nationalism. The first, and most important because the others depended
upon it, was the growth of a common language, usually the European vehicular language, which enabled people to communicate
across tribal linguistic barriers. The notion of a common plight
under colonial rule easily developed, and there came an increasing awareness of very broad racial likenesses among African peoples, who everywhere were controlled by Europeans. The spread
of education increased literacy in the vehicular language, and
with such literacy the African could begin to learn about weak-
nesses in the European past, and could even learn something of
the colonial process, in the course of which he could develop
knowledge of the state itself as distinct from his family or tribal
area. The development of modern communications as part of the
colonial pattern enabled the educated African to communicate to
his fellows, educated and uneducated alike, the loud cry for
uhuru, freedom. It enabled him to point up widely the basic hypocrisy underlying the so-called "civilizing mission" which existed
because European firearms supported European exploitation of
Africa. It enabled him to remind the Europeans that World War
II was fought, in part, to defend people's right to self-determina-
tion, and that by maintaining their colonies they were contra-
dicting their Atlantic Charter and the Charter of the United Nations. So independence, in country after country, finally came.

What followed and accompanied the reactions to changes
wrought in African history by the impact of non-African cultures
was modern African literature, which is inevitably a literature of
self-assertion.

ONE

TRADITIONS

L. Sainville includes in his list of themes of inspiration of African literature the "primacy of the picturesque in traditions and customs" and "fantasy as a projection of the universe.[1] Although he was referring chiefly to tendencies among modern African writers to use traditional motifs and to romanticize the traditional past, Sainville's themes furnish useful categories for classifying African literature in general. Customs and traditions—real or imagined— underlie all our subject. The modern African intellectual is almost passionately aware of traditional and of "bush" Africa, of that past still represented by the village or non-European town, and of the slave trade, colonialism and the historical relationships between Europeans and Africans, and of culture changes. It constantly colors his literary expression, stimulates his nationalism, and feeds fuel to his Africanism.

In this section are included two examples of actual traditional African literature and two examples of modern writings employing traditional motifs. The *Utendi wa Liyongo Fumo,* the Epic of Liyongo the Spear-Lord, based upon Swahili oral traditions, was written down by Muhammad bin Abubakar bin Umar al-Bakari (Muhammad Kijuma) in 1913. The oral tradition of Liyongo is very old: the father of Liyongo Fumo was said to have come from Persia to the Kenya coast of East Africa about the year 1000 A.D.

or earlier and to have carved out a kingdom at the mouth of the Tana River, although Liyongo is claimed as a culture hero also by the waPokomo, Bantu-speaking Negroes living upstream along the Tana. Prins argues that Liyongo might have lived anywhere from the eighth to the thirteenth century, and that he subjugated all the people from Chara to Mwina, imposing a tribute of heads (*kua*)—four slaves from each large village and two from each small one.[2] It is virtually impossible to ascertain Liyongo's exact ancestry, although the various versions of the epic story are relatively consistent in suggesting that the major conflict, over inheritance, was between Liyongo and his cousin, Daud Mringwari, who was the son of Liyongo's father's sister. By an African matrilineal succession, Daud was the rightful heir to the chieftaincy of Shagga, but as Harries says, "Liyongo, as the eldest son, would have succeeded his father, Mringwari I, according to the Arabian law of succession."[3] The waPokomo do not have a matrilineal system of inheritance, so it appears that the internal evidence rules out waPokomo claims to Liyongo. He might, nevertheless, be a culture hero of both the waPokomo and the Swahili based upon a far more ancient folk hero shared by numerous tribal groups in northeastern Kenya and southern Somali Republic.

Tendi or *tenzi* (plurals of *utendi, utenzi*) are intended to be sung or intoned to musical accompaniment before an audience, and as a form were used by the Swahili for inscribing historical poems from the oral tradition, for epics and *hadithi* ("tales"), and for homiletic and didactic poems. In the original the verse form consists of four *vipande* (sections of a verse), the first three rhyming, the fourth carrying a rhyme repeated as a terminal rhyme throughout the poem.[4] For example:

Na mimi ni muislamu   pame na yangu kaumu
    kumwabudu Mkarimu   ni laili wa nahari.
And I am a Muslim   along with my people
    we worship the Good One   by night and by day.

Tumtiile Latifu   na Tumewe Msharafu
    kesho tupate wokofu   tuepukane na sairi.
Let us obey the Beloved   and his Prophet, the Lord
    so tomorrow we may be saved   and keep away from hell.

The second example of African literature from the oral tradition is the set of *oriki* for Lagunju of Ede.° *Oriki*, or "praise names," are heroic verse-forms which are common to monarchic societies across the continent, from the Tswana of Botswana to the Baganda of Uganda and westward to the Yoruba of western Nigeria and the Wolof of Senegal and Gambia. These *oriki*, which form a unified composition more as a result of being focused on a single person than of being structured by a European style, are normally delivered by means of the talking drum. In this they differ slightly from similar praise-names of other cultures where the presentation is through the chanting human voice. In substance and heroic attitude, however, Yoruba *oriki* are virtually the same as praise-name chants in other cultures, for they reflect the basic need within these societies for the rulers, the heroes, and the demigods to be outwardly, unabashedly worshiped and praised.

Oriki celebrate a man because he is powerful and impressive, not necessarily because he is good or beloved. The subject of the following *oriki*, Abidu Lagunju, was a harsh *Timi* (ruler) of Ede during the late nineteenth century and was influential in converting many of his people to Islam. Because of his oppressions he was dethroned and forced into exile, but after seven years he regained his throne and was just as tyrannical as he had been before. So he was deposed again for his cruelty. Nine months after this again he retook his throne and was even more a tyrant than ever, although Reverend Samuel Johnson praised him as "venerable" and "renowned," especially as a "gifted and trusty historian of the Yoruba country."[6] A new civil war broke out and Lagunju was deposed for the last time—in 1892—and he died in exile.

The two modern stories deal with traditional beliefs in the power of spiritual forces. The story of *Le pagne noir*, by the well-known novelist and poet of Ivory Coast, Bernard Dadié, concerns the widespread folktale motif of the "impossible" quest and reveals the strong emphasis upon blood ties and ancestralism in

Ede: Ede is located in western Nigeria on the Oshun River some ten miles west of Oshogbo and approximately forty miles southeast of Oyo. The *ede* tree is common to the area, and the Yoruba town of Ede was referred to as the settlement in the *ede* bush. (5)

African thought.[7] *The Sacrificial Egg*, by the Nigerian novelist
Chinua Achebe, treats what is possibly his favorite topic: the
conflict between traditional and Europeanized Africa, with the
traditional—in this case represented by the spirit-forces bringing
smallpox—succeeding again in injuring the changed African. Both
of these stories exemplify the modern African writer's adaptation
of his people's past to the literary situation of today, and they
reflect as well, possibly, a yearning for the past when magic used
to work, when one's mother was a wise old woman instead of an
ignorant bush-woman, and when God and the gods and the ancestors were continually engaged in the affairs of men, guiding,
helping, protecting, punishing, loving.

(*Swahili*)

UTENDI WA LIYONGO FUMO°:
THE EPIC OF LIYONGO,
THE SPEAR-LORD

I *Liyongo and the waGalla*°

As Liyongo matured, becoming a man,
He truly grew, his features beautiful.
He was strong and tall, erect of bearing.
He became famous in outlying provinces,

Utendi Wa Liyongo Fumo: This version of the *utendi* is combined from
translations by Harries, Steere, and Werner, with the texts reorganized to
locate the *gungu* songs in their logical place. (8)
  waGalla: The Galla (sometimes waKala) are nomadic pastoral peoples
of Ethiopia, Somali Republic, and the Northern Frontier Region of Kenya
who have traditionally been enemies of the Swahili (although not of the
waPokomo, who also claim Liyongo). This element of the epic is possibly
post-sixteenth century, because the Galla previously had little contact with
the Swahili. From about 1550 to 1650 bands of Galla moved south and
eastwards from the Shungwaya-Juba hinterland, destroying the Ozi Kingdom and other Swahili city-states.

And people began to come just to look at this hero.
Some waGalla trekked to the court of Pate,°
Wanting to buy food and to look at Liyongo.
These waGalla, you know, were chiefs in the forest,
Members of ruling clans, each of them equally brave.
The Lord of Pate, the Sultan,° said to them:
"Men of the Galla tribe, have you ever laid eyes on Liyongo?"
The Galla leaders responded plainly:
"This man, Liyongo, who is he?
In our home he's unknown,
Nor have we even heard of him."
The Sultan explained, praising Liyongo to the Galla men:
"Say that a hundred warriors attack him—
They never win, and they run away.
For he is a proper man, with a noble manner like that of a lion,
And as he walks on the face of the earth
For him the night and day are always the same.°
Should he suddenly appear directly in front of you,
Each of you Galla would tremble and cry,
Shiver all over, and urinate from fear.
Let him but stare at you, and straightway you'll faint:
Death would breathe in your teeth from fear in your bellies."
As the men of the Galla listened, they laughed and they joked,
And then they replied: "We too desire to see him."

Pate: Pate Island is located off the coast of Kenya northeast of the mouth
of the Tana River, some 130 miles from the Somali border, and is the
setting for much of the action of this story. From this district come the
Swahilini, the "true" Swahili, and it is the original homeland of Swahili
culture and language. The Pate Kingdom was founded in 1204 and conquered its neighbors, becoming ascendant in the late fourteenth century.
Sultan: This is Daud Mringwari, Mfalume (King) of Shagga on Pate
Island, who wants Liyongo to remain in Galla country—that is, the interior
country of Kenya upstream along the Tana—for fear that he might usurp
the throne. A marriage is later arranged between Liyongo and a Galla
woman, Kundazi. (9)
night and day are always the same: that is, he is so powerful and bold
that he does not fear the night and the evil forces wandering about during
the night.

Liyongo used to live at Ozi,° some distance away
His own house was there in the noble town of Mashaha.°
Girding himself well with his chosen weapons,°
One day he set his face to the trail,
And journeyed swiftly, trekking along the road.
   (If a person leaves Shaka to go as far as Pate,
    It takes four days of rapid travel,
     And this for a good walker, understand.)
Liyongo went to that town of Pate
And, finally reaching the gates,
He placed a horn to his mouth,
But his blowing rent it asunder.
Setting his noble face to the town,
Liyongo went on in his manly way.
For two days he tried, and on the second he entered the place.
Truly blowing the first of his horns,
He startled the folk of Pate.
This horn split apart,
But the Galla men heard it, nevertheless,
So they inquired: "What was that?
Who could have made that terrible noise?"
And the Sultan told them: "Liyongo has come."
Without a delay, Liyongo blew on the second horn,
But this could not hold, and it split apart.
So he took up the third, and panic spread,
The people desperately seeking escape.
The waGalla warrior chieftains all ran away.

Ozi: The Ozi people (and locale) at the mouth of the Tana River. The three old Ozi Kingdoms of the waOzi ("Ozi People" who were Shirazi, descendants of colonists from Benadir on the Somali coast) were Shaka, Mwana, and Ungwana. Liyongo ruled over the principality of Shaka, not the Shagga or Shaka of Pate Island.

Mashaha: possibly the old town of Kwa wangwana wa Mashaha, or Kwa Mwana waMashaha, in the Ozi River forests.

his chosen weapons: His weapons traditionally were the *fumo* (spear), *uta* (bow), *sayufu* (sabre), and *sakini* (cutlass).

II *The Sultan's Plot to Kill Liyongo*[10]

Rumors by thousands° came to the Lord of Shagga,
So he determined to use guile and to kill Liyongo, the Spear-
    Lord.
(The Sultan, I must explain,
Feared that Liyongo would usurp the kingdom,
So he always distrusted the man.)
Aware that they sought a way to kill him,
Liyongo withdrew from Pate, and went to the mainland.

When the Sultan learned he had gone to the forest,
He contacted the Sanye tribesmen,
And the Dahalo people as well.°
The Sultan spoke to the waTwa° people:
"Catch him and tie him up.
Do this, and to his killer I promise to give
Head-cloths and cinctures of cloth for your loins.
Flap the hand-cloth,° and hunt this person
In those wilds and bush where nobody dwells
Save Liyongo alone in the forest.
Go, I tell you, and be secretive and cunning,
And we shall leave him for dead aloft.
He is hiding at Kiyungwa in Ngozi°
In the miserable haunts of waBoni,
Eating wild fruit and the *areca*-nut° of the forest."

Rumors by thousands: that is, that Liyongo was approaching the town
and intended to challenge Daud Mringwari.
contacted . . . well: to seek their help in killing Liyongo. The waSanye, who
live west of and upstream along the Tana River, were original inhabitants of
the valley and ancestors of some Pokomo clans. They are also called
waBoni, waDahalo, and *waTwa.* Most of these peoples are nomadic hunters
or pastoral groups.
waTwa: the Twa people, an alternate term for the waDahalo.
hand-cloth: used by dancers, here suggesting preparatory war-ceremonies;
used also for flushing animals from their hiding-places.
Kiyungwa in Ngozi: text, *ngozi kiyungwa,* the locality of Kiyungwa or
Kiongwe, south of Ras Mtio. This is a slightly ambiguous reference, *ngozi*
also suggesting Pate nobility. *WaNgozi* refers to a clan among the waBoni
in the southern Somali Republic. (11)
areca: genus name of a tropical Asian palm related to betel palm

One day these people said to Liyongo Fumo:
"Now let us eat like the gentle classes,
And have ourselves a delicious *kikoa*-feast,°
The kind of a feast which will always please."
Liyongo replied, "If I come to a sharing-feast,
What shall I, a poor man, be able to pay?"
"For this *kikoa*," they said, "let us eat the fruit of the dum-palm.°
    Each day a different man shall climb
To gather fruit for the others and all to eat."
Liyongo addressed them: "I will do it.
I will get down the ripest of the uppermost branches!"

    Their plans completed, each of them went his way.
One man must climb up alone to gather fruit for the others.
Their secret plan was this:
On the day Liyongo Fumo would climb,
They would kill him with one swift volley of arrows.
So finally everyone made his *kikoa* offering, and only Liyongo
        remained.
"Your time has now come," they informed him:
"Understand this clearly—we want our share of the fruit."
Liyongo replied immediately:
"Select a dum-palm with fruits that you like,
So that I may pluck them down for you."
Walking in single file, seeking a proper tree,
They found a tall enough one and said to the Spear-Lord:
"Here is the tree."
When Liyongo saw that the tree was extremely tall,
He knew that his earlier doubts were confirmed,
Because he was forever cautious
(Even while sleeping he was normally on guard),
And now he realized their intended evil.

    kikoa-feast: a contributory feast for which each guest in turn supplies the food. This occurs partly because of food shortage, sometimes as a potlatch festival for the display of wealth. Here, of course, it is being used by the waSanye and waDahalo to catch Liyongo off guard so they can murder him.
    fruit of the dum-palm: makoma, the fruit of the *mkoma*, which is the *hypaene* or dwarf-palm, and the branched doum-palm.

Telling them, "Wait!" he took arrows from a quiver,
Put one to his bowstring, and brought down the fruit—
An entire cluster from high in the tree,
A cluster of numerous fruits.
The people were gaping, wonder filling their hearts.
They said to each other: "Who can defeat him?
This man is no man: he is more like a *djinn!*°
Liyongo the Spear-Lord cannot be defeated
But escapes with the help of God,
And to contest him will end only in death!"

III *Liyongo's Capture and Escape*

The Sultan spoke to the leading men,° saying to them in secret:
"Proclaim a *gungu*° tourney, a dance for men and women,
And invite Liyongo the Spear-Lord.
I still intend to capture him.
But this is a secret which I have told you,
So if he hears and escapes because you have told him,
I will have every one of you killed!"
Whenever this Sultan intended to kill,
No one could stop him with words or deeds;
And when he spoke, one could be certain
That he would fulfil his word at once.
So the leaders sent invitations, to Liyongo proclaiming:
"We will prepare a *mwao*° dance and all be together!"
And they prepared the *mwao* according to custom.

---

djinn: text, *jini.* The *djinn* are spirits, usually malign, which often take
the form of animals.

leading men: actually the grown men and chiefs of groups subordinate
to Pate, such as the WaSanye, waDahalo, and waTwa.

gungu: a ceremony at which dancing and verse-composing are principal
actvities. In Mombasa the *gungu,* along with a story of Liyongo, is danced
at the grave of Shaha wa Mvita, the founder of a settlement on Mombasa
Island, who claimed Shirazi origin. The *gungu* is danced at weddings in
Zanzibar.

mwao: the dance of the *gungu* tourney.

The Sultan sent his men at arms—a hundred in number,
Marching in order with spears and bows—
And they managed to seize Liyongo the Spear-Lord.
He was put in the prison, shut up in a cell,
With soldiers at the door taking turns to watch him.
Then there was debate whether he ought to be killed.
Some said, "Avoid it, for I am afraid of Liyongo!"
While others explained: "To kill him is stupid,
For he is a city's defense!
Since he is the one who could strive for us,
Make him our leader in this!
So if war should come, he would die honoured
(For he would not run away).
And if he were killed, well enough,
But remaining alive, he would remain our defense."
Thus they agreed, and they went to inform the Sultan,
Who thought: *It is better to kill him.*
He's a danger if spared, certain to plot and to scheme.
And if he became a usurper, I would gnaw my knuckles regret-
*   fully.*
So better for me to have this fellow killed.
He called together his kinsmen to plan the slaying with them,
And they agreed: "Indeed, that's the only possible thing you
    can do!"
They sent to Liyongo a servant who said:
"Death is certain. They have sent me to tell you.
What would you like to have? For I am sent by the Sultan,
And you will receive it, be sure,
As your very last wish in this world.
He has said this, Spear-Lord, and has sent me to tell you:
In the space of three days, understand, you will be killed."
Liyongo replied: "Do not be too sure.
Now go tell the Sultan for me
That I ask for *mwao* and another *gungu* tourney as well."
When the Sultan's man had gone from the cell,
There entered a girl, bringing some food.
Every time Liyongo's mother sent good food to him,

The soldiers would steal it and eat it themselves,
So now he said to Saada, the slave-girl,
Speaking in the secret language of rhymes:
"Greet my mother for me,
And let my mother prepare the following things . . .

The Song to Saada, the Slave Girl

O maiden, I send you because they will trust you.
Tell my mother, who knows little of cunning and guile.
Let her bake me a loaf, inside it a file
To cut through these shackles and break my chains.
Let me climb these walls and break through the roof;
Let me kill enemies and, fighting, laugh them to scorn.
Let me go into the reeds and creep like a cunning snake.
Let me go into the forest and roar like a powerful lion.
I, Liyongo, resemble a lonely tree
Alone in a treeless wilderness.
Without kinsfolk or friends,
I am alone like a sorrowing orphan.
Only my mother remains,
To whose only son's cry
Her answer must be given!"

The girl understood his plan, and his mother made fires
To bake a loaf of bran, and she sent him the bread.
Seeing it was only of bran,° the solders cursed:
"Only a slave would eat bran!
Take it to him, if you wish—go on!"
This bread, understand, was eight pounds in weight.
Inside it the file, and Saada brought it to Liyongo.
Alone in his cell, Liyongo broke open the loaf
And, seeing inside it the file, was filled with joy,
So he rejoiced for his mother and Saada the slave girl.

bran: kiSwahili, *mtama, mawele*—maize husks.

When twilight came, the people made ready for dancing,
According to custom preparing the gongs, the horns, and the
    trumpets.
With the drums and the clapping of hands,
It was just like a wedding, the people all watching.
The floor was bedecked with cushions and silken cloths,
Spread with rugs of golden thread and beautiful silken fabrics,
And they sang the poems amidst the handclapping and drum-
    ming.

MWENGO, THE PRAISE-SINGER:
"From here where I am, let me behold the festive array,
With the players gathered together in noisy joy.
Today is the time of merry sounds: hear them today!
Players of drums and cymbals—today is the day!
Remember Kundazi and the Spear-Lord in their homeland!
Remember his bow and his spears, the arms which he carried!
The bow is his father, or like his mother, nurturing him . . .
I know not what to say or to speak on this day of days!"

LIYONGO, THE SPEAR-LORD:
"Mringwari,° drummers and dancers, come!
You are called by Liyongo the Spear-Lord!
Come! Liyongo the Spear-Lord calls you and his kinsman,
    Shaha Bwana Mwengo!°
Let them gather the graceful dancers skilled in composing enig-
    mas!
With great show, take the young girls and receive the young
    men° with united chorus
Of hand-clappers and singers!"
From the moment Liyongo arose, supressing his rage,

Mringwari: Daud Mringwari, the Sultan of Shagga in Pate.
Shaha Bwana Mwengo: "Shaha" is a Shah or ruler, but in this case it refers to the minstrel, the "ruler" of the dance-tourney. *Mwengo:* echo, answering voice—that is, a praise-singer.
young men: the *gungu*-dancers of Pate. *Gungu* dances were performed
by the men and slave girls, usually the younger ones. At marriage celebrations, young unmarried girls would be dressed up to wait upon the bride-
groom.

Calming himself as he sang, while the youths and the maidens
    were dancing about,
    The people cried out together:
"It is Liyongo the poet, make no mistake:
Liyongo Fumo, the poet who came to the coastland with battle!"

    While the refrains of singing increased, and drumming grew
        louder,
Liyongo was cutting away at his shackles and chains.
While the clapping increased he was steadily filing.
When the clapping had ended, he said to the people:
"Lift up your eyes and see!"
They paused in their dancing and beheld Liyongo, the Spear-
    Lord.
Fear overcame them, and in panic they fled away,
All of them running, leaving no one behind.
Liyongo went forth from the city
And at once he returned to the mainland.

IV   *The Death of Liyongo*

With fear in his heart, Liyongo's son° returned,
And by dusk of the second day he entered the city of Shaka.
He went to his father's house, and Liyongo was joyous in greet-
    ing him.
He welcomed him warmly, gave him a place to rest,
And massaged his limbs and the rest of his body,
For the boy was fatigued from the wearisome journey.
When the boy had rested he went out on the street
To talk and laugh with his friends as they strolled about.
In the folds of his clothing he had hidden the dagger
(Although nobody saw it), for he sought a way to kill his father.°

    Liyongo's son: (in the *Hadithi ya Liongo* it is his nephew) he has been
feted by the Sultan of Pate, who offered the youth his daughter's hand if he
could discover which weapon can kill Liyongo.
    Sought a way . . . father: In *Hadithi ya Liongo* the boy says, "Father,
what is it that can kill you?" And Liyongo replies, "A copper needle. If
anyone stabs me in the navel, I die." (12)

Shairi la Ndoto: The Dream Song[13]

LIYONGO:
I was at home asleep when I had a prophetic dream:
I dreamed I was killed by a kinsman—my father's sister's son.°
Waking suddenly and weak with fear,
My heart refused me, so I called for Kundazi.°
She tiptoed in and took off my shield,
The sword I owned, and even my lantern.
But however they approach, I will always resist!
O when they approach, let my heart be firm:
Let me be strong as a bull vaulting the goat-house!

    Each day as the boy went into the rooms,
Liyongo appeared to be sleeping.
The youth became worried, unable to find a way to do it.
Seeing his father asleep, he would call to him loudly,
Intending to kill him if Liyongo would fail to awake,
But Liyongo the Spear-Lord always awoke at the sound.
The youth would then say: "Give me some food, for I am hungry."
The boy grew more worried and felt overwhelmed,
Yet kept to his purpose as the days sped past.
The Lord of Pate sent him a message which said:
We are making the plans for your wedding day.
When the boy received that letter, his father was sleeping;
His breathing was loud, like thunder in the middle of rains,
And the youth perceived that Liyongo was truly asleep.
Seeing all this, the youth now intended an evil deed,
For he felt a deep longing to have him a wife.
As Liyongo lay sleeping flat on his back,
The son stabbed the dagger deep into his father's navel.
Awaking in pain, Liyongo saw no one, for the boy had fled.

---

   my father's sister's son: that is, Sultan Daud Mringwari, as the instigator
of the murder.
   Kundazi: Liyongo's Galla wife, and the woman who betrays him in alternate versions of the story.

Arising, Liyongo seized bow and arrows and went into the
    center of town.
According to custom, he put a notched arrow to the bowstring,
Sank to one knee, and drew the barbed shaft to its aim.
This place, I must say, was close to the well:
But no one drew water there now, nor woman nor man,
For the news had traveled across the land;
And no one stood looking, for all the people had fled.
Liyongo was standing close by the village well.
The people had stopped drawing water: no one appeared.
To get water for the mosque,° the people of Shaka
Drew water from a pot until all was gone.
Now all the town's water was gone, even that of the jugs,
But relentless Liyongo had placed his arrow to bowstring.
Having buried the people who died of thirst,
Distressed, they called a council of elders.
The palava reached a unanimous decision:
"We must forthwith approach his mother.
If she will help, she can calm him with motherly care."
So they went to his mother, and she agreed to help,
So together they came again outside the city walls.°

Liyongo's mother besought him, singing womanly songs of
    deep lamentation
To lead him to her in sorrow, but the Spear-Lord heard nothing.
Trembling, his mother was afraid to approach him,
So from a distance she observed him and constantly wept.

(None understood that Liyongo the Spear-Lord was dead,
And terror so struck them that they dare not go closer.)

At her place every day his mother would weep,
But not once would Liyongo rise up,
So they thought he was angered and vengeful.

   water for the mosque: that is, for the ritual ablutions required of Muslims
before reciting their prayers.
   outside the city walls: that is, with the rest of the people. They are afraid
to remain inside the city lest Liyongo kill them.

One day on returning his mother explained to them:
"I have no idea what he blames, but anger is holding him:
My son is enraged, for it is not his way to refuse to listen.
He refuses to rise, and I still do not know what wrong our people
      have done.
No, this is never his usual manner:
If I go to him with any request, he hears me at once.
But now he is strangely silent."
      Putting aside her fears, his mother approached him again
And when she saw clearly, a rage swept over her mind.
It was not possible now for Liyongo to kill, even if angry;
He could not have spoken, for he groaned with internal wounds.
His mother, marvelling, said, "A cruel shame it is,
That all in this hour my son has died without hearing my voice!"

      Thus within the span of a day,° he fell a corpse to the earth,
And the throng of people knew that Liyongo was dead.
All of the people drew near: his mother and kin and others,
Looking intently and exclaiming: "It is a dagger!
He has been stabbed in the navel with a dagger of copper!"

They carried him from the town, and quickly they buried him.

The news spread fast until it arrived at Pate,
And when the Sultan heard it, he was filled with joy.[14]

Takhmis ya Liyongo: The Dungeon Song[15]

Although I be sick, when I see war I am well,
As pleased as bridegrooms in wedding processions,

---

      within the span of a day: he was at the well longer than a day, but this
final day includes the action of the meeting of elders and the mother's attempts to speak with Liyongo.

Turning my heart in faith toward God.°
Like a young lion there is nothing I fear
Save disgrace, that enemies might find me hiding in the rear.

Who sways my heart once it has taken strength?
When I strive in battle I recognize no one.
Consider all others as nothing but outcasts.
I draw myself up, cast hatred against the evil,
And slaughter the enemy to please my heart.

Woe to the coward who is fearful and thoughtless;
Death is not chosen, but comes to each person.
He who fears death cannot receive honor,
But experiences only vile destitution
Until death finally comes to remove him.

I am valiant, a lion with claws,
A breaker of prisons and forts by my cunning.
Beating my breast, I leap against evil,
Fearing no bows nor spears that glitter.
Many they are who die, and many who turn and flee.

I would carve out my way with sword and cutlass,
Swinging my weapons both high and low,
Thundering like Heaven with rage,
But my legs are confined in shackles,
And around my neck is welded an iron ring.

It is done: I have finished the five-line stanzas
About Liyongo the Spear-Lord: all are completed.
Who finds a mistake to remove should never be blamed:
Rewards will be his, from our Bountiful God
When the day has come for repayment of good and evil.

Turning . . . God: This verse suggests an element of the Islamic *jihad,*
that death in battle—especially when one is promulgating the true faith of
"submission" (Islam)—brings eternal reward.

(*Yoruba*)

ORIKI (PRAISE NAMES)
FOR LAGUNJU OF EDE°

Adukesi: all the body except the teeth is black,
A hero at sea.
An eagle that kills choice game.
Faithful servant of the great king.°
A stranger becomes a companion only after a while.°
You play with a carving knife and think it is blunt:
Playfully, playfully, but it makes a deep cut.°
It is easy to wrap your maize pap in *ibisere* leaves° when they are
     young,
But when they become old they are rather stiff and hard to handle.
A leopard cub is a hunter.
A grown up leopard is also a hunter.
A single leopard can destroy ten score hunters.
When the leopard° kills, its tail drags playfully on the ground.
Friend of Dipe, confidant of Dahomey:°
One who should be greeted and greeted, is not greeted;

Oriki for Lagunju of Ede: played on the talking drum by Sunmonu Ade-
kanmi, the Are'Ilu of Ede, son of Odubitan. (16)
   great king: refers to the Alafin of Oyo, overlord of Ede. *Alafin* means "owner of the palace"; he was the mightiest chief in Yorubaland until the destruction of Old Oyo in the 1830's, after which Ibadan became the leading
city-state of Yoruba peoples.
   after a while: Lagunju's people required time to reacquaint themselves
with him each time he returned from exile.
   You play . . . deep cut: He is very dangerous: what to him is meaning-
less play is, to his subjects, a matter of life and death.
   ibisere leaves: maize leaves. Lagunju, steadily aging, becomes ever more
difficult for advisors to manipulate and to control.
   leopard: The leopard, a noble, fearsome creature, has little awareness of
its own destructive power. By implication here, the Timi as a human ought
to become aware of his destructiveness.
   Friend of Dipe, confidant of Dahomey: reference to other Yoruba and
related kingdoms. Dipe was a famous man in Ede.

One who should be praised and praised, is not praised.°
The god° who met a man in rags at the market
Smiled and smiled, then burst into laughter.
The god who created a man in rags will also create a garment
    for him.
Cotton wool dare not be careless near fire:
If it is careless, the fire will eat it up.
You cut marks° on the face of the butcher:
Adukesi, you cut marks on the face of the goat thief.
You are like big ripe fruit that fell on a child at midnight.
The *opolo*° frog gazes contemptuously at the man holding a
    knife.
Adesina,° my father: you do not care for another man's property.
Oloro says: "As they are going their own way, they will never
    keep their mouths shut."
They keep on saying: "Father, take the black, and I give you the
    white."
When you take the blue, then I give you the blue-black.°

One who should be greeted . . . is not praised: This refers to the unpop-
ularity of Lagunju among his subjects when he grew tyrannical after the
Alagbara War. Of course, popularity and power have little necessary need
of one another.
    god: Orisha-nla. Reference to the fact that greater powers exist, and
change is possible. An important being (*god*) would naturally laugh at a
ragged beggar, especially because most of those in rags are madmen, thus
ridiculous. At the same time, although a powerful god can ridicule, he is
responsible for the object of his ridicule. Similarly, Lagunju is powerful and
can be tyrannical and scornful of those in his control, yet he possesses the
power to change not only his behavior but the very conditions of existence
for his people.
    You cut marks: reference to the cruel punishments and barbaric "jus-
tice" meted out by Lagunju against the sensible advice of his council and
even of his relatives. After the Alagbara War, Lagunju commonly ordered
executions without due trial, ordered persons to be drowned in the Oshun
River, and ordered *Yagba* marks (three straight lines joining together at
an acute angle at the corner of the mouth) cut on the cheeks of anyone who
offended him.
    Opolo: a frog which is considered to be poisonous, so it is not eaten,
and it naturally has no fear of the hunter's knife. This is praise of a special
sort of power, and at the same time is criticism of Lagunju.
    Adesina: a royal name, meaning "The Crown has opened the way." It
is direct, positive praise—Lagunju is not covetous.
    "*Father, take the black . . . blue-black:* note by Timi Laoye: "The ref-
erence here could not be explained by the praise-singer." (17)

The *Olobu* with his insult.

The *Obagun* who pretends he is forbidden to walk out.

The *Akirun* in his ignorance keeps company with them.

The *Olugbon* said: "I should salute you."

The *Aresa* said: " I should salute you."

You said: "When you get back, tell *Olugbere:* Woe betide him."

You said: "When you get back, tell the *Aresa:* Woe betide him."°

You have yams in the market, *Adukesi.*

And on the farm you have long, long yams.

My father, you have maize with fat-cobs on your forest farm,

You pile up food in the palace.

We asked you why, and you said:

"When the people of Agbale begin their plot,

I shall have food to feed you."

The wind blew at Akesan,°

And only two fruit fell down.

Ayika got to the tree and picked one,

Ayika got there quickly and picked one;

But when Oloro came, there was no fruit left.

So Ayika split his fruit in two,

And gave half to Dejutelegan, son of Sabi.

Ayika split his fruit in two,

Then each of them had half, and Dejutelegan, son of Sabi, had
      a whole fruit.°

It was forbidden to enter the palace of the king with three things,

But *Adukesi* entered the palace with all three.

It was forbidden to enter the palace in working clothes:

He entered the palace in his working clothes.

The Olobu . . . Woe betide him: detractors and enemies of Lagunju.
These are kinglings of equal rank to Timi: *Oloro*—head of Oro Society,
Olobu—Chief of Obu, *Obogun*—Chief of Agun, *Akirun*—Chief of Ikurun,
Ologbon—Chief of Ibom, *Aresa*—Chief of Iresa, *Olugbere*—Chief of Igbere.

   Akesan: a market in Old Oyo, capital of the Yoruba peoples.

   The wind blew . . . a whole fruit: reference to the chieftaincy dispute
which resulted in Abidu Lagunju's being made Timi of Ede after the
throne had been vacant for nine years following Arohanran's death. This
symbolic account does not parallel the actual accession by Lagunju, who
was named Timi by the *Ikolaba* (Chamberlain) and Kingmakers on the advice of Pegba, a prince in the maternal line. In this account, Ayika and
Oloro each got a "fruit," and Lagunju none, but each "gave" Lagunju a
half, so he came out the victor, with more "fruit" (votes) than either opponent. *Dejutelegan* should be *Dojutelegan:* "To put a slanderer to shame."

It was forbidden to enter the palace in a loincloth:
He entered the palace in a loincloth.
It was forbidden to use tobacco on Akesan Market [day]:
He used tobacco on Akesan Market.°
He shaved his head clean and made a pad of iron chains,
And went around Akesan Market six times carrying a big stone
    on his head.°
The king's servant in truth.
An eagle which kills choice game.
A single leopard who destroys ten score hunters.

Satirical Song Against Lagunju°

    In the days of Arohanran,° we were wealthy:
    Each bought at least seven shawls.
    Please note that.
    In the reign of Ajeniju,° we were not too badly off:
    Each bought at least six shawls.
    Please note that.
    In the reign of Lagunju, we are all famished:
    Even foodstuffs are costly and we are underfed.
    Please note that.
        You, Timi, a despised Muslim,
        Are unwanted in Ede; you have to go
        Beyond Oshun River.

It was forbidden . . . Akesan Market: references to the boldness of
Lagunju, who defied prohibitions.
He shaved . . . on his head: people normally weave a small pad of palm-
strips, grass, or cloth, which they place on their head to cushion their
headload. Here Lagunju shaves his head, thus removing all natural cush-
ioning, then uses hard iron as the pad and carries a big stone, so he accordingly demonstrates his strength and power.
Satirical Song Against Lagunju: this is not part of the *oriki*, even though
the latter are critical in places. The first eighteen years of Timi Lagunju's
reign were peaceful, but then came the Alagbara War against the Ijesa
people. Lagunju returned to Ede a victor over the enemy and became
increasingly tyrannical; advised by his council to make amends and to
behave properly, he refused, so the council sent drummers around the city
to drum this poem of criticism against him.
Arohanran: Timi for about three years, after which the throne was vacant
for nine years before Lagunju was selected.
Ajeniju: Bamgbaiye Ajeniju Omo Lalemo, Timi for about twenty-five
years before Arohanran.

Bernard Dadié
(Ivory Coast)

THE BLACK LOINCLOTH[18]

Once upon a time there was a little girl who had lost her mother
on the very day that she was born. The mother's labors had lasted
for an entire week despite the attempts of older village women to
help her with the birth. The first cry of the baby girl coincided
with the final gasp of the mother's breath.

Although the husband gave his wife a fine funeral, time passed,
and the man remarried. On that very day the trials of gentle little
Aïwa began: subjected to constant privation, affronts, beatings,
scoldings, and punitive labor, she nevertheless smiled all the time.
This cheerful demeanor irritated and infuriated the stepmother,
who could continuously dream up new tasks for the child to perform, and new punishments for failure.

Little Aiwa was prettier than any of the other little girls in the
village, which also irritated her stepmother, who loathed that resplendent, captivating beauty. Yet the more she multiplied the
insults and the humiliations, the forced labors° and the priva-
tions, the more Aïwa would smile, appearing even more beautiful as she sang—and that little orphan girl sang wonderfully. She
was beaten for her good humor, for her gentleness, for her courage and for her diligence. She arose before cockcrow, and went to
bed only after the dogs themselves had fallen asleep, and she was
beaten even because of that.

The stepmother never truly knew how to vanquish that little
girl. She searched for a means which could not fail to succeed,
thinking and plotting in the morning when she arose, at noon
while she ate, and in the evening while she was dozing, her eyes
glinting yellow like those of a cunning beast. She sought the means
of ending that young girl's laughter, of stopping her songs, of

labors: text—*corvées,* literally "forced labors."

dulling the splendor of that youthful beauty. So patient yet so ardent was she that one morning she felt she had discovered the perfect method by which she could crush the girl, so going out of her house she snapped,

"*Tiens!* Go wash that black loincloth for me! Wash it wherever you wish, but wash it so that it becomes as white as cotton!"°

Aïwa picked up the black loincloth from the ground at her feet and smiled. But this smile of hers was now her way to hold back any murmuring, complaints, tears, and crying. Even so, this very smile which charmed everyone else aroused the stepmother's wrath, scattering live coals on her heart, so she fell upon the child with even greater violence than was usual. Finally, beaten and bruised, Aïwa snatched up the black cloth and ran away from her tormenter.

After having walked for a moon, Aïwa reached the bank of a stream. She tossed the cloth into it, but the cloth would not become wet even though the water of the creek was perfectly normal, with little fish and some beautiful waterlilies in it. On the steep banks frogs puffed and croaked as if to frighten her, but Aïwa, undaunted, dipped the black cloth once more into the water. Again the water refused to moisten it.° She resumed her journey, singing:

> O Mother, if you should see me on the path:
>> Aïwa-o! Aïwa!
> If you see me on the path to the river:
>> Aïwa-o! Aïwa!
> The black loincloth must become white,
> But the waters refuse to moisten it:
>> Aïwa-o! Aïwa!

cotton: text—*kaolin,* white pottery clay, or by extension white porcelain china.

After having walked . . . refused to moisten it: the motif of the cruel stepmother is common to Old World folk stories. The impossibility of Aïwa's task is increased here by the refusal of the water to moisten the cloth, thus the refusal of waters to engage in unnatural activity. This will emphasize the need for supernatural intervention later.

> The waters ripple like morning light,
> The waters glimmer like happiness,
> So, Mother, if you see me on the path:
> Aïwa-o! Aïwa!

Aïwa set out again, and this time she walked for six more moons.

In front of her, a large silk-cotton tree° lay across the path. In a crotch of the huge trunk was some water, completely yellow and limpid despite the breeze. All about it was a sea of gigantic ants with enormous pincers mounting guard and talking with one another: they came and went, they increased in number, and they passed orders back and forth to one another. Upon the queenly branch pointing a dead finger toward the sky was perched a phenomenal vulture whose wings obscured the sun for leagues and leagues in each direction. Its eyes glittered with flames and lightning, and its talons were like powerful aerial roots dragging along the ground. It had a tremendous beak!

Into the limpid yellow water the orphan girl plunged the black cloth which the other water had refused to moisten.

O Mother, if you should see me on the path:
Aïwa-o! Aïwa!
The path to the spring which will wash the black cloth:
Aïwa-o! Aïwa!
The black cloth which this water of the silk-cotton tree now refuses to wash:
Aïwa-o! Aïwa!

Still smiling as she always did, the girl continued upon her way.

She walked for moons and moons, as many moons as anyone can imagine. She went on day and night, never even lying down to rest, nourishing herself on fruits she gathered at the side of the road and drinking the dew which clung to the leaves of trees.

---

silk-cotton tree: text—*fromager.* This tree, *Ceiba pentandra,* is sacred among most West African village peoples, usually associated with ancestralism or the worship of tutelary spirits or both.

She arrived at a village of chimpanzees, to whom she related her adventures. After listening sympathetically to her for a while, the chimpanzees beat their chests with indignation and told her she could wash the black loincloth in the spring which passed through their village. But the water of this spring, too, refused to moisten the black loincloth.

The orphan again resumed her traveling. Now she came to a place which was truly strange: the path in front of her would open up only to close again behind her. The trees, birds, insects, even the earth, the dead and dry leaves, the lianas and the fruits hanging on the trees all spoke. Within that place, however, there was not a trace of a human being. When she heard herself being called, little Aïwa was thrown into distraction, and she walked and walked but saw that she had not budged an inch despite all the walking. Then, all of a sudden, as if she were shoved and compelled by a prodigious force, she leaped over stages and places and plunged even more deeply into this forest, where an agonizing silence reigned.

In front of her was a beautiful glade and, at the foot of a banana tree a small spring arose from the earth.

The water shimmered and was so clear and pure that it mirrored the sky, the clouds, and the trees of the forest. Falling to her knees and laughing with pleasure, Aïwa threw some of the water on the black loincloth. The cloth became wet. Now on her knees at the bank of the spring, she scrubbed at the black loincloth for two moons, but the cloth remained black. Even when her hands were covered with blisters she continued with her work, but finally she sang out this plea:

> O Mother, come to see me!
> Aïwa-o! Aïwa!
> See me kneeling beside this spring:
> Aïwa-o! Aïwa!
> The black loincloth must become white as cotton:
> Aïwa-o! Aïwa!
> Come see my hands, come see your daughter!
> Aïwa-o! Aïwa!

Scarcely had she finished singing than, behold! there was her mother, who gave her a cloth which was whiter than cotton. She took the black linen from Aïwa and, without saying a word, disappeared in the sky.

When the stepmother saw the white cloth, she gawked with stupefaction. She trembled, not with rage this time, but from fear, for she recognized one of the white cloths which had been used to bury her husband's first wife. Aïwa was smiling, as usual.

She smiled once more now, with that peculiar, strangely haunting smile one sees now and then on the lips of little girls.

Chinua Achebe
(Nigeria)

THE SACRIFICIAL EGG°

[1] Julius Obi set gazing at his typewriter. The fat Chief Clerk, his boss, was snoring at his table. Outside, the gatekeeper in his green uniform was sleeping at his post. You couldn't blame him; no customer had passed through the gate for nearly a week. There was an empty basket on the giant weighing machine. A few palm kernels lay in the dust around the machine, desolate reminders of its former activity.

[2] Julius went to the window that overlooked the great market° on the bank of the River Niger. This market, though still

The Sacrificial Egg: The paragraphs are numbered for easy reference when working with *Critical Exercise I* immediately following. M. J. C. Echeruo writes, "These stories tell of mysteries without presuming to know the explanations to them. If it is in the direction of stories like *Akueke* and *The Sacrificial Egg* that Achebe plans to move in his future fiction, and if he can sustain that independent sympathy, this 'credulousness' which rightly belongs—or used to belong—to the folktale, he would have chosen a form which could enable him to bridge the gulf between the innocence of Amos Tutuola and Ekwensi's sophistication." (19)

the great market: the city of Onitsha, in eastern Nigeria, is the locale of this market and story.

called *Nkwo*, had long spilled over into *Eke, Oye,* and *Afo*° with the coming of civilization and the growth of the town into a big palm oil port. In spite of this encroachment, however, it was still busiest on its original *Nkwo* day, because the deity° who had presided over it from antiquity still cast her spell only on her own day—let men do what they will. It was said that she appeared in the form of an old woman in the centre of the market just before cock-crow and waved her magic fan in the four directions of the earth—in front of her, behind her, to the right and to the left—to draw to the market men and women from distant places. And they came bringing the produce of their lands—palm oil and kernels, kola nuts, cassava, mats, baskets and earthenware pots; and took home many-coloured cloths, smoked fish, iron pots and plates. These were the forest peoples. The other half of the world° who lived by the great rivers came down also—by canoe, bringing yams and fish. Sometimes it was a big canoe with a dozen or more people in it; sometimes it was a lone fisherman and his wife in a small vessel from the swift-flowing Anambara. They moored their canoe on the bank and sold their fish, after much haggling. The woman then walked up the steep banks of the river to the heart of the market to buy salt and oil and, if the sales had been very good, a length of cloth. And for her children at home she bought bean cakes and *mai-mai*° which the Igara women cooked.° As evening approached, they took up their paddles again and paddled away, the water shimmering in the sunset and their canoe becoming smaller and smaller in the distance

Nkwo . . . Eke, Oye, and *Afo:* the days, named after markets (and viceversa). The Igbo week has four days. (20)

the deity: a tutelary spirit whose function is to protect the people from thieves, operating especially through people of the village-group which controls the market. (21)

The other half of the world: riverain *Ijo* peoples.

mai-mai: cooked bean flour.

Igara: Igala, a tribal group living northwest of the Igbo, near the confluence of the Benue and Niger Rivers, and upstream along the Anambara River, which pours into the Niger near Onitsha. The foods referred to derive from the Yoruba peoples of Western Nigeria, and the entire passage suggests the great mixture of ethnic groups at the market, which is paralleled by an equally great number of spiritual forces, some of them antagonistic.

until it was just a dark crescent on the water's face and two dark bodies swaying forwards and backwards in it. Umuru then was the meeting place of the forest people who were called Igbo and the alien riverain folk whom the Igbo called Olu and beyond whom the world stretched in indefiniteness.

[3]Julius Obi was not a native of Umuru. He had come like countless others from some bush village inland. But having passed his Standard Six° in a mission school he had come to Umuru to work as a clerk in the offices of a European trading company which bought palm oil and kernels and sold cloth and metalware. The offices were situated beside the famous market so that in his first two or three weeks Julius had to learn to work within its huge enveloping hum. Sometimes when the Chief Clerk was away or asleep he walked to the window and looked down on the vast anthill activity. Most of these people were not there yesterday, he thought, and yet the market had been as full. There must be many, many people in the world to be able to fill the market day after day like this. Of course they say that not all who came to the great market were real people. Janet's mother, Ma, had said so.

[4]"Some of the beautiful young women you see squeezing through the crowds are not people like you or me but *mammy-wota*° who have their town in the depths of the river," she said. "You can always tell them, because they are beautiful with a beauty that is not of this world. You catch a glimpse of them with the tail of your eye, then they disappear in the crowd."

[5]Julius thought about these things as he now stood at the window looking down on the silent, empty market. Who would have believed that the great boisterous market could ever be quenched like this? But such was the strength of *Kitikpa*,° the incarnate power of smallpox.

Standard Six: elementary school.

mammy-wota: "Mammy-Water," the mermaid, a spirit able to assume animal or human form. Common in the belief system of the Ibibio-speaking and Ijo peoples, she is called *Owu,* but is one of many such spirits. The Igbo people call her *Mmuo mmili,* "Spirit of the Water."

Kitikpa: a spiritual force whose most characteristic mark is smallpox, also called *Ogan'elu,* and at times personified as an old woman, other times as a male deity.

[6]When Umuru had been a little village, some people said, it had been swept and kept clean by its handful of inhabitants. But progress had turned it into a busy, sprawling, crowded and dirty river port, a no-man's-land where strangers outnumbered by far the sons of the soil who could do nothing about it except shake their heads at this gross perversion of their prayer. For indeed they had prayed—who had not?—for their town to grow and prosper. And it had grown. But there was good growth and there was bad growth. The belly does not bulge out only with food and drink; it might be the abominable swelling disease which would end by sending its ill-fated sufferer out of the house even before he was fully dead.

[7]The strangers who had crowded into Umuru came for trade and money ,not in search of gods and elders, for they had those in plenty back home, which was real home.

[8]And as if this did not suffice, the young sons and daughters of Umuru themselves, encouraged by schools and churches, were behaving no better than the strangers.

[9]Such was the state of the town when *Kitikpa* came to see it and to demand the sacrifice the inhabitants had neglected to give to the gods of the soil. He came in confident knowledge of the terror he held over the people. He was an evil deity, and he knew it.° Lest he be offended those he killed were not killed but decorated, and no one dared weep for them. He put an end to the coming and going between neighbors and between villages. They said, "*Kitikpa* is in that village," and immediately it was cut off by its neighbors.

[10]Julius was sad and worried because it was almost a week since he had seen Janet, the girl he was going to marry. Ma had explained to him very gently that he should no longer go to see them "until this thing is over, by the power of Jehovah." (Ma was a very devout Christian convert and one reason why she approved of Julius for her only daughter was that he sang in the church choir.)

Such was the state . . . he knew it: This comment by the author should be considered as a local provincialism rather than as a statement of fact about the Igbo people in general.

[11]"You must keep to your rooms," she had said in hushed tones, for *Kitikpa* strictly forbade any noise or boisterousness. "You never know whom you might meet on the streets. That family has got it." She lowered her voice even more and pointed surreptitiously at the house across the road whose doorway was barred with a yellow palm-frond. "He has decorated one of them already and the rest were moved away today in the big government lorry." (Who you might meet on the streets was of course the dread incarnation himself; if he saw you abroad he would ask you hadn't you heard he was in this town and then . . .)

[12]Janet walked a short way with Julius and stopped; and he stopped. They seemed to have nothing to say to each other yet they lingered on. Then she said goodnight and he said goodnight. And they shook hands, which was very odd, as though parting for the night were something new and grave.

[13]He did not go straight home, because being educated he was not afraid° of whom he might meet. He went to the bank of the river and just walked up and down it. He must have been there a long time because he was still there when the wooden gong of the night-mask° sounded. He immediately set out for home, half walking and half running, for night-masks were not a matter of superstition; they were real. They chose the night for their revelry because like the bat's their ugliness was great.

[14]As Julius hurried home he stepped on something that broke with a slight liquid explosion. He stopped and peeped down at the foot-path. The moon was not up yet but there was a faint light which showed that it would not be long delayed. In this half light he saw that he had stepped on a sacrificial egg. There were young palm fronds around it, like a house where the terrible artist was at work. Someone oppressed by misfortune had brought the offer-

---

he was not afraid: that is, because he went to school, which means that he had at least to pretend to convert to Christianity, for Christian missions operated the schools. As the story suggests, this is shallow faith at best.

night-mask: the mask for a "night spirit" (*Mmuo'anyase*), here referring to the tutelary ancestral spirit whom Kitikpa has come to aid because of the failure of the people to make proper propitiations. The crossroads motif is related to traditional Igbo veneration of the number 4 rather than to Christian influences.

ing to the crossroads in the dusk. And he had stepped on it. He wiped the sole of his foot on the sandy path and hurried away, carrying another vague worry he could not put his finger on. But hurrying was no use now; the fleet-footed mask was already abroad. Its voice rose high and clear in the still, black air like a flaming sword. It was yet a long way away, but Julius knew that distance would vanish before it. So he made straight for the co-coyam farm beside the road and threw himself on his belly. He had hardly done this when he heard the rattling staff of the spirit and a thundering stream of esoteric speech.° He shook all over. The sounds came bearing down on him, almost choking him. And now he could hear the footsteps. It was as if twenty evil men were running together. Panic sweat broke all over him and he was nearly impelled to get up and run. Fortunately he kept a firm hold on himself. In no time at all the commotion in the air and on the earth—the thunder and torrential rain, the earthquake and flood—passed and disappeared in the distance on the other side of the road.

[15]The next morning at the office the Chief Clerk, a son of the soil, spoke bitterly about last night's provocation of *Kitikpa* by the headstrong youngsters who had launched the noisy fleet-footed mask in defiance of their elders, who knew that *Kitikpa* would be enraged, and then . . .

[16]The trouble was that the disobedient youth had never yet experienced the power of *Kitikpa* themselves; they had only heard of it. Soon they knew.

[17]As Julius stood at the window looking out on the emptied market he lived through the terror of that night again. It was barely a week ago but already it seemed like another life, separated from the present by a vast emptiness. This emptiness deepened with the passage of time. On this side of it stood Julius, and on the other Ma and Janet whom the dread artist decorated.

---

he heard . . . esoteric speech: This is actually a description, however slight, of the sound made by masqueraders and their attendants during religious festivals and other ritual appearances of the embodied spirits in Igbo villages.

"The Sacrificial Egg"

The version of this story which we have used is the author's latest, done in October, 1966. In this critical exercise, some of the author's additions, deletions, and substitutions are described. In each instance, determine the function and the significance of the alteration in relation to the passage in which it occurs and to the story as a whole, or to its meaning in relation to matters extraneous to the actual story.

[Par. 1] *Change:* ". . . palm kernels lay desolately in the dust around the machine to remind you . . ." *to:*
   ". . . palm kernels lay in the dust around the machine, desolate reminders of its former activity."

[Par. 2] *Change:* "This market, like all Igbo markets, had been held on one of the four days of the week. But with the coming of civilization . . ." *to:*
   "This market, though still called *Nkwo,* had long spilled over in to *Eke, Oye,* and *Afo* with the coming of civilization . . ."
Change: ". . . the deity that had presided over it from antiquity still cast her spell only on that day." *to:*
   ". . . the deity who had presided over it from antiquity still cast her spell only on her own day—let men do what they will."
Substitution: "But with the coming of the white man" *changed to* ". . . with the coming of civilization . . ."
Change: "*akara*" to "bean cakes"

[Par. 5] *Substitution:* "so empty" *changed to:* "quenched like this."

[Pars. 7, 8, 9] Not in the original.

[Par. 10] Addition of "convert."

[Par. 11] *Addition: from* " 'You must keep to your rooms,' she had said."
   to: " 'You must keep to your rooms,' she had said in hushed tones, for *Kitikpa* strictly forbade any noise or boisterousness."

[Par. 12] Original was much shorter: "Janet walked a short way with him, and they said good night. And they shook hands, which was very odd."

[Pars. 15, 16] Not in the original.

T W O

IMAGES OF AFRICA

Every modern African writer at one time or another in the development of his career has been troubled about the identity of Africa and of himself, a problem aggravated by change, by the depersonalization of Africans, and by the stereotyped images of Africa common among non-Africans. Many African writers grew up in villages of mud or reed-and-wattle huts amidst relatively unclothed or poorly clothed people who were not always very clean in their habits (sometimes with good reason, such as lack of water), who had little conception of sanitation, and who often reasoned and acted illogically because of the misapplication of an "effect" to a "cause." This was the behavior and the life which the writer knew in his youth and accepted as normal. As he grew older, he became educated and partly Europeanized and learned to dislike what the Europeans had done, but he also saw that sometimes European criticism of African behavior was valid—that, for instance, sacrificial offerings were not so pragmatically sound as the use of antibiotics or other European medicines in saving the lives of sick children. Africa, or a small segment of it, contained *his* past, and he loved it even though he had grown away from some African practices and had ceased behaving like a traditionalist. On the other hand, Europeans were obviously wicked and alien (with, for example, the overseas slave trade, colonialism, the color-bar), and he disliked them even though he emulated them and knew that some of their ways were true and good. Aware of these contradictions and confusions in his attitudes toward his own past and toward the Europeans, he could only wonder what was true and what was false about Africa itself, and what was his personal role in the midst of such contrary values.[1] Underlying everything persisted that question of identification.

What is the *real* Africa to the writer? Is it a lush green jungle inhabited by laughing, innocent noble savages who are pure because they are untouched by the more complex and therefore evil life of Europe and Asia? Practically no modern African writer openly proclaims this sort of romanticism in its entirety, although now and then several of them skirt its borders. Certainly the novelist Nazi Boni of Upper Volta, in *Crépuscule des temps anciens,* falsifies African tradition through his characterization of Souroumantérhé, as the Nigerian Cyprian Ekwensi romanticizes the traditional village and its "purifying" effects upon even the corrupt Africans portrayed in *Jagua Nana.*

If not the homeland of primeval innocence, is Africa the land of mystery and the ever-exotic, containing mighty secrets which, if ever revealed to non-Africans, will completely alter the course of human history, will upset or debunk the highly vaunted European technology, and will arouse among men of the world profound respect—nay, reverence—for the wisdom of traditional Africa? "Africa the Mysterious" like "Africa the Innocent" is a recurrent theme in the modern literature and the new folklore of the continent, and it takes several distinct forms. Diop's dancer "begins" the world all over with her wonderful magic, and Senghor must hide the real truth of his totemic soul from the outside to protect himself and to get along with Others, the non-Africans. Even the natural change from nighttime to daylight is seen, perhaps correctly, as a miraculous transformation by Rabéarivelo; and Clark, listening to the drumming of rain at night, feels secure in the knowledge that protective rituals have been enacted.

As Thomas has said, referring to what others might call the self-fulfilling prophecy:

The *presentification* of the past by a consecrating ritual assures the permanence of the mythical event, which, lived with faith as much as force, gives an illusion of eternity to the subject in question.[2]

Thus the mysterious is sacred, related to the eternal if only through illusion, and is maintained through religious practice so that it becomes unassailable. One who seriously questions the validity of claims falling in this category of Africanism is invariably treated either like a colonialist-racist or a traitor to his people.

Is Africa, on the other hand, not necessarily a continent of innocent noble savages nor of mysterious forces, but simply the homeland of men and women who, like Ranaivo's young woman, behave and believe according to a basically realistic attitude toward themselves and life? Is it the home of fools like Mabel Dove-Danquah's Nana Adaku, who is ridiculously confused by his own combination of lechery and conspicuous display of wealth: Is it Medhen's Ethiopia—home, like it or not, though progress rots and peasants die? Or is Africa all these things, the romanticized and the faked, the real and the beautiful, the mysterious and the commonly known, and more, much more?

Abioseh Nicol

(Sierra Leone)

THE CONTINENT THAT LIES WITHIN US[3]

Africa, you were once just a name to me,
But now you lie before me with sombre green challenge
To that loud faith of freedom° (life more abundant)

loud . . . freedom: reference to romanticized notions of Africa, and the grandiose ideas of African independence common to the zealous African students who have been away from home for some time.

Which we once professed, shouting
Into the silent, listening microphone;
Or, on a London platform, to a sea
of white, perplexed faces, troubled
With secret Imperial doubt,° shouting
Of you with a vision euphemistic
As you always appear
To your lonely sons in alien shores ...
(Then in my wistful exile's mind
The dusty East End lane would vanish
In a grey mental mist, leaving behind
A warm, shimmering image of you.)

The hibiscus blooming in shameless scarlet,
And the bougainvillea in mauve passion
Entwining itself around strong branches;
The palm trees standing like tall, proud, moral women
Shaking their plaited locks against
The cool, suggestive evening breeze;
The short twilight dwindling;
The white, full moon turning its round gladness
Towards the swept open space
Among the trees; there will be
Dancing there tonight,° and in my brimming heart
Plenty love and plenty laughter.

Oh, I am tired of sausages and mast
With trifle and cream to follow,
Of clay-brown tea in breakfast cups,
And "Please return your trays here."

doubt: Many of the injustices of the colonial system described by im-
passioned student orators were thought by the European audience to be
exaggerations, although at the same time the listeners often possessed
germs of doubt about the colonial system itself.
    tonight: during the nights of the full moon, throughout most of West
Africa the villagers engage in "Moonlight Play," consisting of dances,
drumming, singing, the telling of folktales and, now and then, some love-
making.

I am tired of grim-faced, black-coated men
Reading the *Financial Times* with impersonal fear,
of slim City typists, picking their sandwich lunches
like forlorn sparrows, in chromium milk bars;
Of unfulfilled men shouting the racing editions
As I buy my ticket to Camden Town, N.W. 1.

I am tired of crouching over the spluttering gas fire
In this my lone bed-sitter;
Of queuing up for cheap lamb chops,
At two for one-and-three.°

The only thing I am not tired of
Is the persistent kindness
Of you too few who are not afraid
Of my blank dusky strangeness.

But now I am back,
Gazing at the sophistication of your brave new cities
Whose very names hold promise—
Dakar, Bathurst, Cotonou,
Lagos, Accra, and Bissau;
Monrovia, Freetown, Libreville,
Freetown is really in my mind.°

Go up-country, so they say,
To see the real Africa;°
For whoever you may be,
That is where you come from;
Go for bush, inside the bush,°

one-and-three: that is, one shilling and three-pence.
Freetown is really in my mind: double meaning: author's home is in
Freetown, Sierra Leone, and "Freetown" suggests independence.
the real Africa: that is, relatively unchanged by colonialism and missionary endeavors.
bush: the country, more specifically the forest. *Go for bush* is pidgin
English meaning "Go out to the country," or "to behave like a country
villager."

There you'll find your hidden heart,
Your mute, ancestral spirit.

And so I went, hopeful on my way.

   But now you lie before me, passive, actual
With your unanswering green challenge:
Is this all you are?
This long, uneven red road, this occasional succession
Of huddled heaps of four mud walls
And thatched falling grass roofs,
Sometimes ennobled by a thin layer
Of white plaster, and covered with dull, silvery,
Slanting, corrugated zinc.
Those patient faces on weather-beaten bodies
Bowing under heavy market loads.
The pedalling cyclist wavers by
On the wrong side of the road,
As if uncertain of this new emancipation.
The squawking chickens, the pregnant she-goats
Lumber awkwardly with fear across the road,
Across the windscreen view of my four-cylinder kit-car.°
An overladen lorry° speeds madly onwards,
Full of produce, passengers, with driver leaning
Out into the swirling dust to pilot his
Swinging, obsessed vehicle along.
Beside him on the raised seat his first-class
Passengers, clutching and timid, but he drives on
At so, so many miles per hour, peering out with
Bloodshot eyes, unshaven face, and dedicated look:
His motto painted across—"Sunshine transport,"

---

kit-car: a military vehicle, similar to a Land-Rover or Jeep, used for
rough-country transportation.
   lorry: Such lorries (trucks) used as buses and for cargo transport in
Africa are called "Mammy Wagons" because they often haul village women
to markets, and are inscribed with sayings usually in English but often in
vernacular languages.

                                                        "We get you
There quick, quick." "The Lord is my Shepherd"—
(The red dust° settles down on the green leaves)
I know I shall not want, my Lord,
Though I have reddened your green pastures,
It is only because I have wanted so much
That I have always been found wanting.
   From South and East and from my West
(The sandy desert° holds the North)
We have looked across a vast continent and
Dared to call it ours. You are not a country,
Africa, you are a concept, which we all
Fashion in our minds, each to each, to
Hide our separate years, to dream our separate dreams.

Only those within you who know their circumscribed
Plot, and till it well with steady plough
Can from that harvest then look up
To the vast blue inside of the enamelled bowl of sky
Which covers you and say, "This is my Africa," meaning
"I am content and I am happy. I am fulfilled within,
Without and roundabout. I have gained the little
Longings of my hands, my heart, my skin, and the soul
That follows in my shadow."°
I know now that is what you are, Africa,
Happiness, contentment and fulfilment,
And a small bird singing on a mango tree.

red dust: Most African soil is laterite, rusty-red in color.
desert: that is, the Sahara.
   the soul / That follows in my shadow: a common belief, differing only
in fairly slight detail, throughout equatorial Africa is that a person's
"shadow" or semi-invisible second self which follows a person everywhere
in life is actually the repository of one's soul or vital substance.

Abdoul Kader Kéré

(Upper Volta)

PAYS NATAL[4]

Je naquis dans un pays
Aux levers de soleils si beaux
Aux couchers si flamboyants
Partout, où que l'on soit
La nature offrant à portée
De la main sa beauté,
Ses énigmes, ses mystères.
D'interminables champs de mil ou de riz
Coulent l'ondoiement de leur or le long
De tortueux sentiers;
Au-delà, la brousse, la savane
A hautes herbes, domaine
Des animaux qui, depuis
La stupide hyène jusqu'au
Majestueux lion, ornent
Nos fables lors des nocturnes veillées.

NATIVE LAND

I was born in a land
Of such beautiful sunrises
Of such flaming sunsets
Everywhere, wherever you may be
Nature offering within
Reach her beauty,
Her enigmas, her mysteries.
Unending fields of millet or of rice
Roll the undulation of their gold along
Meandering paths;
Beyond, the bush, the high-grassed
Savanna, domain
Of animals which, from
The stupid hyena to the
Majestic lion, adorn
The stories we tell at night.

Jean-Joseph Rabéarivelo°
(Malagasy Republic)

FLUTISTES[5]

Ta flûte,
    tu l'as taillée dans un tibia de taureau puissant,
    et tu l'as polie sur les collines arides
    flagellées de soleil;
    sa flûte,
    il l'a taillée dans un roseau tremblotant de brise,
    et il l'a perforée au bord d'une eau courante
    ivre de songes lunaires.

Vous en jouez ensemble au fond du soir,
    comme pour retenir la pirogue sphérique
    qui chavire aux rives du ciel;
    comme pour la délivrer
    de son sort:
    mais vos plaintives incantations
    sont-elles entendues des dieux du vent,
    et de la terre et de la forêt,
    et du sable?

Ta flûte
    tire un accent où se perçoit la marche d'un taureau furieux
    qui court vers le désert

Rabéarivelo: a Hova (middle class) of the Imerina people of Madagascar.

FLUTE PLAYERS

Your flute
   you carved from the shin-bone of a mighty bull
   and you polished it on the arid hillsides
   scourged by the sun;
   his flute
   he cut from a reed trembling in the breeze
   and he cut its holes on the bank of a flowing stream
   drunken with moonlight dreams.°

You play them together at deepening twilight
   as if to steady the round canoe
   which capsizes at the shores of the sky;
   as if to deliver it
   from its fate:
   but your plaintive incantations
   are they heard by the gods of the wind
   and of the earth and of the forest
   and of the sand?

Your flute
   draws out a tone in which is felt the tread of an angry bull
   running toward the desert

   moonlight dreams: reference to beliefs about *volana* or "Moon"—upon
death, the dead acquire the name of the moon, thus have been exalted to
sacred beings. The moon's appearance in the water suggests the appearance of the dead with their power to injure, by punishing the living.
Gabriel Razafintsambaina has said of the poet in "Tribute to Rabéarivelo":
"The high plains of Imerina are for him a tower from which he translates
his cosmic vision of the world; it is a fairyland where he sees the sky
admiring itself in the ocean and the ocean sending the image of the earth
back to the sky." (6)

et en revient en courant,
brûlé de soif et de faim,
mais abattu par la fatigue
au pied d'un arbre sans ombre,
ni fruit, ni feuilles.
Sa flûte
est comme un roseau qui se plie
sous le poids d'un oiseau de passage—
non d'un oiseau pris par un enfant
et dont les plumes se dressent,
mais d'un oiseau séparé des siens
qui regarde sa propre ombre, pour se consoler,
sur l'eau courante.

Ta flûte
et la sienne—
elles regrettent leurs origines
dans les chants de vos peines.

and returning, running,
burning with thirst and with hunger,
but broken by fatigue
at the foot of a tree without shadow,°
nor fruit, nor leaves.
His flute
is like a reed which bends
under the weight of a passing bird—
not of a bird caught by a child
and whose feathers are ruffled,
but of a bird separated from its flock
who looks at his own shadow, for consolation,
on the flowing stream.

Your flute
and his—
they long for their beginnings
in the songs of your sorrows.

a tree without shadow: a tree without a "shadow" is one which gives no shade, and also one—by extension—with no soul or vital substance, thus one which cannot give good things to the needy.

TRADUIT NO. 3°

La peau de la vache noire est tendue,
tendue sans être mise à sécher,
tendue dans l'ombre septuple.

Mais qui a abattu la vache noire
morte sans avoir mugi, morte sans avoir beuglé,
morte sans avoir été poursuivie
sur cette prairie fleurie d'étoiles?

La voici qui gît dans la moitié du ciel.
Tendue est la peau
sur la boîte de résonance du vent
que sculptent les esprits du sommeil.

Originally in Hova, translated into French by the author. (7)

TRANSLATION NO. 3:

SACRIFICE AND REBIRTH

The hide of the black cow° is stretched,
stretched without being staked to dry,
stretched in the sevenfold° shadow.

But who has slaughtered the black cow
dead without having bellowed, dead without having lowed,
dead without having been chased
on that prairie flowered with stars?

Here she° is lying in the half° of the sky.
Stretched is the hide
on the sounding box of the wind
that is carved by the spirits of sleep.°

the black cow: black cattle are slaughtered because they are a *fady* or taboo beast, bringing poverty, the black color being compared with fields ruined by locust swarms. Black, furthermore, is a slave color: at the feast of the turning of corpses, a black ox is slaughtered to remove any evil destiny.

sevenfold: seven symbolizes evil to be removed in the renunciation of a taboo act; seven is a number of disaster, a fatal number, thus *sevenfold* here suggests a shadow which is utterly destructive and which—were it able—would maintain darkness and death forever.

she: that is, *volana,* "Moon."

half: Malagasy cosmology holds that the world is square and exists on a horizontal plane, thus has four equal sides and directions.

spirits of sleep: spiritual forces in the ascendancy when one is sleeping—especially the dead, who appear in dreams to remind the living of religious duties and, at times, to avenge themselves on the living if the latter are ill-behaved. *Dreams,* therefore, are reminders of realities which will occur.

Et le tambour est prêt
lorsque se couronnent de glaïeuls
les cornes du veau délivré
qui bondit
et broute les herbes des collines.

Il y résonnera,
et ses incantations deviendront rêves
jusqu'au moment où la vache noire ressuscitera,
blanche et rose,
devant un fleuve de lumière.

Léopold Sédar Senghor
(Senegal)

NUIT DE SINE°

Femme, pose sur mon front tes mains balsamiques, tes mains
   douces plus que fourrure.
Là-haut les palmes balancées qui bruissent dans la haute
   brise nocturne
A peine. Pas même la chanson de nourrice.
Qu'il nous berce, le silence rythmé.
Ecoutons son chant, écoutons battre notre sang sombre,
   écoutons
Battre le pouls profond de l'Afrique dans la brume des
   villages perdus.

Nuit de Sinê: Sinê-Salum is a region between the Sinê and Salum Rivers
in Senegal, originally settled by the Serer people, Senghor's tribal group.
(8)

And the drum is ready
when crowned with gladiolus
are the horns of the newborn calf
who cavorts
and grazes on the grass of the hills.

It will reverberate there,
and its incantations will become dreams
until the black cow arises from the dead,
white and pink,°
before a river of light.

NIGHT OF SINE

Woman, rest on my brow your soothing hands, your hands
    softer than fur.
Up above the swaying palm trees scarcely rustle in the
    high night breeze.
Not even a lullaby.
Let the rhythmic silence cradle us.
Let us listen to its song, let us listen to the beat of
    our dark blood, let us listen
To the deep pulse of Africa beating in the midst of
    forgotten villages.

white and pink: suggest reference to *Dabarà* cattle which are used to
heal people suffering from possession by spirits, at a ceremony called
bilo. Dabarà are sacred cattle, called the Cattle of *Zanahary* (God). The
evil of dying and of the night thus is removed by the Moon, who gives
birth to the Sun and to light, which changes the darkness into *white* and
pink like sacred coral, which was *fady* or taboo and reserved for Imerina
royalty as proof of their descent from the deified Vazimba.

Voici que décline la lune lasse vers son lit de mer étale
Voici que s'assoupissent les éclats de rire, que les conteurs
    eux-mêmes
Dodelinent de la tête comme l'enfant sur le dos de sa mère
Voici que les pieds des danseurs s'alourdissent, que
    s'alourdit la langue des chœurs alternés.

C'est l'heure des étoiles et de la nuit qui songe et
S'accoude à cette colline de nuages, drapée dans son long
    pagne de lait.
Les toits des cases luisent tendrement. Que disent-ils,
    si confidentiels, aux étoiles?
Dedans le foyer s'éteint dans l'intimité d'odeurs âcres
    et douces.

Femme, allume la lampe au beurre clair, que causent autour
    les ancêtres comme les parents, les enfants au lit.
Ecoutons la voix des anciens d'Elissa. Comme nous exilés
Ils n'ont pas voulu mourir, que se perdît par les sables
    leur torrent séminal.
Que j'écoute, dans la case enfumée que visite un reflet
    d'âmes propices
Ma tête sur ton sein chaud comme un dang au sortir du feu
    et fumant

Now the weary moon sinks toward her bed in the quiet sea
Now the bursts of laughter grow sleepy, the
    story-tellers themselves
Are nodding their heads like babies on the backs of their mothers°
Now the feet of the dancers grow heavy, and heavy the
    voices of the alternating choruses.

This is the hour of stars and of the night who dreams
And reclines on the hill of clouds, wrapped in her long
    milky cloth.
The roofs of the huts gleam tenderly. What do they
    say, so confidentially, to the stars?
Inside, the fire dies out among intimate smells bitter
    and sweet.

Woman, light the lamp of clear oil, that the Ancestors
    may gather about and talk like parents when children
    are sleeping.
Let us listen to the voices of the Ancients of
    Elissa. Like us, exiled,
They did not want to die and let the torrent of their
    seed be lost in the desert sands.°
Let me listen in the smoky hut where welcome spirits
    visit,
My head on your breast which is warm like a *dang*°
    just taken steaming from the fire,

like babies on the backs of their mothers: African women carry their
infants strapped upon their backs with a wide piece of cloth. This early
experience, having a profound effect on most Africans, is analogous to the
poet's suggested relationship of the adult with his "Mother" Africa.
   Woman . . . desert sands: reference to Senghor's family, who originated
in the village of Elissa in upper Portuguese Guinea. Migration and colonialism have cut him off from his ancestral home, but the ties of the
family through ancestralism are more important than those of people to
land.
   dang: Wolof for a kind of *couscous* (variant, *kuskus*), which is a pep-
pered, coarse flour-ball sometimes cooked in meat broth as a dumpling,
or steamed in a basket over broth.

Que je respire l'odeur de nos Morts, que je recueille et
   redise leur voix vivante, que j'apprenne à
Vivre avant de descendre, au-delà du plongeur, dans les
   hautes profondeurs du sommeil.

LE TOTEM[10]

Il me faut le cacher au plus intime de mes veines
L'Ancêtre à la peau d'orage sillonnée d'éclairs et de foudre
Mon animal gardien, il me faut le cacher
Que je ne rompe le barrage des scandales.
Il est mon sang fidèle qui requiert fidélité
Protégeant mon orgueil nu contre
Moi-même et la superbe des races heureuses.

Let me breathe the smell of our Dead, let me recall and
repeat their living voice, let me learn to
Live before descending, deeper than a diver,° into the
lofty depths of sleep.

THE TOTEM

I must hide him deep in my veins
The Ancestor° with the skin of a tempest streaked by
lightning and thunder
My Guardian-Animal,° I must hide him
Lest I burst the dam of scandals.
He is my faithful blood who requires fidelity
Protecting my naked pride against
Myself and the insolence of happy races.

descending deeper than a diver: This suggests Ndyadyane Ndyaya,
mythical head of all Wolof peoples, who mysteriously rose from the depths
of a lake to bring peace, then returned to the waters. (9)
   Ancestor: reference especially to the spiritualized human ancestor who
possesses the power of sky-gods, which can be transmitted in part to the
living descendants.
   Guardian-Animal: This is the actual *totem.* A totem is the spirit of an
animal, usually, considered to have aided a founding ancestor in a critical
moment at the beginning or early part of the clan's history, or considered
spiritually related to the members of the clan. Among the Wolof (Senghor
is Serer, a related group), each clan group has totem animals: Diop, the
crown bird; Njai, the lion; Touré, the frog, etc. The totem in the poem
suggests the real self of the poet, as distinct from the artificial, Europeanized
surface of the acculturated African.

Bernard Dadié

(Ivory Coast)

HOMMES DE TOUS LES
CONTINENTS[11]

Je sors des nuits éclaboussées de sang

Regardez mes flancs
Labourés par la faim et le feu
Je fus une terre arable
Voyez ma main calleuse,
   noire
à force de pétrir le monde.
Mes yeux brûlés à l'ardeur de l'Amour.

J'étais là lorsque l'ange chassait l'ancêtre,
J'étais là lorsque les eaux mangeaient les montagnes
Encore là, lorsque Jésus réconciliait le ciel et la terre,
Toujours là, lorsque son sourire par-dessus les ravins
Nous liait au même destin.

   Hommes de tous les continents
Les balles étêtent encore les roses
dans les matins de rêve.

Sorti de la nuit des fumées artificielles
Je voudrais vous chanter
Vous qui portez le ciel à bout de bras
   Nous
qui nous cherchons dans le faux jour des réverbères.

Je connais moi aussi
Le froid dans les os, et la faim au ventre,
Les réveils en sursaut au cliquetis des mousquetons

MEN OF ALL CONTINENTS

I emerge from blood-spattered nights.

Look at my flanks
Plowed by hunger and fire
I was an arable land
See my callused hand,
    black
from ever working the world.
My eyes burned by the fire of Love.

I was there when the angel drove out the ancestor
I was there when the waters consumed the mountains
Also there, when Jesus reconciled heaven and earth
Still there, when his smile above the ravines
Bound us together in the same destiny.

    Men of all continents
Bullets still behead the roses
in the mornings of dreams.

Having left the night of artificial hopes
I would sing to you
You who hold heaven within reach
    We
who seek ourselves in the false dawn of the streetlamps.

I too know
Of cold in the bones, of hunger in the belly,
Of waking up startled by the clatter of carbines

Mais toujours une étoile a cligné des yeux
Les soirs d'incendie, dans les heures saoules de poudre.

Hommes de tous les continents
Portant le ciel à bout de bras,
Vous qui aimez entendre rire la femme,
Vous qui aimez regarder jouer l'enfant,
Vous qui aimez donner la main
Pour former la chaîne,

Les balles étêtent encore les roses
dans les matins de rêve.

David Diop
(Senegal)

AFRIQUE, A MA MERE[12]

Afrique mon Afrique
Afrique des fiers guerriers dans les savanes ancestrales
Afrique que chante ma grand'Mère
Au bord de son fleuve lointain
Je ne t'ai jamais connue
Mais mon regard est plein de ton sang
Ton beau sang noir à travers les champs répandu
Le sang de ta sueur
La sueur de ton travail
Le travail de l'esclavage

But a star has always given a wink
On evenings of fires, in the hours drunk with gunpowder.

Men of all continents
Holding heaven within reach
You who like to hear a woman laugh,
You who like to watch a child play,
You who like to offer your hand
To form a chain

Bullets still behead the roses
in the mornings of dreams.

AFRICA (TO MY MOTHER)

Africa my Africa
Africa of proud warriors in the ancestral savannas
Africa of whom my Grandmother sings
On the bank of her distant river
I have never known you°
But my eyes are full of your blood
Your beautiful black blood splashed across the countryside
The blood of your sweat
The sweat of your labor
The labor of slavery

I have never known you: Diop was born in Bordeaux, France, of a Senegalese father and a Camerounaise mother, and came to know Africa less through childhood experience than through secondary contact and, later, through visits to West Africa. He says that "the poet must strengthen the best of himself with what reflects essential views of his nation, and his poetry will become 'national.' . . . it will become a message for all, a message of brotherhood that crosses all borders and barriers." (13)

L'esclavage de tes enfants
Afrique dis-moi Afrique
Est-ce donc toi ce dos qui se courbe
Et se couche sous le poids de l'humilité
Ce dos tremblant à zébrures rouges
Qui dit oui au fouet sur les routes de midi
Alors gravement une voix me répondit
Fils impétueux cet arbre robuste et jeune
Cet arbre là-bas
Splendidement seul au milieu de fleurs blanches et fanées
C'est l'Afrique ton Afrique qui repousse
Qui repousse patiemment obstinément
Et dont les fruits ont peu à peu
L'amère saveur de la liberté.

A UNE DANSEUSE NOIRE[14]

Négresse ma chaude rumeur d'Afrique
Ma terre d'énigme et mon fruit de raison
Tu es danse par la joie nue de ton sourire
Par l'offrande de tes seins et tes secrets pouvoirs

The slavery° of your children
Africa tell me Africa
Is this you this back that bends
and is crushed under the burden of humiliation
This trembling back with red lacerations
which says yes to the whip° on the midday roads?
Then gravely a voice answers me
Impetuous son that young and strong tree
That tree over yonder
splendidly alone amidst white and faded° flowers
That is Africa your Africa which grows again
Which grows again patiently obstinately
and whose fruits acquire little by little
the bitter taste of liberty.

TO A BLACK DANCER

Black woman my warm clamor of Africa
My land of mystery and my fruit of reason
You are the dance in the naked joy of your smile
Through the offering of your breasts and your secret powers

slavery: overseas slavery, especially transatlantic slavery, and colonialism in Africa itself.

whip: The "whip" of European colonialism in Africa is symbolized by this image drawn from the *corvée* or forced labor of Africans under colonial systems.

white and faded: suggesting the theme of the decline of the Western European powers and the ascendancy of the colored races of mankind.

Tu es danse par les légendes d'or des nuits nuptiales
Par les temps nouveaux et les rythmes séculaires
Négresse triomphe multiplié de rêves et d'étoiles
Maîtresse docile à l'étreinte des koras
Tu es danse par le vertige
Par la magie des reins recommençant le monde
Tu es danse
Et les mythes autour de moi brûlent
Autour de moi les perruques du savoir
En grands feux de joie dans le ciel de tes pas
Tu es danse
Et brûlent les faux dieux sous ta flamme verticale
Tu es le visage de l'initié
Sacrifiant la folie auprès de l'arbre-gardien
Tu es l'idée du Tout et la voix de l'Ancien.
Lancée grave à l'assaut des chimères
Tu es le Verbe qui explose
En gerbes miraculeuses sur les côtes de l'oubli.

You are the dance by the golden legends of wedding nights°
In the new times and the age-old rhythms
Black woman manifold triumph of dreams and of stars
Docile mistress in the embrace of the *kora*°
You are the dance by vertigo
By the magic of loins recreating the world
You are the dance
And the myths flame around me
Around me the wigs of the learned
In bonfires of joy in the heaven of your steps.°
You are the dance
And false gods burn under your vertical flame
You are the dance of the initiate
Sacrificing his folly under the Guardian-Tree°
You are the idea of the All° and the voice of the Ancient°
Hurled solemn to assault delusions
You are the Word° which explodes
In miraculous showers of light on the shores of oblivion.

Black woman . . . wedding nights: lines 1-5 emphasize the ritual function of the dance and dancer. Dance is the sovereign expression of African
art "because, through it are synthesized rhythm, melody, word and gesture
in the human body, space and duration. It is also the most dramatic cultural expression because it is the only one where Man—as a refusal of Nature's determinism—wishes not only to be free, but wishes freedom *to the
limit,* therefore *it is the only mystical expression of African religion."*—
E. Mveng (15).

kora: a stringed instrument similar to a harp with a varying number of
strings (usually twelve), used especially in Senegal as accompaniment to
song and to dance.

You are the dance . . . the heaven of your steps: The dance, which restores vital power to the onlooker who has been endangered by over-exposure
to European culture, reveals that Europeanism ("wigs," suggesting arti-
ficiality, "of the learned") is merely falsehood, the "myths" of those who
worship false gods.

the initiate . . . Guardian-Tree: reference to the coming-of-age initiation
ceremony or *rites de passage* in which the male child is circumcised and
the female undergoes clitoridectomy, after which the youths are no longer
children but adults.

All: God, or the High God.

Ancient: the spiritualized ancestors, who possess numerous powers over
the living and are the final repositories of village wisdom.

Word: the concept of the *Word* as giving life to practical and ritual
realities is common among Negro African peoples. (16)

Assoi Adiko
(Ivory Coast)

LE DANSEUR[17]

L'incendie du tam-tam
Dans ses veines
L'incendie du tam-tam
Dans son cœur.

Le buste penché
Et courte haleine
Il ruisselle de sueur
Il frémit d'impatience
Il est subjugué
Travesti par les transes.

Les grelots à ses pieds
Noirs et agiles
Vibrent à l'unisson
Des tambours battant
Il saute, il virevolte
Il frissone, il frétille.

C'est la danse,
Et de la danse,
C'est lui le Phénix
Et le géant.

THE DANCER

> The fire of the tom-tom
> in his veins
> The fire of the tom-tom
> in his heart.
>
> His chest inclined
> And short of breath
> He streams with sweat
> He shudders with frenzy
> He is overcome
> Masked by terrors.
>
> Bells on his black
> And agile feet
> Shake in unison
> With beating drums.
> He leaps, he wheels,
> He shudders, he quivers.
>
> It is the dance,
> And of the dance,
> He is the Phoenix°
> And the Giant.°

Phoenix: The Phoenix, which is consumed in fire from the ashes of which it arises with renewed youth, symbolizes the magical quality of the dance, which ritually restores vitality.

Giant: The Giant symbolizes the power possessed by the dancer's magic.

Ses muscles
D'ébène moiré
S'auréolent
Du rythme sacré
Il crée la vie
Intense et folle
Pour narguer
la mort . . .
Toujours immortelle.

J. P. Clark

(Nigeria)

NIGHT RAIN[18]

What time of night it is
I do not know
Except that like some fish
Doped out of the deep°
I have bobbed up bellywise
From stream of sleep
And no cocks crow.

It is drumming° hard here
And I suppose everywhere

fish doped out of the deep: a common fish-catching technique in equatorial Africa is to drop paralyzing drugs into the water to stun the fish, which then float to the surface and can be gathered easily into the boat.

drumming: the "drumming" of the rain, the activity, and then the rest it produces become analogous in the poem to actual night drumming and the peace of mind induced by its assurance that mankind is protected through regular enacting of proper rituals. As Mveng has said, "the drum (in the full sense of the word) is the *logos* of our culture, identifying itself with the human condition it expresses."—E. Mveng. (19)

His muscles
Of glistening ebony
Shine with the glory
Of the sacred rhythm.
He creates life
Intense and wild
To mock and taunt
death . . .
Forever immortal.

Droning with insistent ardour upon
Our roof-thatch and shed
And through sheaves slit open
To lightning and rafters
I cannot quite make out overhead
Great water drops are dribbling
Falling like orange or mango
Fruits showered forth in the wind
Or perhaps I should say so
Much like beads I could in prayer tell
Them on string as they break
In wooden bowls and earthenware
Mother is busy now deploying
About our roomlet and floor.
Although it is so dark
I know her practised step as
She moves her bins, bags, and vats
Out of the run of water
That like ants° filing out of the wood
Will scatter and gain possession
Of the floor. Do not tremble then,
But turn, brothers, turn upon your side

ants: termites.

Of the loosening mats
To where the others lie.
We have drunk tonight of a spell
Deeper than the owl's or bat's°
That wet of wings may not fly.
Bedraggled upon the *iroko*,° they stand
Emptied of hearts, and
Therefore will not stir, no, not
Even at dawn° for then
They must scurry in to hide.
So let us roll over on our back
And again roll to the beat
Of drumming all over the land
And under its ample soothing hand
Joined to that of the sea
We will settle to sleep of the innocent and free.

the owl's or bat's: Witches take the form of these creatures. This cleansing
spell created by nature (and symbolically by positive ritual in drumming)
affects one even more solemnly than so-called "black" magic of witchcraft
or sorcery.
  iroko: a very tall tree (*Chlorophora excelsa*) with strong, coarse-grained
wood. The *iroko* is a common symbol of strength.
  at dawn: At dawn, bats and owls find dark hiding places; similarly,
witches, who take these forms, are often not effective in daylight. Accordingly, this night of cleansing rain and symbolic drumming is a night
during which one is safe from witches and other evil creatures.

GIRL BATHING[20]

Her basket of cassava° set away from reach
Of a log basking smooth on the beach,
She wades gingerly up to her high
Girdled hips, her underskirt lapping her thigh
Like calyces a corn. And as she ducks
Under, with deft fingers plucks
Loose her hair, the sweat and dirt long dried in every pore
Fall off her back, and in their place once more
The unguent flow of limbs, the fresh
Warm smell of her flesh.
O girl of erect and rearing breast,
So ripe with joy for the blest,
Splash, your teeth flashing pearls, in the whirlpool
You have made, its lively cool
Waters lambent through your veins,
A tonic at the core of your bones.
And striding back to land, neat
On sands golden at your feet,
How irridescent breaks all
Your porcelain skin to tattoo beads of coral!°

cassava: genus *Manihot,* family *Euphorbiaceae,* a tuberous plant grown in West and Equatorial Africa as a staple food. The cassava tubers are usually washed in a stream to remove the milky, poisonous juices, and the remaining starch is cooked and eaten with pepper sauces.
coral: sacred and ceremonial stone, often designating nobility or a titled person.

Tshakatumba
(Republic of the Congo)

MESSAGE A MPUTU ANTOINETTE,
FILLE DE LA BROUSSE,
AMIE DE MON ENFANCE[21]

Sœur africaine sœur noire
toi qui ne connais ni Damas ni Mac Kay
toi qui doit apprendre Césaire et Senghor
toi ignorante des bornes de ton continent
et à chaque crépuscule vas puiser l'eau
telle une déesse antique
arborant un sourire édénique
à l'unique source des alentours
c'est pour toi avant tout que je peine
c'est pour toi que le froid me transit
sœur de sapotille sœur aimant
l'Afrique sera le fruit de notre entente.

Gazelle infatigable
qui parcours à la chute du jour
les buissons calmés du bois mort tu ramasses
ô négresse! sœur sans artifice
ta beauté m'émeut ta beauté m'enchante
comme l'onde bleue mijotant
dans tes entrailles insondables

MESSAGE TO MPUTU ANTOINETTE,
GIRL OF THE BUSH,
FRIEND OF MY CHILDHOOD

African sister black sister
you who do not know Damas or Mackay
you who must learn Césaire and Senghor°
you who are ignorant of the boundaries of your continent
and in the half-light go to draw water
like an ancient goddess
wearing an Edenic smile
at the only spring in the neighborhood
it is for you above all that I labor
it is for you that the cold benumbs me
sister of the sapodilla° tree loving sister
Africa will be the fruit of our accord.

Tireless gazelle
who wanders at the close of day
through the hushed thickets of dead wood you gather
O black woman! guileless sister
your beauty touches me your beauty enchants me
like the blue wave simmering
in your unfathomable depths

Damas . . . Senghor: Negro poets who have celebrated the beauties of Negro women: Claude Mackay of the United States, Léon Damas and Aimé Césaire of the French West Indies, and Léopold Sédar Senghor of Senegal.

sapodilla: tropical evergreen. Since she is a means of growth, the black woman is linked with the sapodilla and, later, the lokumé trees. The trees symbolize constant growth.

Voir amarré sous les lianes entrelacées
amarré un continent en transe
où les tam-tams scandent rythment la vie
O tendre amie dans le géant lokumé incruste:
L'Afrique sera ce qu'ensemble nous la ferons.

Tsegaye Gabre Medhen
(Ethiopia)

OURS[22]

Time-old
Highland of highlands°
Ancient
Where all history ends
Where all rainbows meet.

Deep-throated giant
In whom
Forever is buried
Duplicates, of
The ten messages of Moses°—
Mighty earth
Highland of highlands
On your head
Wind blew
In your chest
Life fluttered

Highland of highlands: Ethiopia.
The ten messages of Moses: the Commandments. Besides the Amhara peoples who are traditionally Christian, having been converted in the third century, Ethiopians have a long history of contact with Judaism through the Falashas.

To see moored beneath the intertwined lianas
a continent moored in a trance
where the tom-toms beat out the rhythm of life
O loving friend in the giant encrusted lokumé:
Africa will be what together we make it.

In your belly
Progress rotted
Under your feet
Peasants died.
Hail
Roof of mother Africa
Worshipped idol of liberty
Whose age-old freedom
Cost overwhelming blood
Cost rituals of war—
Ancient highland
With your feet
In the sea
Your head
In the clouds.
Feature of volcanoes
Of erosions, valleys
Green, deserts.
Land of landscapes
Of labouring peasants
Land of warriers
Of churches, kings, history
Of reviving intrigue
Like fangs of serpents—
Highlands of highlands
Man cannot unmake
What you were

Unlearn
What he knew of your glory
Unfeel
What he lived in your shame.
Time-old.
Alone, aloof
Shading the desert
Dusting the heavens—
Ancient.
Your mother-guardian°
"Stretching her hands
In supplication to God"
Since time unheard of.
Your valiant sons
Sharpening their swords
Since time unheard of.
Your priests chanting
In prayers and curses
Since time unheard of—
Highland of highlands
We, your children
Admire you
For your past.
Fear you
For your injustice.
Nag you
For what you could have been.
Serve you
For better ends.
Respect you
For you are ours.
Love you
For what you are—

mother-guardian: reference to Mary, wife of Joseph; as the Virgin Mother of Christ (*Theotokos*), she is the mediator of grace between God and man. (23)

Time-old.
Slow
In change
Sure
In your steps
Cunning
In your freedom.
Courage
Is your challenge
Patience
Is your pass-word—
Ancient.
Rugged
Imposing cliffs
Characteristic
Of your defiance.
Chains of anarchy
Symbolic
Of your decadence.
Time-old
With your eyes
In today's date
Your feet
In pre-historic.
Home of buried walls
Symbolic
Of your age.
Home of
Songs of war
Characteristic
Of your lonesomeness.
Time-old
Highlands of highlands
Ancient
Where all history ends
Where all rainbows meet.

Tsegaye Gabre Medhen
(Ethiopia)

BAD DAYS[24]

Around what seemed the parched lips
of a hunger-silenced child,
fat, oily flies paraded.
They say those were the bad days,
when the northern soil was shaded
by the death cloud of locusts;
they say those were the days
when what was left of life
was more dead than alive,
except for the flying visitation
that eclipsed the light of sun.
When the shadow of doom knocked at every door,
and on every roof perched
overfed fowls screaming madness,
when paralyzed eyes gazed
for a hope that was not there,
and blotted-out eyes
made caves for fat flies.
When every floor was swarmed
by plague-emitting rats,
and the air was abused
by the stink of man's flesh,
when the northern winds blew in death
and mothers' breasts yielded pestilence.

They say those were the bad days,
when fat, oily flies paraded
around what seemed the parched lips
of a hunger-silenced child.

Flavien Ranaivo
(*Malagasy Republic*)

CHANSON DE JEUNE FEMME[25]

Pleutre
le jeune homme qui habite là-bas
près de l'aire-où-l'on-dépique-le-riz;
comme deux pieds de bananiers
de part et d'autre du fossé du village,
nous nous regardons,
nous sommes amants,
mais il ne veut m'épouser.
Jalouse
sa concubine que j'aperçus avant-hier au lavoir
en descendant le sentier contre le vent.
Elle était fière;
était-ce parce qu'elle portait un lamba épais
et affublée de coraux
ou parce qu'ils sont nouveaux conjoints?
Ce n'est pourtant pas la bourrasque
qui aura raison du frêle roseau,
ni la grosse pluie éphémère
au passage d'un nuage
qui surprendra outre mesure
le bœuf bleu.

SONG OF A YOUNG WOMAN

No-good heel
the young man who lives down there
near the rice-threshing floor;
like two feet of the banana tree
each on a side of the village ditch,
we gaze at each other,
we are lovers,
but he will not marry me.
Jealous
his concubine whom I saw the day before yesterday at the wash-
    house
as I came down the path against the wind.
She was haughty;
was it because she wore a heavy *lamba*°
and was dolled up with coral°
or because they have just gotten together?
It will take more than a squall
to break the frail reed,
or a sudden downpour
from a passing cloud
to surprise excessively
the blue ox.°

   lamba: a kind of shawl, serving as a blanket and a shroud, usually made
of wild silk or cotton, and nowadays a symbol of Malagasy independence.
   coral: coral is (or was) reserved for Imerina royalty as proof of their
descent from the deified Vazimba.
   blue ox: Blue is generally a sacred and thus a *fady* or taboo color, as
the "blue hill," *Ambohimanga,* is a mystic town and source of Imerina
strength, a royal town, the birthplace of Imerina kings and queens; similar
is the "blue forest," *Analamanga,* in the Imerina highlands. The *blue ox*
here is a symbol of strength and courage.

Je suis étonnée;
le grand rocher stérile
brava la pluie diluvienne
et c'est dans l'âtre que crépitent
les mauvais grains de maïs.
Tel ce fumeur de renom
qui prisa du tabac
quand il n'eut plus de chanvre à brûler.
Pied de chanvre?
—Germe dans l'Andringitra,
s'effrite dans l'Ankaratra,
n'est plus que cendres chez nous.
Flatterie perfide
un peu stimule l'amour
mais lame a deux tranchants;
pourquoi changer ce qui est nature?

—Si vous êtes triste de moi,
mirez-vous dans l'eau du repentir,
vous y déchiffrerez un mot que j'ai laissé.
Adieu, gyrin perplexe,
je vous donne bénédiction:
luttez contre le caïman,
voici des victuailles et trois fleurs de nénuphar
car longue est la route.

I am amazed;
the large, barren rock
braved the waters of the deluge
and it is on the hearth
that the bad kernels of corn crackle.
Like that notorious smoker
who took snuff
when he had no more hemp to burn.°
A stalk of hemp?
—It springs up in Andringitra,
it is used up in Ankaratra,
among us it is nothing but ashes.
False-hearted flattery
somewhat stimulates love
but a sword has two edges;
why try to change nature?

—If you are sad about me,
look at yourself in the water of repentance,
you'll make out a word I left there.
Goodbye, confused whirligig-beetle,
I give you my blessing:
wrestle your own crocodile,°
here is food and three waterlilies
for the way is long.

---

hemp: a drug, particularly hashish, made from the leaves of the *Cannabis* plant; marijuana.
crocodile: Crocodiles are *fady* or taboo creatures because ancestral spirits dwell in them, making them sacred. If a crocodile enters a village, it is fed and addressed as "Grandfather" or "Grandmother" and the people ask its blessing. One means of trial by ordeal was for a man to swim across a river of crocodiles. If he swam across and back, he was considered innocent, because the spiritualized ancestors and the gods in the form of crocodiles had spared him. What the woman suggests here is that her oafish lover is "guilty" of having ignored her, passing by what is so readily available to make a kind of liaison which she, the speaker, considers stupid.

Mabel Dove-Danquah
(Ghana)

ANTICIPATION[26]

Nana Adaku II, Omanhene° Akwasin, was celebrating the twentieth anniversary of his accession to the stool° of Akwasin.° The capital, Nkwabi, was thronged with people from the outlying towns and villages.

It was in the height of the cocoa season, money was circulating freely and farmers were spending to their hearts' content. Friends who had not seen one another for a long time were renewing their friendship. They called with gifts of gin, champagne or whiskey, recalled old days with gusto and before departing imbibed most of the drinks they brought as gifts. No one cared, everyone was happy. Few could be seen in European attire; nearly all were in Gold Coast costume. The men had tokota sandals on their feet, and rich multi-colored velvet and gorgeous, hand-woven kente° cloths nicely wrapped round their bodies. The women, with golden ear-rings dangling, with golden chains and bracelets,° looked dignified in their colorful native attire.

The state drums were beating paeans of joy.

It was four o'clock in the afternoon and people were walking to

---

Omanhene: the male ruler of the Akan state, appointed originally by *Ohemmaa* or the Queen Mother.

stool: among the Akan peoples, the stool contained the spirit of its owner, or was the material symbol of the State. A stool of an Omanhene was usually of carved wood covered with gold leaf or silver leaf.

Akwasin: this main character represents the author's brother-in-law, Nana Ofori Atta I of Kibi, King of Abuakwa, elder brother to Joseph Boakye Danquah.

kente: the toga-like attire of the Akan peoples.

golden chains and bracelets: Gold was the sacred and favorite metal of the Ashante.

the state park where the Odwira° was to be staged. Enclosures of palm leaves decorated the grounds.

The Omanhene arrived in a palanquin under a brightly-patterned state umbrella, a golden crown on his head, his kente studded with tiny golden beads, rows upon rows of golden necklaces piled high on his chest. He wore bracelets of gold from the wrists right up to the elbows. He held in his right hand a decorated elephant tail which he waved to his enthusiastic, cheering people. In front of him sat his "soul,"° a young boy of twelve, holding the sword of office.

After the Omanhene came the Adontehene,° the next in importance. He was resplendent in rich green and red velvet cloth; his head band was studded with golden bars. Other chiefs came one after the other under their brightly-colored state umbrellas. The procession was long. The crowd raised cheers as each palanquin was lowered, and the drums went on beating resounding joys of jubilation. The Omanhene took his seat on the dais with the Elders. The District Commissioner, Captain Hobbs, was near him. Sasa,° the jester, looked ludicrous in his motley pair of trousers and his cap of monkey skin. He made faces at the Omanhene, he leered, did acrobatic stunts; the Omanhene could not laugh; it was against custom for the great Chief to be moved to laughter in public.

The state park presented a scene of barbaric splendor. Chiefs and their retinue sat on native stools under state umbrellas of diverse colors. The golden linguist° staves of office gleamed in the sunlight. The women, like tropical butterflies, looked charming in

Odwira: "cleansing" or "purification," a festival occurring at the end of the Akan year and celebrating, usually, the yam harvest. It was held most often in October (Akan: *Berampono*) in the southern Akan States.

"soul": This refers to the Omanhene's *okrafo,* "soul-bearer," so called because the Omanhene had projected his actual soul (*kra*) to a person he loved dearly. The *okrafo* became an extremely sacred person in the State; later, *okrafo* became a court title among the Ashante.

Adontehene: the commander of the main body of the army in the Ashante state.

Sasa: Sasa here is a proper name. It refers to a spirit, usually of a special animal (certain members of the antelope family) which must be given funeral rites and funeral laments if killed.

linguist: the *Okyeame* (pronounced *Awch-yah-meh*), or spokesman for the Omanhene, who carried a long staff of office.

their multi-colored brocaded silk, kente and velvet, and the
Oduku headdress, black and shiny, studded with long golden pins
and slides. Young men paraded the grounds, their flowing cloths
trailing behind them, their silken plaited headbands glittering in
the sun.

The drums beat on.

The women are going to perform the celebrated Adowa
dance.° The decorated calabashes make rhythm. The women run
a few steps, move slowly sideways and sway their shoulders. One
dancer looks particularly enchanting in her green, blue and red
square kente, moving with the simple, charming grace of a wild
woodland creature; the Chief is stirred, and throws a handful of
loose cash into the crowd of dancers. She smiles as the coins fall
on her and tinkle to the ground. There is a rush. She makes no
sign but keeps on dancing.

The Omanhene turns to his trusted linguist:

"Who is that beautiful dancer?"

"I am sorry, I do not know her."

"I must have her as a wife."

Nana Adaku II was fifty-five and he had already forty wives,
but a new beauty gave him the same new thrill as it did the man
who is blessed—or cursed—with only one better half. Desire again
burned fiercely in his veins; he was bored with his forty wives. He
usually got so mixed up among them that lately he kept calling
them by the wrong names. His new wife cried bitterly when he
called her Oda, the name of an old, ugly wife.

"This dancer is totally different," thought the Chief; "she will
be a joy to the palace." He turned round to the linguist:

"I will pay one hundred pounds for her."

"She might already be married, Nana."°

"I shall pay the husband any moneys he demands."

The linguist knew his Omanhene: when he desired a woman
he usually had his way.

"Get fifty pounds from the chief treasurer, find the relatives,

Adowa dance: This is the special dance at *Odwira* and *Adae* ceremonies,
and at royal funerals. It is performed usually by women under the leadership of the *Adowahemmaa,* a titled elder woman.

Nana: "Grandfather," or even "Father," as to a monarch and head of
the State.

give them the money and when she is in my palace tonight I shall give her the balance of fifty pounds.° Give the linguist staff to Kojo and begin your investigations now."

Nana Adaku II was a fast worker. He was like men all over the world when they are stirred by feminine charm: a shapely leg, the flash of an eye, the quiver of a nostril, the timbre of a voice, and the male species becomes frenzy personified. Many men go through this sort of mania until they reach their dotage. The cynics among them treat women with a little flattery, bland tolerance, and take fine care not to become seriously entangled for life. Women, on the other hand, use quite a lot of common sense: they are not particularly thrilled by the physical charms of a man; if his pockets are heavy and his income sure, he is a good matrimonial risk. But there is evolving a new type of hardheaded modern woman who insists on the perfect lover as well as an income and other necessaries, or stays forever from the unbliss of marriage.

By 6 P.M. Nana Adaku II was getting bored with the whole assembly and very glad to get into his palanquin. The state umbrellas danced, the chiefs sat again in their palanquins, the crowd cheered wildly, the drums beat. Soon the shadows of evening fell and the enclosures of palm leaves in the state park stood empty and deserted.

The Omanhene had taken his bath after dusk and changed into a gold and green brocaded cloth. Two male servants stood on either side and fanned him with large ostrich feathsrs as he reclined on a velvet-cushioned settee in his private sitting room. An envelope containing fifty golden sovereigns was near him. He knew his linguist as a man of tact and diplomacy and he was sure that night would bring him a wife to help him celebrate the anniversary of his accession to the Akwasin Stool.

He must have dozed. When he woke up the young woman was kneeling by his feet. He raised her onto the settee.

"Were you pleased to come?"

"I was pleased to do Nana's bidding."

"Good girl. What is your name?"

---

fifty pounds: about $140.00.

"Effua, my lord and master."

"It is a beautiful name, and you are a beautiful woman, too. Here are fifty gold sovereigns, the balance of the marriage dowry. We will marry privately tonight and do the necessary custom° afterward." Nana Adaku II is not the first man to use this technique. Civilized, semi-civilized, and primitive men all over the world have said the very same thing in nearly the same words.

"I shall give the money to my mother," said the sensible girl. "She is in the corridor. May I?" The Chief nodded assent.

Effua returned.

"Nana, my mother and other relatives want to thank you for the hundred pounds."

"There is no need, my beauty," and he played with the ivory beads lying so snugly on her bosom.

"They think you must have noticed some extraordinary charm in me for you to have spent so much money," she smiled shyly at the Omanhene.

"But, my dear, you are charming. Haven't they eyes?"

"But, Nana, I cannot understand it myself."

"You cannot, you modest woman? Look at yourself in that long mirror over there."

The girl smiled mischievously, went to the mirror, looked at herself. She came back and sat on the settee and leaned her head on his bosom.

"You are a lovely girl, Effua." He caressed her shiny black hair, so artistically plaited.

"But, my master, I have always been like this, haven't I?"

"I suppose so, beautiful, but I only saw you today."

"You only saw me today?"

"Today."

"Have you forgotten?"

"Forgotten what, my love?"

"You paid fifty pounds . . . and married me two years ago."[28]

necessary custom: quite a bit more elaborate than the Omanhene's payment here of the *ayeyode* or gift presentation and the *afa-yide* or consolation fee, which ironically is paid *only* on the occasion of a girl's *first* marriage. (27)

THREE

MIDDLE PASSAGE

A kiSwahili proverb says:

Ungeenda juu, Kiboko, makazi yako ni pwani.
Although you go upcountry, Hippopotamus, your real home is at
the coast.

Perhaps this is a useful comment on the proper habitat and role
of the hippopotamus (or of the King, the possessor of the slave-
whip, the *kiboko* made of hippo hide), and perhaps it is simply
pessimistic. But, more deeply, the proverb says that the voyager
never really loses his roots and the conditioning of his childhood,
no matter how far he might travel. It is an admonition to the
wanderer that he remember and, presumably, respect his traditions and his source, and as such it stresses the old and time-
tested (or time-worn), the status quo, even though it recognizes
the fact that people move into stages of the new and the different.
The proverb also suggests that social and cultural change involv-
ing new automatic responses from the individual is well-nigh impossible, so that he who attempts to change himself is a fool. As
the hippo does not change essentially by going upcountry, neither
does the villager experience utter newness in learning matters
European, although outwardly he might appear to be quite
different from what he was.

Mphahlele has said that the white world

. . . still battles for the soul of the African. I think the educated black man, frustrations notwithstanding, will yet emerge tough as tried metal from all this debris of colonial systems the West has thought fit to dump in Africa. How much of all this the African will find of some use in the scrapyard, and how much of his past, is still a big question. . . . The white man has detribalized me. He had better go the whole hog. He must know that I'm the personification of the African paradox, detribalized, Westernized, but still African—minus the conflicts.[1]

Although Mphahele's arguments are particularly germane to the South African situation, they nonetheless apply generally. What links Africans together at the present time, what helps to overcome at least part of their struggle amongst themselves in ideology if not in politics, is the commonalty of historical experience, the sharing of similar goals, and the same general racial background. This is as it has always been, although the awareness of common experience has increased with the spread of education, and an increasing knowledge of the historical situation (slavery plus colonialism plus missionary education) has added details which were not and could not have been recognized in a traditionally African cultural evolution. This has aroused in many educated Africans a self-consciousness, a sense of humiliation, and a feeling of reaction against those who "wronged" Africa and Africans, as well as a sense of social disorganization and personality disorientation because of the conflict of cultures. For conflicts exist, despite the confident words of Mphahlele.

A number of African writers describe the combination of being African within (like Senghor in "Totem") and partly European on the outside, and they express the conflicts aroused by such awareness. Mabel Joloaso Segun, for example, wrote in "Conflict":

> Here we stand
> Infants overblown,
> poised between two civilisations,
> finding the balance irksome,
> itching for something to happen,
> to tip us one way or the other,

> groping in the dark for a helping hand
> and finding none.
> I'm tired, O my God, I'm tired
> I'm tired of hanging in the middle way—
> but where can I go?[2]

This poet suggests the forlorn case of many educated Africans: she feels like an "infant" waiting for a guide out of the darkness, a guide which obviously the colonial power with its "civilizing mission" could not furnish. This sense of confusion because of cultural change, of belonging neither to coast nor to upcountry, constitutes a literary "middle passage" which thus far has remained unresolved and which itself is a subject intriguing to many writers. Interest in change becomes almost compulsive, the writer knowing that something has happened to Africa and to Africans, but asking constantly: *What was it? How did it happen? Why must it be so?* and *What does it mean?*

David Rubadiri

(Malawi)

STANLEY MEETS MUTESA°

> Such a time of it they had
> The heat of the day
> The chill of the night
> And the mosquitoes
> That day and night   5

Stanley Meets Mutesa: Henry Morton Stanley, journalist and explorer, on April 4, 1875, arrived at Rubaga, the capital of the Baganda in present-day Uganda, whose king or *Kabaka* was Mutesa I. (3)

Trailed the march bound for a kingdom.°
The thin weary line of porters
With tattered dirty rags
To cover their backs
The battered bulky chests   10
Perched on sweating shaven heads;
The sun fierce and scorching
Its rise their hope
And its fall their rest;
Sweat dripped off their bodies   15
Whilst clouds of flies
Clung in thick clumps
On their sweat-scented backs,
Such was the march
And the hot season just breaking   20
Each day a weary pony° dropped
Left for the vultures on the plains,
Each afternoon a human skeleton collapsed°
Left for the hyenas on the plains,
But the march trudged on   25
Its khaki leader in front

bound for a kingdom: this has a double meaning. Concretely it refers to the safari bound for the Kingdom of Buganda. But it refers also to something like the "kingdom of God," which Stanley wished to bring to the Baganda. Since 1848, Arab and Swahili-speaking traders had been visiting Buganda from Zanzibar, and when Stanley visited the Kingdom, Mutesa was nominally Muslim. Capt. J. H. Speke, the first European explorer to visit the Baganda, had suggested that missionaries be sent to Mutesa, an idea repeated much more emphatically by Stanley.

pony: actually donkeys were brought along as riding animals for the Europeans, Stanley, Edward and Francis Pocock, and Frederick Barker, and few donkeys were lost on the safari.

Each afternoon a human skeleton collapsed: This is exaggerated, although the safari nevertheless did encounter difficulties. Of 356 porters hired at Zanzibar, 247 remained when the safari reached Ituru, but of those lost some eighty-nine or ninety had deserted.

He the spirit that inspired
He the beacon of hope.°

Then came the afternoon of a long march
A hot and hungry march   30
The Nile and the Nyanza°
Like a grown tadpole
Lay azure
Across the green countryside,
They had arrived in the promised land.   35

The march leapt on
Chaunting, panting
Like young gazelles to a waterhole.
Hearts beat faster
Loads felt lighter   40
Cool soft water
Lapt their sore feet,
No more
The dread of hungry hyenas
Or the burning heat of sand on feet   45
Only tales of valour,
Song, laughter and dance
When at Mutesa's court
In the evening
Fires are lit.   50

The village looks on behind banana groves
Children peer with round eyes behind reed fences,

beacon of hope: that is, always confident that the safari would reach its objective. This is ironic insofar as Stanley was a notorious driver of his men, and his "inspiring" of them was too often through brutality and force rather than behaviour in the least degree spiritual or uplifting. As Stanley said in his *Autobiography,* "The selfish and wooden-headed world requires mastering, as well as loving charity." (4)

Nyanza: actually Lake Victoria, source of the White Nile. This is an erroneous picture of events: Stanley sailed to Baganda in a boat from the southeast side of Lake Victoria.

That was the welcome—
No women to wail a song
Or drums to greet the white ambassador,°   55
Only a few silent nods
From a few aged faces
Only a rumbling peal of drums
To summon Mutesa's court to parley:
You see, there were rumours   60
Tales and rumours at court
Rumours and tales round the countryside:
That was expected
Mutesa was worried.°

The reed gate is flung open   65
The crowd watches in silence
But only a moment's silence
A silence of assessment—
The tall dark tyrant steps forward
He towers over the thin bearded whiteman   70
Then grabbing his lean white hand
Manages to whisper
"Mtu Mweupe karibu"°
White man you are welcome
The gate of reeds closes behind them   75
And the west is let in.°

ambassador: Stanley figuratively was the "ambassador" of the white people or Europeans, but not literally an ambassador for a government. He was
seeking the source of the Nile.

Mutesa was worried: this is somewhat exaggerated, for Mutesa was quite
confident of himself and knew well ahead of time that Stanley's safari was
no invading army. Stanley said that the Kabaka "soon heard of the presence
of my boat on the lake, and despatched a flotilla to meet me." The leader
of the flotilla took Stanley to Usavara, where thousands of people met him,
and he was interrogated by officials for over an hour before he was permitted
to see Mutesa. (5)

"Mtu Mweupe karibu": "A white person is nearby," literally, from Swahili:
mtu = person; *mweupe* = white; *karibu* = near.

the west is let in: Stanley's visit to Mutesa marked the beginning of
European intrusion among the Baganda. In 1877, agents of the Church
Missionary Society arrived in Uganda, and in 1879 the French Roman
Catholic White Fathers arrived.

CRITICAL EXERCISE II

"Stanley Meets Mutesa"

The version of this poem which we have used is the author's latest, revised in 1964 for inclusion in D. Cook's anthology of East African writings. In this critical exercise, the author's additions, deletions, and substitutions are described. In each instance, determine the function and the significance of the alteration in relation to the passage in which it occurs and to the poem as a whole, or to its meaning in relation to matters extraneous to the actual story.

[Lines 4–6] *Substitution.* Original reading:
> And the mosquitoes that followed.
> Such was the time and
> They bound for a kingdom.

[Line 7] *Substitution.* Original "carriers" changed to "porters."

[Lines 11–18]. *Substitution.* Original reading:
> That kept on falling off their shaven heads.
> Their tempers high and hot
> The sun fierce and scorching
> With it rose their spirits
> With its fall their hopes
> As each day sweated their bodies dry and
> Flies clung in clumps on their sweat-scented backs.

[Line 24] *Substitution:* "hyenas" for original "Masai."

[Line 28] *Substitution:* "beacon" for original "light."

[Line 29] *Substitution:* "long" for original "hungry."

[Line 30] *Deletion:* "it was" deleted from original
> A hot and hungry march it was;

[Line 32] *Substitution:* Original reading:
> Lay like two twins
> Azure across the green countryside.

[Line 35] *Addition:* entire line added.

[Line 37] *Addition:* "panting" added. Original reading:
> The march leapt on chaunting

[Lines 41–42] *Substitutions:*   Original reading:
      As the cool water lapt their sore soft feet.
[Line 45] *Addition:*   entire line added.
[Line 47] *Addition:*   entire lined added.
[After line 50] *Deletion:*
      No more the burning heat of the day
      But song, laughter and dance.
[Line 52] *Addition:*   "with round eyes."
[Line 54] *Substitutions* and *deletions:* Original reading:
      No singing women to chaunt a welcome.
[Line 57] *Addition:*   "a few."
[Lines 60–64] *Substitution:*   Passage was one line in original.
   Original reading:
      For the country was not sure.
[Line 69] *Substitution:*   "dark tyrant" for original "black king."

Mbelle Sonne Dipoko
(Cameroon)

TO PRE-COLONIAL AFRICA[6]

So did the waves arrive,
swimming in like hump-backed divers
with their finds from faraway seas.

Glittering, their liquid lustre gave the illusion of pearls,
as shorewards they shoved up mighty canoes
that looked like the carcasses of drifting whales.

Our sight misled us
when the sun's glint on the spear's blade
passed for lightning,
and the gunfire of conquest the thunderbolt that razed the forest.

So did our days change their robes
from the hide of leopard skin
to prints of false lions
that fall in tatters
like the wings of a whipped butterfly.

Lenrie Peter
(Gambia)

PARACHUTE[7]

Parachute men say
The first jump
Takes the breath away;
Feet in the air disturbs
Till you get used to it.

Solid ground
Is now where you left it.
As you plunge down
—Perhaps head first—
As you listen to
Your arteries talking,
You learn to sustain hope.

Suddenly you are only
Holding an open umbrella
In a windy place.
As the warm earth
Reaches out to you,
Reassures you
The vibrating interim is over,

You try to land
Where green grass yields,
And carry your pack
Across the fields.

The violent arrival
Puts out the joint.
Earth has nowhere to go:
You are at the starting point;

Jumping across worlds
In condensed time—
After the awkward fall,
We are always at the starting point.

HOMECOMING[8]

The present reigned supreme
  Like the shallow floods over the gutters
Over the raw paths where we had been,
  The house with the shutters.

Too strange the sudden change
  Of the times we buried when we left
The times before we had properly arranged
  The memoirs that we kept.°

Our sapless roots have fed
  The wind-swept seedlings of another age.
Luxuriant weeds have grown where we led
  The Virgins to the water's edge.°

There at the edge of the town
  Just by the burial ground
Stands the house without a shadow°
  Lived in by new skeletons.

That is all that is left
  To greet us on the home coming
After we have paced the world
  And longed for returning.

Too strange . . . that we kept: reference to the eagerness for change and the consequent carelessness about previous cultural behavior—that which is to be lost through social change; and the reversal of this attitude when one is abroad and able to view one's past culture from a different perspective, then returns home and perceives the changes.

Luxuriant weeds . . . to the water's edge: suggesting leading the innocents to a sacrificial offering; change has resulted in loss of the good and the growth of the unwanted, the "weeds."

shadow: soul, the vital spirit.

Emile Ologoudou
(Dahomey)

LA FLAMBEE[9]

Je revins
comme
l'oiseau
dans
les
premiers frissons du soir;
dans
les rues
on jetait des tracts:
dernier cri des hommes;
les journaux
avaient paru
pour une dernière fois,
feuilles frémissantes
sur la houle des passions,
tangible était alors
le néant de tout ce que nous désirâmes!

THE BLAZE

I returned
like
the bird
in
the
first chill of evening;
in
the streets
they were throwing pamphlets:
the last word of mankind;
the newspapers
had appeared
for the last time,
leaves rustling
on the swell of passions,
tangible then was
the nothingness of all that we desired.

Kwesi Brew
(Ghana)

A PLEA FOR MERCY[10]

We have come to your shrine to worship—
We, the sons of the land.°
The naked cowherd has brought
The cows safely home,
And stands silent with his bamboo flute
Wiping the rain from his brow.
As the birds brood in their nests
Awaiting the dawn with unsung melodies,
The shadows crowd on the shores
Pressing their lips against the bosom of the sea;°
The peasants home from their labours
Sit by their log fires
Telling tales of long ago.
Why should we, the sons of the land,
Plead unheeded before your shrine,
When our hearts are full of song
And our lips tremble with sadness?
The little firefly vies with the star,
The log fire with the sun°

We have come . . . sons of the land: This is a poem of double intent, that which is "worshipped" being a tutelary spirit on one hand and, on the other, the European culture to which the African was forced to conform and show respect. "A plea for mercy" accordingly indicates that the treatment of the earth-born has been too harsh, and the poet in successive images develops the simplicity of the African supplicant before the spiritual being, all of which is ironic in its second aspect, for the African need "plead" for nothing from strangers on his home soil.

shadows . . . sea: suggesting the departed dead and, by extension, the millions of slaves taken from the Guinea Coast of West Africa.

sun: in Twi this is *Owia,* the symbol of *'Nyame,* the High God, whose spirit-power is reflected and symbolized by lesser sources of light.

The water in the calabash°
With the mighty Volta.°
But we have come in tattered penury
Begging at the door of a Master.

Gabriel Okara
(Nigeria)

PIANO AND DRUMS[11]

When at break of day at a riverside
I hear jungle drums telegraphing
the mystic rhythm, urgent, raw
like bleeding flesh, speaking of
primal youth and the beginning,
I see the panther ready to pounce,
the leopard snarling about to leap
and the hunters crouch with spears poised;

And my blood ripples, turns torrent,
topples the years and at once I'm
in my mother's lap a suckling;
at once I'm walking simple
paths with no innovations,
rugged, fashioned with the naked
warmth of hurrying feet and groping hearts
in green leaves and wild flowers pulsing.°

calabash: a long-necked gourd.
Volta: the major river coursing southeastwards through Ghana.
When at break of day . . . wild flowers pulsing: That is, the sound of
drums arouses memories of his (and Africa's) "childhood," before he was
aware of the Europeanism induced by the British colonialists. This motif of
a "simple" African past is an aspect of *négritude* which is not very valid:
Africans were no more simple or innocent than any other peoples on the
earth.

Then I hear a wailing piano
solo speaking of complex ways°
in tear-furrowed concerto;
of far-away lands
and new horizons with
coaxing diminuendo, counterpoint,
crescendo. But lost in the labyrinth
of its complexities, it ends in the middle
of a phrase at a daggerpoint.°

And I lost in the morning mist
of an age at a riverside keep
wandering in the mystic rhythm
of jungle drums and the concerto.

Christopher Okigbo
(Nigeria)

LUSTRA,° Part IV of
HEAVENSGATE

(i)

So would I to the hills again,
so would I
to where springs the fountain,
there to draw from;

complex ways: that is, the ways of the Europeans.
   it ends . . . at a daggerpoint: The suggestion here is that colonialism, despite its complexities (good and bad), was not a completing process of socio-cultural and personal change, but a killing process which left the African at a halfway point between worlds and cultures.
   Lustra: At one level the entire poem is a mythical projection of a personal experience of the poet; *Lustra* concerns the poet's move to purify himself after profound experiences which leave a sense of taint. (12)

and to hilltop clamber,
body and soul
whitewashed in the moondew,
there to see from.

So would I from my eye the mist,
so would I
thro moonmist to hilltop
there for the cleansing.

Here is a new laid egg,
here a white hen at midterm.

(ii)

Thundering drums and cannons°
in palm grove:
the spirit is in ascent.

I have visited,
on palm bean imprinted
my pentagon°—

I have visited, the prodigal°. . .

In palm grove,
long drums and cannons:
the spirit in the ascent.

---

drums and cannons: the sounds associated with a traditional West African (particularly Igbo) religious festival.

pentagon: five-angled plane figure, here probably used like *pentagram*, suggesting a personal magical talisman, symbol, and print.

prodigal: This return to the village during a religious festival to make a sacrifice (*new laid egg* and *white hen*) suggests the previous separation of the poet from his sources, and emphasizes his desire to be "purified" through a return to those sources.

(iii)

And the flower weeps
　　unbruised,
Lacrimae Christi,

for him who was silenced;

　　whose advent
dumb bells in the dim light celebrate
　　with wine song:

Messiah will come again,
After the argument in heaven;
Messiah will come again,
Lumen mundi . . .

Fingers of penitence
bring
to a palm grove
vegetable offering
with five
fingers of chalk.°

And the flower weeps . . . fingers of chalk: "The third strophe of *Lustra,*
if we ignore its weeping flower sentimentalism and the 'Lacrimae Christi,'
is a fine expression of poetic optimism in terms of the Christian Messianic
hope. It is, above all, a prayer: the poet has done his *confiteor deo* and is
penitent at heart." (13)

Efua Sutherland

(Ghana)

NEW LIFE AT KYEREFASO°

Shall we say,
Shall we put it this way,

Shall we say that the maid of Kyerefaso, Foruwa,° daughter of
the Queen Mother,° was as a young deer, graceful in limb? Such
was she, with head held high, eyes soft and wide with wonder.
And she was light of foot, light in all her moving.

Stepping springily along the water path like a deer that had
strayed from the thicket, springily stepping along the water path,
she was a picture to give the eye a feast. And nobody passed her
by but turned to look at her again.

Those of her village said that her voice in speech was like the
murmur of a river quietly flowing beneath shadows of bamboo
leaves. They said her smile would sometimes blossom like a lily
on her lips and sometimes rise like sunrise.

The butterflies do not fly away from the flowers, they draw
near. Foruwa was the flower of her village.

So shall we say,
Shall we put it this way,

Kyerefaso: pronounced *chair-ay-fáh-so*, a difficult crossing over a perilous
stream; related to *kyere,* to show, instruct, relate. (14)

Foruwa: (*Foriwa*) "Deer Woman," a proper name for a princess of the
Akan royal family.

Queen Mother: The *Ohemmaa* or female king among the Ashante was
considered to be the daughter of the Moon, the owner of the State. The
Moon (*Amowia,* "Giver of the Sun") was the female aspect of *'Nyame,* the
High God, and gave birth to the Sun (*Owia*), who is male. The King or
Omanhene, representing the Sun, is the ruler of the State, which is
"owned" by the Queen Mother. Queen Mothers were responsible for inno-
vation, progress, morality of youth, and were the patronesses of agriculture.
(15)

That all the village butterflies, the men, tried to draw near her
at every turn, crossed and crossed her path? Men said of her, "She
shall be my wife, and mine, and mine and mine."

But suns rose and set, moons silvered and died and as the days
passed Foruwa grew more lovesome, yet she became no one's
wife. She smiled at the butterflies and waved her hand lightly to
greet them as she went swiftly about her daily work:

> "Morning, Kweku
> Morning, Kwesi
> Morning, Kodwo"

But that was all.

And so they said, even while their hearts thumped for her:

> "Proud!
> Foruwa is proud . . . and very strange."

And so the men when they gathered would say:

"There goes a strange girl. She is not just stiff-in-the-neck
proud, not just breasts-stuck-out, I-am-the-only-girl-in-the-village
proud. What kind of pride is hers?"

The end of the year came round again, bringing the season of
festivals. For the gathering in of corn, yams and cocoa there were
harvest celebrations. There were bride-meetings, too. And it came
to the time when the *Asafo*° companies should hold their festival.
The village was full of manly sounds, loud musketry and swelling
choruses.

The pathfinding, path-clearing ceremony came to an end. The
Asafo marched on toward the Queen Mother's house, the women
fussing round them, prancing round them, spreading their cloths
in their way.

Asafo: a "society" or "company," usually of dancers and celebrants of
sacred festivals, especially the path-clearing festival. *Asafo* formerly were
the military companies and executive body of the central authority of the
Akan State. In the past, young men trained for war in the *asafo* companies;
in peacetime, they performed municipal work, built markets, collected
taxes, were responsible for law and order. *Asafo* companies were organized
according to *ntoro* (see below) rather than age-groups.

"*Osee!*"° rang the cry. "*Osee!*" to the manly men of old. They crouched like leopards upon the branches.

> Before the drums beat
> Before the danger drums beat, beware!
> Before the horns moaned
> Before the wailing horns moaned, beware!

They were upright, they sprang. They sprang. They sprang upon the enemy. But now, blood no more! No more thundershot on thundershot.

But still we are the leopards on the branches. We are those who roar and cannot be answered back. Beware, we are they who cannot be answered back.

There was excitement outside the Queen Mother's courtyard gate.

"Gently, gently," warned the *Asafo* leader. "Here comes the Queen Mother.

> Spread skins of the gentle sheep in her way.
> Lightly, lightly walks our Mother Queen.°
> Shower her with silver,
> Shower her with silver for she is peace."

And the Queen Mother stood there, tall, beautiful, before the men and there was silence.

"What news, what news do you bring?" she quietly asked.

"We come with dusty brows from our pathfinding, Mother. We come with tired, thorn-pricked feet. We come to bathe in the

Osee!: a title given, especially to men of the Bosommuru *ntoro* (spirit-group), considered the first *ntoro* given to mankind. The Bosommuru is a river in Akyem and was nicknamed *Asafodie,* suggesting the looting by the king of that *ntoro.* Among totem animals of this spirit-group were the leopard and the python, both of which are referred to in this story.

Mother Queen: the Queen Mother traditionally was considered (or desired) to be calm and peaceful, her body delicately beautiful. Because she is the Moon on Earth, silver is her metal and symbolic color. As the exponent of all feminine matters, she cares for women, birth, marriage, family life, agriculture, peace and gentleness, and beauty.

coolness of your peaceful stream. We come to offer our manliness to new life."°

The Queen Mother stood there, tall and beautiful and quiet. Her fanbearers stood by her and all the women clustered near. One by one the men laid their guns at her feet and then she said:

"It is well. The gun is laid aside. The gun's rage is silenced in the stream. Let your weapons from now on be your minds and your hands' toil.°

Come, maidens, women all, join the men in dance for they offer themselves to new life."

There was one girl who did not dance.

"What, Foruwa!" urged the Queen Mother, "will you not dance? The men are tired of parading in the ashes of their grandfathers' glorious deeds. That should make you smile. They are tired of the empty croak: 'We are men, we are men.'

They are tired of sitting like vultures upon the rubbish heaps they have piled upon the half-built walls of their grandfathers. Smile, then, Foruwa, smile.

Their brows shall now indeed be dusty, their feet thorn-pricked, and 'I love my land' shall cease to be the empty croaking of a vulture upon the rubbish heap. Dance, Foruwa, Dance!"

Foruwa opened her lips and this was all she said: "Mother, I do not find him here."

"Who? Who do you not find here?"

"He with whom this new life shall be built. He is not here, Mother. These men's faces are empty; there is nothing in them, nothing at all."

"Alas, Foruwa, alas, alas! What will become of you, my daughter?"

"The day I find him, Mother, the day I find the man, I shall come running to you, and your worries will come to an end."

new life: that is, the "new life" of the forthcoming New Year, which follows the harvest festivals.

It is well . . . your hands' toil: ceremonial invocation following the war ceremonies. War was traditionally considered to be a calamity. During war, the Queen Mother and the royal wives (*mmaamu*) daily performed the *twe-mmommomme* rites of wailing and prayer for the restoration of normal life and peace.

"But, Foruwa, Foruwa," argued the Queen Mother, although in her heart she understood her daughter, "five years ago your rites were fulfilled. Where is the child of your womb? Your friend Maanan married. Your friend Esi married. Both had their rites° with you."

"Yes, Mother, they married and see how their steps once lively now drag in the dust. The sparkle has died out of their eyes. Their husbands drink palm wine the day long under the mango trees, drink palm wine and push counters across the draught-boards all the day, and are they not already looking for other wives? Mother, the man I say is not here."

This conversation had been overheard by one of the men and soon others heard what Foruwa had said. That evening there was heard a new song in the village.

> There was a woman long ago,
> Tell that maid, tell that maid,
> There was a woman long ago,
> She would not marry Kwesi,
> She would not marry Kwaw,
> She would not, would not, would not.
> One day she came home with hurrying feet,
> I've found the man, the man, the man,
> Tell that maid, tell that maid,
> Her man looked like a chief,
> Tell that maid, tell that maid
> Her man looked like a chief
> Most splendid to see,
> But he turned into a python,
> He turned into a python°
> And swallowed her up.

rites: the *Beragoro* puberty rite, a festival lasting about seven days to celebrate the change of a girl into a marriageable woman. (16)

python: one Akan origin myth tells of the python (*onini*) which came from Nyame, the High God, and lived in the sacred Bosommuru River. This python taught the first people how to procreate their own species, so people of the Bosommuru *ntoro* (spirit-group) revere pythons. The implica-

From that time onward there were some in the village who
turned their backs on Foruwa when she passed.

> Shall we say,
> Shall we put it this way,

Shall we say that a day came when Foruwa with hurrying feet
came running to her mother? She burst through the courtyard
gate; and there she stood in the courtyard, joy all over. And a
stranger walked in after her and stood in the courtyard beside
her, stood tall and strong as a pillar.° Foruwa said to the aston-
ished Queen Mother:

"Here he is, Mother, here is the man."

The Queen Mother took a slow look at the stranger standing
there strong as a forest tree,° and she said:

"You carry the light of wisdom° on your face, my son. Greetings, you are welcome. But who are you, my son?"

"Greetings, Mother," replied the stranger quietly. "I am a worker. My hands are all I have to offer your daughter, for they are all
my riches. I have traveled to see how men work in other lands. I
have that knowledge and my strength. That is all my story."

> Shall we say,
> Shall we put it this way,

strange as the story is, that Foruwa was given in marriage to the
stranger.

---

tion here is that Foruwa seeks a man with special qualities, an ideal, but
when she encounters him he will be not actually a man nor a god, but
rather a great snake who will take her into his body as she had hoped to
take the great fertility spirit into hers. In simple words, they are saying
that Foruwa is foolish to expect a man to be able to have the powers of
sexual potency and love which a spirit possesses, but they miss the point
of her argument: she is not thinking solely of sex nor of love, but of new
growth and development from the older ways to a newer and better society.

*tall and strong as a pillar, strong as a forest tree, carry the light of wis-
dom:* characteristics of the sacred python.

There was a rage in the village and many openly mocked, saying, "Now the proud ones eat the dust."

> Yet shall we say,
> Shall we put it this way,

that soon, quite soon, the people of Kyerefaso began to take notice of the stranger in quite a different way.

"Who," some said, "is this who has come among us? He who mingles sweat and song, he for whom toil is joy and life is full and abundant?"

"See," said others, "what a harvest the land yields under his ceaseless care."

"He has taken the earth and molded it into bricks. See what a home he has built, how it graces the village where it stands."

"Look at the craft of his fingers, baskets or *kente*,° stool or mat, the man makes them all."

"And our children swarm about him, gazing at him with wonder and delight."

Then it did not satisfy them any more to sit all day at their draughtboards under the mango trees.

"See what Foruwa's husband has done," they declared; "shall the sons of the land not do the same?"

And soon they began to seek out the stranger to talk with him. Soon they too were toiling, their fields began to yield as never before, and the women labored joyfully to bring in the harvest. A new spirit stirred the village. As the carelessly built houses disappeared one by one, and new homes built after the fashion of the stranger's grew up, it seemed as if the village of Kyerefaso had been born afresh.

The people themselves became more alive and a new pride possessed them. They were no longer just grabbing from the land what they desired for their stomachs' present hunger and for their present comfort. They were looking at the land with new eyes, feeling it in their blood, and thoughtfully building a permanent and beautiful place for themselves and their children.

"*Osee!*" It was festival-time again. "*Osee!*" Blood no more. Our

---

kente: the traditional cloth of the Akan-peoples, worn usually much like a Roman toga.

fathers found for us the paths. We are the roadmakers. They bought for us the land with their blood. We shall build it with our strength. We shall create it with our minds.

Following the men were the women and children. On their heads they carried every kind of produce that the land had yielded and crafts that their fingers had created. Green plantains and yellow bananas were carried by the bunch in large white wooden trays. Garden eggs,° tomatoes, red oil-palm nuts warmed by the sun were piled high in black earthen vessels. Oranges, yams,° maize filled shining brass trays and golden calabashes. Here and there were children proudly carrying colorful mats, baskets and toys which they themselves had made.

The Queen Mother watched the procession gathering on the new village playground now richly green from recent rains. She watched the people palpitating in a massive dance toward her where she stood with her fanbearers outside the royal house. She caught sight of Foruwa. Her load of charcoal in a large brass tray which she had adorned with red hibiscus danced with her body. Happiness filled the Queen Mother when she saw her daughter thus.

Then she caught sight of Foruwa's husband. He was carrying a white lamb° in his arms, and he was singing happily with the men. She looked on him with pride. The procession had approached the royal house.

"See!" rang the cry of the *Asafo* leader. "See how the best in all the land stands. See how she stands waiting, our Queen Mother. Waiting to wash the dust from our brow in the coolness of her peaceful stream. Spread skins of the gentle sheep in her way, gently, gently. Spread the yield of the land before her. Spread the craft of your hands before her, gently, gently.

Lightly, lightly walks our Queen Mother, for she is peace."

garden eggs: eggplant.
yams: Yams are not sweet potatoes but very large tubers which are one of the staple foods of West Africa.
white lamb: suggesting the white sheep which is used in major ancestral sacrifices among the Akan peoples.

Abioseh Nicol

(*Sierra Leone*)

THE DEVIL AT YOLAHUN
BRIDGE[17]

[1]Sanderson twirled his fountain-pen slowly round between the
fingers of one hand and drummed with the other on the desk be-
fore him. His eyes wandered to the distant green hills of
Kissiland° that marked the boundary between his district and the
next. He looked again at the form in front of him, printed on
Crown Agents' paper, and read it to himself for the tenth time.
"District Officer's Annual Report West African Colonial service
(Confidential)." The blank space below looked wider than ever.
Since McPherson, his Senior District Officer,° had gone home on
leave, he had kept postponing writing it. He had received a gen-
tle reminder from Headquarters' Secretariat a few days ago. He
felt he really must get down to it this afternoon.

[2]"Momoh!" he shouted. The young West African clerk came
out of the adjoining office.

[3]"Bring me all the Annual Reports you can lay your hands
on."

[4]"There are about fifty, sir," Momoh said, with some trepida-
tion, "but I can bring them all if you want them," he added hastily.

[5]"Bring the past ten years, then."

[6]When the Reports arrived he glanced through them. He
could not believe that anyone bothered to read them. What
would happen, he wondered, if he sent, say, the 1936 Report ver-
batim with the name of a sub-chief altered here and the name of

---

Kissiland: The setting here is upcountry Sierra Leone, near the Liberian
and Guinean borders. Kissiland, "land of the Kissi," overlaps the borders. (18)
   District Officer: the English colonial officer in charge of an administrative
district.

a village there;° or, say, a blank form with some cryptic remark like "Confidentially (as requested) the Africans have not changed much over the past year, but my fellow Europeans in the station have altered beyond belief. Pale hesitant inexperience, for example, in many cases has slowly but steadily given way to an incredible sunburnt competence."

[7]No, wit was not appreciated in high places. Could he start on an historical note? Or on an anthropological one? He decided against that. He had better stick to the familiar essential things° instead—new roads, the increase in trade, and the shift of the young from the village to the towns. Now to begin.

[8]"Excuse me, sir, I have not yet read out to you your appointments for the week." Momoh had appeared through the doorway and was standing in front of his desk.

[9]Sanderson suppressed a cry of impatience as he remembered that he had impressed on the clerk the importance every Monday morning of reminding him of his week's appointments. He could easily look them up himself, but he was trying to train Momoh to a high pitch of secretarial efficiency and, besides, it gave him a secret pleasure to pretend he was a vast administrator with numerous and important appointments. Momoh himself enjoyed the whole business intensely. He was a short, stocky youth with an alert face and boyish enthusiasm. His breast-pocket was always full of finely sharpened pencils and fountain-pens with different coloured ink.°

[10]"All right, Mr. Momoh, read them out."

What would happen . . . the name of a village there: a suggestion that colonial history remains very much the same. This furthermore suggests the colonialist falsification of African history and the development of false stereotypes about Africans and Negroes in general.

essential things: these "essential things" benefit the European but mean destruction of African traditions.

finely sharpened . . . coloured ink: a doubly-pointed image: to the usual European, the African's carrying a large number of pens to show he has "book" is ridiculous ostentatiousness, demonstrating the necessity of the European presence and its "civilizing mission"; to the African, it is simply the sign of one's tremendous pride in the possession of an ability which is good not merely because Europeans possess it but because it gives a man powers which in oral traditions he can never have.

[11]Momoh cleared his throat and read in a slightly sing-song voice. First, there was the annual inspection of the local secondary school. This was run by a nervous, leathery Irish priest and it had to be inspected every year before receiving the Government grant.° The inspection was a formality; for education officers came round from time to time during the year to see that the standards were maintained. Then there was the semi-official engagement, the following night, to lecture to the local African club.

[12]"Will you be there, Mr. Momoh?" Sanderson asked him, and at once regretted doing so lest his clerk should regard it as an official command.

[13]"Oh, yes, I shall be there, certainly, sir," Momoh said earnestly. "Things like that," he continued, "contribute to a man's uplift of the mind."

[14]"Well, I don't think this will," Sanderson remarked drily. "Still, continue." On Thursday there was to be the visit of the P. W. D.° Headquarters' engineer. Momoh had put into operation the simple procedure required—the rest-house to be got ready, the file for maintenance and repair of Government buildings to be gone through, and new requirements determined or invented; the Government lorry to be made ready in case that of the visiting engineer broke down on the way to Kissy or when returning from it. Sanderson looked through the list, initialled his approval, and asked Momoh the name of the engineer.

[15]"Mr. O. E. Hughes, sir," Momoh replied, with a slight smile which puzzled Sanderson at the time, but which he remembered afterwards. One of our Celtic brethren, Sanderson thought to himself. Aloud he said, "Right. Thank you very much," dismissing the clerk.

[16]"Now, about Hughes," he said, half aloud to himself.

[17]He could not place him; the name did not sound familiar. Must be new, he thought, and decided to look him up in the most

This was run . . . the Government grant: This suggests one of the many links between Christian missionaries and the colonialists.
P. W. D.: Public Works Department.

recent Senior Staff List. He ran his finger down the column of the
Senior P. W. D. Staff until he came to the Hs. Ah, there it was,
Hughes, Oluyemi Egbert. Oh, that was it, he was an African.
That was why he had never heard of him before. He whistled
softly to himself. By Jove, there might be complications. Usually, visiting members of the senior staff were taken to the European Club° in the evenings they spent in Kissy. He began to go
through the list of members in his mind one by one, trying to picture what their reactions would be to an African guest. Then he
wondered for a moment, a little shamefacedly, whether it was not
he who had started making excuses and finding reasons before
anything happened. But no, he decided, it was his duty to make
sure beforehand that there were no incidents, because if there
were he would have to make a report and probably bear the un-
spoken blame from Headquarters. He wondered whether it
would not be wiser to ask old Mr. Thomas, the Senior African
clerk, to entertain Hughes. At last he made a decision—he knew
what he would do. He would ask Hughes to dinner at his bungalow and he would ask Hounslow, the agent of a large firm, to
make up a third. Hounslow was English but born in East Africa,
son of a Kenya settler. He would show by that that he had no
prejudice. With the problem solved he turned to work with a
lighter heart but with a mild sense of dissatisfaction.

  [18]Hughes arrived promptly after lunch. He was a tall man,
probably in his early thirties, with a small military moustache,
close-cropped hair, very dark skin, and even, white teeth, but he
was completely unsmiling, and very polite. He shook hands with
Sanderson, accepted a seat, refused a cigarette, and got down to
business almost immediately. He listened to Sanderson carefully,
made notes, and asked one or two questions. Sanderson called to
Momoh to bring in the files. The clerk brought them in, put them
down, and was going away when Sanderson stopped him suddenly, remembering his smile of pride, and introduced him to
Hughes, who smiled pleasantly and briefly, shook hands and

  European Club: a club restricted to white Europeans, excluding Africans
especially.

turned back to the files. Sanderson found this politeness and efficiency uncomfortable at first, and tried to soften the atmosphere with a joke here and there. But Hughes either did not understand or pretended he did not understand. At the end of a couple of hours most of the work was finished, and Sanderson asked Hughes what he might be doing that night. Then, feeling that the African engineer might regard it as an unwarrantable intrusion into his privacy, he added hastily, "because I'd like you to come to dinner with me."

[19]"Yes, thank you, that will be nice," Hughes answered, putting away his notes and getting up. Sanderson was a little disappointed that he had not shown more enthusiasm. Hang it all, he thought, I don't suppose many Europeans would ask him as I have done, but perhaps he is political° and is accepting out of a sense of duty. Besides, he probably guesses why I asked him to come to the bungalow. "You are sure you can manage it, by the way," he said aloud.

[20]"Oh, yes, thank you, that will be very nice," Hughes repeated. "I'll go and see the other official buildings now, and will be with you this evening. Good-bye, then, for the present," he added. Sanderson walked with him to the door and they shook hands again while Momoh looked on admiringly.

[21]Hounslow appeared at eight at Sanderson's bungalow and mixed himself a drink. He shouted through the door to Sanderson who was changing in his bedroom.

[22]"Is anyone else coming to-night?"

[23]"Hughes, the new assistant engineer," Sanderson shouted back.

[24]"What's he like? Does he come from Swansea, look you, man?"

[25]"No, he is an African—Mr. Oluyemi Egbert Hughes."

[26]There was a pause.

[27]"Are you there, Hounslow?" Sanderson asked anxiously after a while.

---

political: in this context it means "inclined to maintain good relations with those of his professional class."

[28]"Yes, I am," Hounslow replied through the door. "Why didn't you tell me this before?"

[29]"Because, frankly, I wasn't sure whether you'd come."

[30]"Are you afraid, Sanderson, of facing an educated black alone?"

[31]"No, not at all, but I thought it would be good experience for you, my lad. It will correct some of your slave-driving ideas."

[32]"I am afraid he and I won't find much to say to each other," Hounslow replied. "Pity the club's closed to-night or I would have escaped before he arrived."

[33]Sanderson opened the door and entered the lounge-cum-dining-room. "The club's closed?"

[34]"Yes," Hounslow said, "a peculiar situation has arisen. We've run out of drinks through bad management," he added. "Why, were you going to take your Mr. Hughes there?"

[35]"The idea had occurred to me," Sanderson said, feeling relieved and somewhat guilty.

[36]"There's no end to what you wallahs° in the Administration will do to show your damned official broad-mindedness." He lit a cigarette and sank moodily into a chair. "I wish I had brought my black missus° with me," he added, smiling reminiscently. "She's a fine girl, you know," he continued enthusiastically. "Don't know what I'd do without her."

[37]"No, you certainly aren't bringing her: Mr. Hughes looks very respectable. And you're going to behave nicely to him, too."

[38]"Yes, teacher. Is he political?"°

[39]"I shouldn't wonder," Sanderson answered. "They all are, these chaps, you know, although they've got to conceal it when they're in the Service."

wallahs: "Wallah" is from Hindi for "person in charge"; a person engaged in a specific service which tends to control his behaviour so that he is easily identifiable by his profession—in this case, it suggests "busybody."

missus: bedpartner or concubine, not wife. This indicates the sort of fraternizing or tolerance of the "natives" which was manifested in the behaviour of the Europeans. Hounslow's "missus" would be an African always "in her place," thus a "good one," unlike Hughes, who is possibly not so controllable.

political: here means "involved in politics," especially nationalist independence movements.

[40]"Shouldn't be surprised if he supplies copy to nationalist newspapers. However, we must move with the times," Hounslow said resignedly. "He'll probably get drunk and start smashing bottles," he added hopefully.

[41]In fact, they were all a little unsober before the evening was out. Olu Hughes appeared looking very smart in a light tropical suit and a black bow-tie.

[42]"Oh, I forgot to tell you not to dress," said Sanderson.

[43]"Oh, that's all right," Hughes replied.

[44]Hounslow and Hughes were introduced to each other. The African said, "How do you do."

[45]Hounslow nodded. Neither shook hands. Sanderson mixed them drinks and made conversation about his garden.

[46]They moved over to the other side of the room and sat down to chop.° Sanderson waited for Hughes to begin before he himself started. Hughes waited for Sanderson because the latter was more senior in the Service, and in any case the array of knives and forks was a little confusing. Hounslow began as soon as the *hors d'oeuvres* were placed in front of him. Then Sanderson put his knife and fork on his plate and passed Hughes the salt. Hughes took it and began to eat. Hounslow concentrated on the food and ate gloomily and slowly, now and again addressing a remark to Sanderson. Hughes, perhaps noticing this, turned slightly to Sanderson and spoke to him exclusively of his afternoon's work. Towards the end of the meal Hounslow, talking about rising prices, turned to Hughes and said, "How are your people managing, Mr. Hughes, with all these rising prices? I suppose they're finding European food and clothes not quite so easy to maintain as they thought, eh?"

[47]Hughes chewed his food silently for a few minutes. The silence became unbearable. Hounslow, beginning to frown, thinking he had been snubbed, was going to repeat his question in a louder voice. Sanderson, thinking the African was annoyed, was preparing to say something tactful. Hughes sipped some water, then, turning to Hounslow, said, "Yes, they are finding European

chop: food, or the meal.

food and clothes hard to maintain." Then he continued eating. Hounslow was not sure whether sarcasm was meant, and searched the African's face unsuccessfully for a sign. Sanderson said something about the rise in the cost of living hitting all class- es, high and low, except the very rich, of course. "Among which I dare say none of us is numbered. Let's go in and sit in more com- fortable chairs and have coffee."

[48]Hounslow decided to relax, for he did not want to be boor- ish. Moreover, he was curious to know what Africans really thought; for he had never had the opportunity of talking to an Af- rican in such an atmosphere of equality. He addressed questions now and again to Hughes about what Africans thought on this or that matter, until the latter replied quietly that he was afraid he had been so busy lately that he had rather lost touch with the opinions of his people. Hounslow glanced sharply again to see whether any offence had been meant. Trouble is, he said to him- self, you can never tell when these educated natives mean to be insolent or not. They all wear this damned mask of politeness, have not the courage of their convictions. But as the evening wore on and another bottle of whisky was opened, the atmo- sphere became more convivial. Sanderson turned to Hughes sud- denly and said, "You trained at home, didn't you? I mean in Brit- ain. Where were you? London?"

[49]"Yes, I was in London for most of the time, at one of the big Polytechnics near Oxford Circus. I lived in digs at Cricklewood and came up to the College every morning by bus."

[50]"Did you have good digs?" Sanderson asked.

[51]Old Varsity men swapping reminiscences, Hounslow thought, a little contemptuously, stretching himself out on the chair easily. He will soon ask him 'What was your first fifteen like?' and the darkie will say, 'Actually the forwards were not bad, a bit slow at passing perhaps, but not bad at all; we once drew with Rosslyn Park.'°

[52]He helped himself sternly to some more whisky.

What was . . . with Rosslyn Park: references to the game of rugby, a common English sport.

[53]"I found a room eventually," Hughes answered, "after having several doors slammed in my face. It was quite a comfortable room and the landlady was a blonde, decent soul."

[54]Sanderson smiled. "What a turn of phrase you have," he said. "But seriously, apart from the lodgings problem, did you enjoy your time in England?"

[55]"Well, I didn't at first," admitted Hughes, "but later on I wasn't sure. It's the uncertainty of one's reception in England that confuses a lot of us. Sometimes you are welcomed with open arms by nice people. But on the other hand you get sudden rebuffs. Or what is worse, people simply avoid you as if you had some infectious disease. They are just cold and distant."

[56]Sanderson filled his glass slowly. "I know what you mean," he said, sipping his glass and then holding it up to the light. "I worked in London, too, for a few months, and I found people very cold and distant. I often wondered whether there was something wrong with me. People behave very strangely in cities, you know, Hughes. They tend to be secretive and shy as a protection against the vastness surrounding them. And anything stranger than usual, like a man with a dark complexion, makes it even more so."

[57]Hounslow chuckled. "By Jove, you are quite the Oxford man, Sanderson," he said. "You'll theorize your way to heaven and find it hellish when you get there." He laughed at his own words, and then his brow swiftly darkened with heavy anger. "You've got nothing to complain about," he said to Hughes. "Nor you either," turning to Sanderson. "I was the disappointed one in England. I grew up in Kenya and we thought of England as home all the time, and our old man told us all sorts of stories of the English countryside and our heritage. But when I went there to school nobody seemed to bother about the things we held dear." He stretched himself on the chair. "I don't suppose it was a good school," he continued, "but it was a public school all right. Headmasters' Conference and all that. It was well boosted in all the colonies, and there were special cheap rates for the holidays for boys whose parents were overseas. My father was a self-made man and left school early, and when he heard about this school he

thought he would make up to us educationally for what he himself had missed."

[58]"Did you go back to East Africa when you left school?" Sanderson asked.

[59]"No, I stayed on a little longer. But things were never quite the same. I worked for a time with a big exporting firm, but didn't like it particularly. Some of the chaps there thought I was a bit of a Blimp. They thought I was too narrow. People seemed to have changed so since my father's generation, whose ideas were what we colonials had. I mean white colonials, of course," he added hastily.

[60]"And how did you find it changed from what you had expected?" Hughes asked conversationally.

[61]"Oh, in all sorts of ways," Hounslow answered after a short pause, during which he had debated whether to admit Hughes freely into the conversation and had decided that for free and easy social purposes the African could be an honorary white man for an evening. "In all sorts of ways," he repeated reflectively, nodding his head. "Do you know," he said, tapping Sanderson's knee, "that one evening a chap tried to elbow me out of the way at the end of a show, during the National Anthem? I was standing at the end of a row, and the fellow gave me lip. Said I was to move on as he had a bus to catch, and not to block the gangway. Of course I refused to move and stood at attention. The chap leaned over and said into my ear, 'Company at ease!' in a terribly common accent. I stood unflinching and he and his gang climbed over the seats and clattered out. Must have been Communists, of course. At the end of the 'King'° I rushed down the foyer looking for him to knock him down. But by then they had gone. Things like that made me sad," he said, leaning back. "No, the old country is not the same. Too much talk of freedom, equality and democracy, and not enough doing things."

[62]"I don't think they are as bad as that," put in Sanderson, feeling things were rather up to him. "You'll find things have changed in the larger cities, but curiously enough, London itself

'King': the British national anthem, "God Save the King."

and the country-side remain always unchanged. What did you really think of London?" he said, turning to Hughes.

[63]"Ah, London was full of wonders for me. It was the organization of everything and the clockwork efficiency which amazed me. You English are efficient. I used to go for walks at night and watch the traffic lights changing to yellow, to red, to green, to yellow again all through the night. When I was studying hard for exams I would go out at two to three in the morning to clear my brain before going to bed. Once I saw a huge motor lorry stop at a crossroad early when the lights were against it. There was no one about, not even a policeman in sight, and I was in the shadow. But he stopped just because the lights were against him. That's what I call organization and a sense of the right thing. I never shall forget that moment. Further—that moment summarized London and the English for me." There was a pause for a few moments, and the other two looked obviously impressed. Hughes shut his eyes slightly and thought again of the Cricklewood Broadway he had so often loved but hated sometimes with a weary homesickness in the grey winter. "To London," he said, suddenly raising his glass.

[64]"To London," the others murmured. "God bless her!"

[65]"But mind you, I was glad to be back home," Hughes added after a while, fearing they might think him a "black Englishman," which he most dreaded. "There are things a man can do in this country which he cannot do in England."

[66]"For example?" Hounslow asked, with some interest.

[67]"Well, you can start things single-handed, and finish them before your own eyes here, while you'd have to be a genius to do that in England."

[68]"I don't know about beginning and finishing things here," Sanderson began.

[69]"I've built a bridge here," Hughes interrupted. "I came by this district last year, about four miles from here, on the Yolahun road, and there was a dry stream-bed which people used as a short cut to the big market in the dry season, but in the rains the stream was too swift for them to ford and it took them about two hours to make a detour to cross it farther up on a swinging rope

bridge. In fact, that's why for generations you'd have a small famine in this district during the rains, because most people simply
did not bother or could not travel properly to the large town to
sell their crops and buy food. I simply couldn't understand why
nobody had thought of building a bridge there before. Perhaps
they thought of it during the rains, but forgot about it in the dry
season. That often happens in this country. Or, again, people may
simply have accepted it."

[70]"So *you* built that bridge! I wondered about it," Sanderson
said. "I thought it was the army, but it looked too permanent for
them."

[71]"I expect it's improved things quite a lot now, hasn't it?"
Hughes asked with some triumph.

[72]Sanderson wondered whether it was kinder to leave the
truth unsaid, because in fact the bridge was seldom used by villagers and then only by motor transport. Someone had been
drowned years ago at that point, and the local legend had it there
was a water-spirit° there during the rains.

[73]"Yes, I think it has improved things," he said aloud.

[74]"That's much sooner than I expected," Hughes said. "Do
you know that some years ago someone was drowned there? And
people think there is a devil round there during the rains. In fact,
I had to hire a more powerful medicine-man to sacrifice a chicken
on the site and pour some rum on the ground before the labourers
would begin."

[75]"As you know," said Hounslow with jovial politeness, "we
prefer champagne. Break a bottle of the stuff over the prow of a
ship as she slides off her slipway, just to appease the old gods.
Same as you, old man; same as you."

[76]"Of course, I had the chicken and the rest of the rum for
dinner that evening," Hughes said, trying to show that he had

---

water-spirit: probably *dyinganga,* Mende for a *djinn*-type spirit. M. Mc-
Culloch says: "When, during the month of September, the river Jojoima
overflows its banks, it is believed that if the *dyinganga* of the river is not
propitiated the whole area may be flooded." (19) The water-spirit here acts
similarly, although it presumably required only the one standard propitiation
of a white chicken, rum libations, and prayers.

treated the whole thing as a piece of whimsy to humour his work-men and had never for a moment taken it seriously. At the same time he thought Hounslow had been patronizingly polite, trying to compare it with an English custom. He had himself seen a new ship being launched at a shipyard, and had been awed by it. Of course, the ceremony bore no comparison with the blood of a white chicken and the rum poured out by a simple misguided na-tive. In fact, in the launching on Clydeside there had even been a milord about. He had had him pointed out. It bore no compari-son. Anyhow, he thought, perhaps I am too sensitive.

[77]"I envy you chaps—engineers, doctors, agriculturalists and so on," Sanderson said. "You begin things, you finish them, and you see the result. But we never do. We never even know if we've begun. Nor when we finish. We never really know whether we are just redundant."

[78]Hughes was touched. "Oh, no, no," he cried, "you adminis-trators, white or black, will always be needed to plan things and to manage men. When we are old and finished, then there is an end to us as engineers. Then we begin to learn your job, to ad-minister. But I must go," he said, springing up. "I've got to set off early to-morrow, and I know you will forgive me." He shook hands with both, and swiftly disappeared in spite of Sanderson's protesting that he could put him up for the night. And Hounslow pressed the other man's whisky on him, to take just one more for the road.

[79]After the African had left, Hounslow strolled up and down the room, stumbling a little. Then he stopped suddenly in front of Sanderson, who was slowly puffing a pipe. "Do you know," he said, in a voice of such tiredness that the other glanced up swiftly —"do you know that apropos of what you said a few minutes ago, I am beginning to feel particularly redundant in this damned country!" He sat down and rested his head on the edge of the table, with his body sprawling loosely in the chair.

[80]"But you are not an Administrator," Sanderson said, "you are the senior agent of a very prosperous firm."

[81]"No, I'm feeling *de trop* in a different sort of way, especially when I meet educated natives like our mutual friend here this

evening. They brought us up as children saying that Africa was a white man's country, and that for centuries to come we were to help and teach the black man slowly and certainly what it had taken us hundreds of years to gain. But here in my own lifetime I see these people trained to do all sorts of things, and the trouble is they sometimes do them well. Mind you, I don't say they are as good as we are. They can never be that."

[82]"Yes," said Sanderson swiftly, "just as we couldn't be them if we tried. We and they are both different, but good in our separate ways."

[83]"Yes, yes, I suppose you've got to say that in your position," Hounslow replied. "But whatever you say, I don't think they can do it in a generation, old man; they'll crack up when things go bad. That chap Hughes, for example, was frightened of the water-juju:° I could see it in his face." He filled his glass himself and emptied it. "All the same, old man, they make us feel useless —damned useless. You Whitehall chaps can't see that you are trying to put us, your own kith and kin, out into the cold. You'd be surprised how hard I found it to get this job. And now Headquarters is talking about training African assistant managers. As if I didn't know what they meant! Why are you always trying to be fair, you Johnnies? Always pushing us out into the cold?" He burst into tears. Sanderson tried first not to notice; then gave it up, went over and stood by him, putting his hand on Hounslow's shoulder. "Don't you think the country is big enough for Hughes and you and me? Hughes has to be here because it's his country. You are here because no man can do everything in his own country. I think this idea of a man's country belonging to him is a phase we all pass through. *We* passed through it fifty years ago. Only his country-side and the profitless patches in his country belong to any man. The fat of the land is to whoever can get it, and whoever that is then tries to belong to the country even more than those whose heritage it was. It is by this eternal recruitment

---

water-juju: water-spirit. *Juju* is a deprecatory term used by Europeans to refer to African religious beings, practices, and the religions themselves.

of the fittest alien that great nations and privileged classes survive. And that is why you'll always be here if you are good enough, Hounslow, and for no other reason."

[84]The other man had been listening with attention. "I wish I'd been educated your way, Sanderson. I wish I knew what words meant and could use them. But I gather it's a case of the survival of the fittest." The wind rose and fell, rattling the windows.

[85]"So you think there will be room for all of us?" he said, getting up and stretching. "I doubt it; you only have to read the local rag. But it is not a bad country, all said and done. A man can see results in it sometimes."

[86]"To Africa," Sanderson toasted gravely.

[87]"Yes, yes, to Africa: white man's country and black man's too." Hounslow nodded, sipping. "A last one before I go, one for the road, so to speak," he added, nodding all the time as if comforted but only half convinced. Sanderson picked up the bottle. But it was empty. "Never mind," Hounslow said thickly, "we'll have it in soda." He was feeling tired, sad, and then happy.

[88]Sanderson filled the glasses. And the little pearly bubbles clung to the side of the glasses to burst to the surface. They tickled Hounslow's nostrils, and he grimaced happily.

[89]"Whom shall it be to this time?" Sanderson asked.

[90]"To you, to you, old man," Hounslow said affectionately. "To you, old man, and me," he chuckled.

[91]"And Olu Hughes, too?" Sanderson added.

[92]"Yes, him too," Hounslow agreed. "In fact, to all good chaps everywhere. 'For we are jolly good fellows'," he hummed as he searched for his car key.

[93]Sanderson saw him off from the small courtyard in front of his bungalow. "Are you sure you will be able to drive yourself home?" he asked him.

[94]"Positive, old man, I can drive home blindfolded. Give us a shove, there's a good fellow."

[92]Sanderson heaved and pushed for a while before the car broke into life and careered off. It headed in the opposite direction from the town, and Sanderson shouted to Hounslow to stop

and turn round. But the car was soon lost to sight, although the sound could be heard in the distance. Sanderson went indoors with misgivings and wearily prepared for bed.

[96]Hounslow put the car into gear and roared up a hill. The throb of the engine filled him with an exultant power, as did an occasional gust of wind. He knew where he was going and he felt his head strangely clear. After about fifteen minutes he slowed down and stopped. He bent over his wheel and listened to the shrill call of the cicadas and the deep bass croaking of the frogs; these would stop suddenly sometimes and an eerie silence filled the heavy air. He left the head-lamps on and walked forward slowly in the broad beam of light to examine the bridge more closely. It was an ordinary one but strong, concrete, and with a simple, hard grace. He stood in the middle of it and jumped up and down, as if half hoping it would break. He leaned over one side and watched the growing waters between the rocks. He threw a twig in on one side and rushed over to the other side to see it appear, laughing with pleasure when it did so. Then he walked slowly back to his car.

[97]And Olu Hughes, standing by the shadows, where he had hidden when he had first heard the car, marvelled that Hounslow had not detected his presence, his heart had been beating so loudly. He had walked far out of town to come and see the bridge he had fashioned with love and care. He had come in the dark of night, defying the dark to show himself that he was not afraid of the water-spirit. He had been strangely pleased and a little puzzled at the look on the white man's face as he strode past slowly.

[98]It leaped suddenly into the middle of the road and stood there, poised, dazzled by the light from the head-lamps. Hounslow sat quickly upright in the driver's seat to watch it. Hughes restrained a startled cry and gazed with fascination. It was a curious beast. It had the shape of an antelope but was reddish-brown on the back and white underneath, with a sharp boundary-line between the two colours as if it had been swimming and washed off its colour. It had slender curved horns on a head held proudly and supported on a delicate neck. It had black vertical

stripes down each buttock and one on its back continuing to the tail. It stood there for a few long seconds. Hounslow then sounded his horn sharply and the beast bounded high into the air and forward, to be lost as suddenly as it had appeared, like a secret memory.

[99]"Oh, it's only a red-buck," Hounslow shouted aloud, as he thought, to himself. He started the car, reversed carefully into the side of the road, and turned round and drove back steadily to town.

[100]It was, after all, only a red-buck, an impala, that they were afraid of, Hughes meditated as he climbed on to the bridge. He put the small spirit-level he always carried about with him on one of the railings and shone his torch on it. He nodded with satisfaction as he watched the air-bubble oscillate and settle in the centre; and then, reluctantly, he started to walk back to the rest-house. He stopped suddenly, held out his hand a moment or so, and then broke into a steady run. For the rain had begun to fall in single heavy drops like the slow, quiet weeping of a woman proud, proud to distraction for an only son, yet vaguely afraid.

"*The Devil at Yolahun Bridge*"

The version of this story which we have used is the author's early version, which he published in *Blackwood's Magazine* in 1953. He rewrote the story as a novelette in 1965 and published the revision in *Two African Tales* (Cambridge: Cambridge University Press, 1965), pp. 35–76. In the present critical exercise, some of the author's changes are described, others quoted from the novelette form of the story. In each instance, determine the function and significance of the alteration in relation to the passage in which it occurs or which it develops, and to the story as a whole, or to its meaning in relation to matters extraneous to the story.

The author's Foreword to *Two African Tales* can be useful to the student and critic, and might be considered a possible guide to interpretation of materials in this exercise:

These stories were written some years ago and have now been modified for my young friends to give them an impression of what happened when we were colonial countries under the rule of Europeans. They owe something to European writers like E. M. Forster, Joyce Cary, Graham Greene, and Evelyn Waugh, all of whom I admire and who, themselves, wrote about similar situations. However, being both black and African, I was then on the other side of the fence and perhaps saw things somewhat differently.

Since our national independence, much has changed for the better. White and black people can now more easily be friends and equals in many parts of Africa.

But even in the colonial past, it was sometimes possible for them to respect each other.

I hope these two stories show that.

                                                                A. N.

London, 1965.

CRITICAL EXERCISE III

[Pars. 1–9] These paragraphs become seven pages of printed novella. The paragraph 11 reference to the school inspection is developed into six pages of printed text.

[Par. 11] reference to the planned lecture to the local African club, is developed into the following copy:

Sanderson's talk had been on Roman Britain. He had chosen this because he felt it to be strictly non-controversial, and in fact the whole thing was a rehash of a talk he'd given on an Army education course. He soon however found himself in deep waters. First, when an old retired African schoolmaster had got up and fiercely argued the dates of the Roman landings, Sanderson agreed with him hastily, and the old man had sat down again muttering and glaring like a man who had nearly been cheated of the truth had he not been more vigilant. The journalist next stood up and asked with guile, "Did Mr. Sanderson say that Roman Britain was like Kissiland today?"

"Yes, in some ways," Sanderson answered guardedly.

"The speaker means that we are 2,000 years behind Britain, no doubt."

"I do not," Sanderson replied.

"Anyway he means we are centuries behind Britain, I take it," the journalist said, sitting down.

"I meant nothing of the sort," Sanderson said rather sharply.

The journalist stood up again.

"I must have misunderstood the speaker then," he said heavily. "But whilst I am about it may I ask one or two things?" he said, turning to the African Chairman.

The latter was indecisive and started "I am afraid we haven't time...."

The journalist ignored him and turned again to Sanderson, rapidly opening a folded piece of paper in his hand and harangued the meeting for five minutes on British Imperialism. Some members looked embarrassed. Some were secretly pleased, and some looked sternly at Sanderson to see how he was taking it. Sanderson with crossed legs and folded arms smiled and fastened his eyes determinedly on his notes lying on the table near him. He did not reply. After the journalist there was silence. Then the old schoolmaster got up again and asked whether any Roman remains had been discovered recently in Britain, and whether the British Government intended to return them to their rightful heirs and owners, the present Italian people. Sanderson ruffled his notes and smiled into them, trying to hide his face.

Such Roman remains as had been found, he explained, were mainly mosaic pavements, broken pottery, and Roman roads, and ditches. "It might well prove impracticable to return these," he added.

The meeting eventually ended peaceably. The young wife of a junior clerk moved a charming vote of thanks, speaking, Sanderson noticed, directly and seemingly impromptu. (pp. 54–56)

[Par. 18] *changes* in the description of Hughes: He was a tall youngish man . . . with a small, army moustache. . . .

[Par. 20] *changes:*

> "I'll go and see the other official buildings you mentioned, but will be free this evening." He is asking me because he hasn't the courage to take me to their club, Jones thought; these blighters, he probably wants a new refrigerator, too. Ah, well! "Goodbye then, for the present," he said to Sanderson. (p. 59)

[Par. 35] original "somewhat guilty" changed to "a little ashamed."

[Pars. 36 and 37] *deleted.* Deletion of copy: "He lit a cigarette . . . without her," so in the novelette there is no reference to Hounslow's "black missus."

[Par. 45] "Hounslow nodded" *changed to* "The Kenya white nodded." (p. 61)

[Par. 48] *changes:*

Sanderson turned to Hughes suddenly and said, "You trained at home, didn't you? I mean in Britain. Where were you? London?"

changed to

Sanderson turned to Jones suddenly and said, "Look here, Ola, do you chaps hate us? I mean us, the English?" (p. 63)

Immediately following this is a long passage on the race situation:

Although feeling warm with the good fellowship and whisky a trace of guardedness crept over Jones' face. Sanderson noticed it and said, "Oh, of course this is all off the record. We are speaking as man to man. I mean to say, I would regard you as a member of my class, both here and in England. But in general are we hated?"

"I don't think so," said Jones, "at least, not continuously."

"You would admit that we are hated, then," Hounslow said, coming in, "sometimes anyhow?" He leant back feeling he had scored.

"Don't you hate us too sometimes?" Jones countered, smiling.

"The psychologists say it's a good thing to hate well and to love well. After all, it's the hatred of the things evil which make the great social reformers, but to return to the point, do you dislike us?"

"Well, you are sometimes very proud, you know," Jones answered. "One might not dislike you, but whoever he is, white or black, everybody likes to see a proud man humbled occasionally. I don't mind you personally," he said hurriedly. "Good heavens, no, nor you either, Mr. Hounslow."

"Call me Hounslow, old fellow. But tell me seriously, do you think you chaps can run this country without our help? The white man has a stake in this country, and he's done as much for it in a generation as you haven't done for centuries."

"How do you know it's the white man and not the age we live in which has done the miracle? How do you know that we couldn't have done it ourselves, given the opportunity in this age?"

"Ah, I thought you would say that." Hounslow leaned forward, "but how then do you explain the presence in the middle of this century of naked tribesmen on the Jos Plateau and of the naked Masai in East Africa drinking the blood of their cattle; that is, all the savagery in places in Africa where the white man has not spread his influence?"

Jones replied mildly and without heat, "There are more Europeans in Jos than in any other place in Nigeria, and there are more Europeans in Kenya than there are in any other country in East Africa. I suppose those are well established statistical facts, are they not?" he said, turning to Sanderson.

"I believe so," the latter replied; he continued after a pause, "although to counterbalance the backwardness of the Plateau people and the Masai a great many advances have otherwise been made there and elsewhere."

"Oh, quite so," said Jones, "quite so."

The conversation halted for a while in polite silence. An air of reasonableness hung in the atmosphere.

Hounslow felt obscurely worsted by the African but rescued by Sanderson. He did not like the situation too well but he contented himself with a noisy sip to express insouciance. (pp. 63–65)

Text now returns to old end of Par. 48 and Par. 49.

[Par. 54] *added*, after ". . . in England:":

". . . Did you get to know us well?" Sanderson asked. "Did you for instance stay with an English family?"

"I had an invitation once, from some church people, and I nearly went, but in the end I decided not to, because I am not particularly religious, and besides, my friends told me that English families would be patronising to me and would call the neighbors to come and see me at close quarters, like a strange beast."

"Oh but come, come Jones, surely that's nonsense, you didn't believe that, did you? We used to have an Indian friend to come and stay regularly and we usually asked our friends to meet him, simply because it was the custom. And besides we were afraid he would be bored with just our company. You must realise an Englishman's home is his castle, you know, and when he lets down the drawbridge for you to come, you may be sure he likes you, and not for all the world would he do it otherwise, much less ask you a second time. You really didn't believe what your friends told you, did you?" (pp. 65–66)

[Par. 76] "a simple misguided native" *changed to* "a simple misguided African." (p. 71)

Adelaide Casely-Hayford

(Sierra Leone)

MISTA COURIFER[20]

Not a sound was heard in the coffin-maker's workshop, that is to say, no human sound. Mista Courifer, a solid citizen of Sierra Leone, was not given to much speech. His apprentices, knowing this, never dared address him unless he spoke first. Then they only carried on their conversation in whispers. Not that Mista Courifer did not know how to use his tongue. It was incessantly wagging to and fro in his mouth at every blow of the hammer. But his shop in the heart of Freetown° was a part of his house. And, as he had once confided to a friend, he was a silent member of his own household from necessity. His wife, given to much speaking, could outtalk him.

"It's no use for argue wid woman," he said cautiously. "Just like 'e no use for teach woman carpentering; she nebba sabi for hit de nail on de head. If 'e argue, she'll hit eberyting but de nail; and so wid de carpentering."

So, around his wife, with the exception of his tongue's continual wagging like a pendulum, his mouth was kept more or less shut. But whatever self-control he exercised in this respect at home was completely sent to the wind in his official capacity as the local preacher at chapel, for Mista Courifer was one of the pillars of the church, being equally at home in conducting a prayer meeting, superintending the Sunday school or occupying the pulpit.

His voice was remarkable for its wonderful gradations of pitch. He would insist on starting most of the tunes himself; conse-

---

Freetown: Freetown, the capital of Sierra Leone, was a colony of freed slaves captured by the British from slavers operating during the nineteenth century. The dominant class were creoles—freed slaves—and the steadily ascending class were the up-country people, including Mr. Courifer and his family.

quently, they nearly always ended in a solo. If he happened to pitch in the bass, he descended into such a *de profundis* that his congregations were left to flounder in a higher key; if he started in the treble, he soared so high that the children stared at him openmouthed and their elders were lost in wonder and amazement. As for his prayers, he roared and volleyed and thundered to such an extent that poor little mites were quickly reduced to a state of collapse and started to whimper from sheer fright.

But he was most at home in the pulpit. It is true, his labors were altogether confined to the outlying village districts of Regent, Gloucester and Leicester, an arrangement with which he was by no means satisfied. Still, a village congregation is better than none at all.

His favorite themes were Jonah and Noah° and he was forever pointing out the great similarity between the two, generally finishing his discourse after this manner: "You see, my beloved Breben, den two man berry much alike. All two lived in a sinful and adulterous generation. One get inside am ark; de odder one get inside a whale. Day bof seek a refuge fom de swelling waves.

And so it is today, my beloved Breben. No matter if we get inside a whale or get inside an ark, as long as we get inside some place of safety—as long as we can find some refuge, some hiding place from de wiles ob de debil."

But his congregation was by no means convinced.

Mr. Courifer always wore black. He was one of the Sierra Leone gentlemen who consider everything European to be not only the right thing, but the *only* thing for the African, and having read somewhere that English undertakers generally appeared in somber attire, he immediately followed suit.

He even went so far as to build a European house. During his short stay in England, he had noticed how the houses were built and furnished, and had forthwith erected himself one after the approved pattern—a house with stuffy little passages, narrow little staircases and poky rooms, all crammed with saddlebags and carpeted with Axminsters. No wonder his wife had to talk. It was so hopelessly uncomfortable, stuffy and unsanitary.

Jonah and Noah: symbols for the case of African culture being almost "swallowed up" by European culture.

So Mr. Courifer wore black. It never struck him for a single moment that red° would have been more appropriate, far more becoming, far less expensive and far more national. No! It must be black. He would have liked blue black, but he wore rusty black for economy.

There was one subject upon which Mr. Courifer could talk even at home, so no one ever mentioned it: his son, Tomas. Mista Courifer had great expectations for his son; indeed, in the back of his mind he had hopes of seeing him reach the high-water mark of red-tape officialism, for Tomas was in the government service. Not very high up, it is true, but still he was in it. It was an honor that impressed his father deeply, but Tomas unfortunately did not seem to think quite so much of it. The youth in question, however, was altogether neutral in his opinions in his father's presence. Although somewhat feminine as to attire, he was distinctly masculine in his speech. His neutrality was not a matter of choice, since no one was allowed to choose anything in the Courifer family but the paterfamilias himself.

From start to finish, Tomas's career had been cut out, and in spite of the fact that nature had endowed him with a black skin and an African temperament, Tomas was to be an Englishman. He was even to be an Englishman in appearance.

Consequently, once a year mysterious bundles arrived by parcel post. When opened, they revealed marvelous checks and plaids in vivid greens and blues after the fashion of a Liverpool counter-jumper, waistcoats decorative in the extreme with their bold designs and rows of brass buttons, socks vying with the rainbow in glory, and pumps very patent in appearance and very fragile as to texture.

Now, Tomas was no longer a minor and he keenly resented having his clothes chosen for him like a boy going to school for the first time. Indeed, on one occasion, had it not been for his sister's timely interference, he would have chucked the whole collection into the fire.

---

black . . . red: throughout most of equatorial Africa the soil is red laterite. The wearing of black suggests too extreme an imitativeness for black-skinned people. Imitation of the British was a common behavior among those who could manage it; Freetown Africans were especially noted for it.

Dear little Keren-happuch, eight years his junior and not at all attractive, with a very diminutive body and a very large heart. Such a mistake! People's hearts ought always to be in proportion to their size, otherwise it upsets the dimensions of the whole structure and often ends in its total collapse.

Keren was that type of little individual whom nobody worshipped, consequently she understood the art of worshipping others to the full. Tomas was the object of her adoration. Upon him she lavished the whole store of her boundless wealth and whatever hurt Tomas became positive torture as far as Keren-happuch was concerned.

"Tomas!" she said, clinging to him with the tenacity of a bear, as she saw the faggots piled up high, ready for the conflagration. "Do yah! No burn am oh! Ole man go flog you oh! Den clos berry fine! I like am myself too much. I wish"—she added wistfully—"me na boy; I wish I could use am."°

This was quite a new feature which had never struck Tomas before. Keren-happuch had never received a bundle of English clothes in her life, hence her great appreciation of them.

At first Tomas only laughed—the superior, daredevil, don't-care-a-damn-about-consequences laugh of the brave before the deed. But after hearing that wistful little sentence, he forgot his own annoyance and awoke to his responsibilities as an elder brother.

A few Sundays later, Tomas Courifer, Jr., marched up the aisle of the little Wesleyan chapel in all his Liverpool magnificence accompanied by a very elated little Keren-happuch whose natural unattractiveness had been further accentuated by a vivid cerise costume—a heterogeneous mass of frill and furbelows. But the glory of her array by no means outshone the brightness of her smile. Indeed that smile seemed to illuminate the whole church and to dispel the usual melancholy preceding the recital of Jonah and his woes.

Do yah . . . I could use am: This is Krio, a form of pidgin English spoken in Freetown. (21) The meaning here: "Don't! Don't burn them! Father will flog you! Those clothes are very good! I like them myself very much. I wish I were a boy. I wish I could wear them."

Unfortunately, Tomas had a very poor opinion of the government service and in a burst of confidence he had told Keren that he meant to chuck it at the very first opportunity. In vain his sister expostulated and pointed out the advantages connected with it—the honor, the pension—and the awful nemesis upon the head of anyone incurring the head-of-the-family's ire.

"Why you want leave am, Tomas?" she asked desperately.

"Because I never get a proper holiday. I have been in the office four and a half years and have never had a whole week off yet. And," he went on vehemently, "these white chaps come and go, and a fresh one upsets what the old one has done and a newcomer upsets what he does and they all only stay for a year and a half and go away for four months, drawing big fat pay all the time, not to speak of passages, whereas a poor African like me has to work year in and year out with never a chance of a decent break. But you needn't be afraid, Keren, dear," he added consolingly, "I shan't resign, I shall just behave so badly that they'll chuck me and then my ole man can't say very much."

Accordingly, when Tomas, puffing a cigarette, sauntered into the office at 9 a.m. instead of 8 a.m. for the fourth time that week, Mr. Buckmaster, who had hitherto maintained a discreet silence and kept his eyes shut, opened them wide and administered a sharp rebuke. Tomas's conscience was profoundly stirred. Mr. Buckmaster was one of the few white men for whom he had a deep respect, aye, in the depth of his heart, he really had a sneaking regard. It was for fear of offending him that he had remained so long at his post.

But he had only lately heard that his chief was due for leave, so he decided there and then to say a long good-by to a service which had treated him so shabbily. He was a vociferous reader of halfpenny newspapers and he knew that the humblest shop assistant in England was entitled to a fortnight's holiday every year. Therefore it was ridiculous to argue that because he was an African working in Africa there was no need for a holiday. All his applications for leave were quietly pigeonholed for a more convenient season.

"Courifer!" Mr. Buckmaster said sternly. "Walk into my private office, please." And Courifer knew that this was the beginning of the end.

"I suppose you know that the office hours are from 8 a.m. till 4 p.m. daily," commenced Mr. Buckmaster, in a freezing tone.

"Yes, er—Sir!" stammered Courifer with his heart in his mouth and his mouth twisted up into a hard sailor's knot.

"And I suppose you also know that smoking is strictly forbidden in the office?"

"Yes, er—er—Sir!" stammered the youth.

"Now hitherto," the even tones went on, "I have always looked upon you as an exemplary clerk, strictly obliging, punctual, accurate and honest, but for the last two or three weeks I have had nothing but complaints about you. And from what I myself have seen, I am afraid they are not altogether unmerited."

Mr. Buckmaster rose as he spoke, took a bunch of keys out of his pocket and, unlocking his roll-top desk, drew out a sheaf of papers. "This is your work, is it not?" he said to the youth.

"Yes, er—er—Sir!" he stuttered, looking shamefacedly at the dirty, ink-stained, blotched sheets of closely typewritten matter.

"Then what in Heaven's name is the matter with you to produce such work?"

Tomas remained silent for a moment or two. He summoned up courage to look boldly at the stern countenance of his chief. And as he looked, the sternness seemed to melt away and he could see genuine concern there.

"Please, er—Sir!" he stammered. "May—I—er—just tell you everything?"

Half an hour later, a very quiet, subdued, penitent Tomas Courifer walked out of the office by a side door. Mr. Buckmaster followed later, taking with him an increased respect for the powers of endurance exercised by the growing West African youth.

Six weeks later, Mista Courifer was busily occupied wagging his tongue when he looked up from his work to see a European man standing in his doorway.

The undertaker found speech and a chair simultaneously. "Good afternoon, Sah!" he said, dusting the chair before offering it to his visitor. "I hope you don't want a coffin, Sah!" which was a deep-sea lie, for nothing pleased him more than the opportunity of making a coffin for a European. He was always so sure of the money. Such handsome money—paid, it is true, with a few ejaculations, but paid on the nail and without any deductions whatsoever. Now, with his own people things were different. They demurred, they haggled, they bartered, they gave him detailed accounts of all their other expenses and then, after keeping him waiting for weeks, they would end by sending him half the amount with a stern exhortation to be thankful for that.

Mr. Buckmaster took the proffered chair and answered pleasantly: "No, thank you, I don't intend dying just yet. I happened to be passing, so I thought I should just like a word with you about your son."

Mr. Courifer bristled all over with exultation and expectation. Perhaps they were going to make his son a kind of undersecretary of state. What an unexpected honor for the Courifer family. What a rise in their social status; what a rise out of their neighbors. How good God was!

"Of course you know he is in my office?"

"Oh, yes, Sah. He often speaks about you."

"Well, I am going home very soon and, as I may not be returning to Sierra Leone, I just wanted to tell you how pleased I should be at any time to give him a decent testimonial."

Mr. Courifer's countenance fell. What a comedown!

"Yes, Sah," he answered, somewhat dubiously.

"I can recommend him highly as being steady, persevering, reliable and trustworthy. And you can always apply to me if ever such a thing be necessary."

Was that all! What a disappointment! Still, it was something worth having. Mr. Buckmaster was an Englishman, and a testimonial from him would certainly be a very valuable possession. He rubbed his hands together as he said: "Well, I am berry much obliged to you, Sah, berry much obliged. And as time is short and we nebba know what a day may bring forth, would you mind writing one down now, Sah?"

"Certainly. If you will give me a sheet of paper, I shall do so at once."

Before Tomas returned home from his evening work, the testimonial was already framed and hanging up amidst the moth-eaten velvet of the drawing room.

On the following Monday morning, Courifer Jr. bounced into his father's workshop, upsetting the equilibrium of the carpenter's bench and also of the voiceless apprentices hard at work.

"Well, Sah?" ejaculated his father, surveying him in disgust. "You berry late. Why you no go office dis morning?"

"Because I've got a whole two months' holiday, Sir! Just think of it—two whole months—with nothing to do but just enjoy myself!"

"Tomas," his father said solemnly, peering at him over his glasses, "you must larn for make coffins. You get fine chance now."

Sotto voce: "I'll be damned if I will!" Aloud: "No, thank you, Sir. I am going to learn how to make love, after which I am going to learn how to build myself a nice mud hut."°

"And who dis gal you want married?" thundered his father, ignoring the latter part of the sentence altogether.

A broad smile illuminated Tomas's countenance. "She is a very nice girl, Sir, a very nice girl. Very quiet and gentle and sweet, and she doesn't talk too much."

"I see. Is dat all?"

"Oh, no. She can sew and clean and make a nice little home. And she has plenty sense; she will make a good mother."

"Yes, notting pass dat!"

"She has been to school for a long time. She reads nice books and she writes, oh, such a nice letter,"° said Tomas, patting his breast pocket affectionately.

"I see. I suppose she sabi° cook good fashion?"

"I don't know. I don't think so, and it doesn't matter very much."

---

mud hut: villagers throughout most of West Africa build their houses of packed mud walls with grass roof-thatch. The mud hut is certainly not status housing.

nice letter: Among urbanized educated young West Africans much courtship was and still is conducted through the exchange of love letters.

sabi: understands how (to).

"What!" roared the old man; "You mean tell me you want married woman who no sabi cook?"

"I want to marry her because I love her, Sir!"°

"Dat's all right, but for we country, de heart and de stomach always go togedder. For we country, black man no want married woman who no sabi cook! Dat de berry first requisitional. You own mudder sabi cook."

That's the reason why she has been nothing but your miserable drudge all these years, thought the young man. His face was very grave as he rejoined: "The style in our country is not at all nice, Sir. I don't like to see a wife slaving away in the kitchen all times to make good chop for her husband who sits down alone and eats the best of everything himself, and she and the children only get the leavings. No, thank you! And besides, Sir, you are always telling me that you want me to be an Englishman. That is why I always try to talk good English to you."

"Yes, dat's right. Dat's berry good. But I want make you *look* like Englishman. I don't say you must copy all der different way!"

"Well, sir, if I try till I die, I shall never look like an Englishman, and I don't know that I want to. But there are some English customs that I like very much indeed. I like the way white men treat their wives; I like their home life; I like to see mother and father and the little family all sitting down eating their meals together."

"I see," retorted his father sarcastically. "And who go cook den

---

1 love her, Sir: Marriage in traditional Africa was based almost everywhere upon practical considerations—the character and housewifely abilities of the girl—rather than upon love. In contrast, the European has traditionally confused love and sex, or love and marriage. In this and the following passage the author ironically reveals that Tomas, Jr., has actually become Europeanized, but that such change is considered shockingly impractical to his father, who hitherto had overemphasized Europeanization but now is stressing African virtues. Suggested is that, whereas Courifer, Sr., had been somewhat imbalanced in favor of assimilating European culture, the son perhaps of necessity must be imbalanced in an inverse ratio, if only that balance of any sort be reached. In fact, however, there is no real "balance" between two divergent cultures.

meal? You tink say wid your four pound° a month, you go able hire a perfessional cook?"

"Oh, I don't say so, Sir. And I am sure if Accastasia does not know how to cook now, she will before we are married. But what I want you to understand is just this, that whether she is able to cook or not, I shall marry her just the same."

"Berry well," shouted his father, wrath delineated in every feature, "but instead of building one mud hut you better go one time build one madhouse!"

"Sir, thank you. But I know what I am about, and a mud hut will suit us perfectly for the present."

"A mud hut!" ejaculated his father in horror. "You done use fine England house wid staircase and balustrade and tick carpet and handsome furnitures. You want to go live in mud hut? You ungrateful boy, you shame me, Oh!"

"Dear me, no, Sir. I won't shame you. It's going to be a nice clean spacious mud hut. And what is more, it is going to be a sweet little home, just big enough for two. I am going to distemper the walls pale green, like at the principal's rooms at Keren's school."

"How you sabi den woman's rooms?"

"Because you have sent me two or three times to pay her school fees, so I have looked at those walls and I like them too much."

"I see. And what else you go do?" asked his father ironically.

"I am going to order some nice wicker chairs from the Islands° and a few good pieces of linoleum for the floors and then—"

"And den what?"

"I shall bring home my bride."

Mr. Courifer's dejection grew deeper with each moment. A mud hut! This son of his—the hope of his life! A government officer! A would-be Englishman! To live in a mud hut! His disgust knew no bounds. "You ungrateful wretch!" he bellowed; "You go disgrace me! Yo go lower your pore father! You go lower your position for de office!"

---

four pound: at that time, before World War II, worth approximately $16.20.

the Islands: The Canary Islands.

"I am sorry, Sir," retorted the young man. "I don't wish to offend you. I'm grateful for all you have done for me. But I have had a raise in salary and I want a home of my own which, after all, is only natural, and"—he went on steadily, staring his father straight in the face—"I may as well tell you at once, you need not order any more Liverpool suits for me."

"Why not?" thundered his irate parent, removing his specs lest any harm should befall them.

"Well, I am sorry to grieve you, Sir, but I have been trying to live up to your European standards all this time. Now I am going to chuck it once and for all. I am going back to the native costume of my mother's people, and the next time I appear in chapel it will be as a Wolof."°

The very next Sunday the awful shock of seeing his son walk up the aisle of the church in pantaloons and the bright loose overjacket of a Wolof from Gambia, escorting a pretty young bride the color of chocolate, also in native dress, so unnerved Mista Courifer that his mind suddenly became a complete blank. He could not even remember Jonah and the whale, nor could his tongue possess one word to let fly, not one. The service had to be turned into a prayer meeting.

Mista Courifer is the local preacher no longer. Now he only makes coffins.

Tom Chacha
(Tanzania)

ROAD TO MARA[22]

The day was hot and humid. The air had the stillness of death. Somewhere in the distance, a bell rang. The girl listened. The shrills from the small schoolchildren had swallowed the ringing, but the girl knew it was four o'clock in the evening.

She walked slowly, almost reluctantly, from her village. Her

Wolof: Negro peoples of Senegal and Gambia in West Africa.

left arm relieved the right one of the small bundle she was carrying. That bundle securely stuck under her armpit was all the
property she owned in this world. Walking on that firm and dusty
road was not pleasant. When an old green bus, groaning as if in
great pain, appeared, the girl was happy. She waved to stop it.

"Mara?" shouted the driver.

Without answering, she got in, sat up, rather stiffly, and looked
about. On her right were seated three other passengers: an old
man in a stained old coat, a woman of indeterminate age and a
young man. The woman smiled. The young girl, feeling rather
embarrassed, returned the smile. No word passed between them.

"This must be Bena, Father," the young man said.

"Can't you keep your eyes off the girls?" the old man whispered
in a strong questioning tone. He eyed Bena; frowned; and bit his
lower lip. How could a young girl like Bena travel alone without
an elderly companion? The old man's eyes caught those of the
woman. In the moment when their eyes met the old man knew
that she was thinking the same thing as himself.

This is one of those spoilt modern girls, the old man seemed to
be saying. *She's probably going to be a common prostitute in the
town.*

The woman, sensing the old man's thoughts, looked at Bena
again. Her lips were parted; not in a smile this time, but with a
mixture of pity and embarrassment. To her, Bena was a symbol
of shame to all respectable women. She realized that Bena lacked
something. She did not have the tribal markings on her face. Bena
did not wear the iron rings on her neck. Instead she had a cross.
On her arms, the tribal multi-coloured beads were replaced by
a small gold watch.

"The town is ruining our young girls," the woman whispered
into the ear of the old man.

"Sure," the old man answered, nodding his head.

It was only the young man who looked at Bena with admiration.
As she got into the bus, he had watched her swaying her hips with
every breath he took. Bena was young and beautiful. Her hair
was soft and coal-black. Her eyes, kind and tender. Her lips
tempting, and her full sharp breasts inviting. The young man
tried to smile at Bena but the smile didn't come off. He looked at

Bena. Bit his fingernails. Lit a cigarette. He seemed to transmit a message through his eyes to her as if saying, *I am with you. I know precisely what you are feeling. Don't worry. I am on your side.* His face was then as inscrutable as everybody else's.

The machine was the only thing with any life; it, at least, showed her respect. The black wheels kept on turning beneath Bena. The seat kept rocking her. And the passengers kept on harassing her with their stares. Outside, the rolling hills swept by. Soon, signs of the town began to dot the road: a board with "Welcome to Mara" in big letters loomed up and disappeared. This encouraged Bena. It gave her confidence and hope about the friendly town.

When they reached Mara, the bus parked in front of the Mara Blue Bar and Restaurant. The passengers got out. The old man and his family stood for a second or two in complete silence, their faces now openly showing pity, contempt and embarrassment at seeing such a young girl alone in a strange town. The young man winked at Bena and gave her a broad smile. His farewell was well meant.

Bena stood with her eyes roving across the drab untidy town; across the rows of *dukas,*° all so quiet; across the moving people; all so quiet too, unconcerned about anything. She transferred her bundle to her other hand. She walked up and down the pavement. Looked at every man who passed by but she did not see Gatimu. The crowds frightened her. The shrill cries of the boys playing in the street annoyed her because they reminded her of her younger brothers back home. She envied the carefree children on the roadside. Here she was, a stranger in a lonely town. Her man, Gatimu, did not come to meet her. Where could he be?

The juke-box in the bar was playing a good number. The music was soft and inviting. She went in. All eyes turned towards her as she stepped into the bar. She held her bundle more tightly. Her eyes were fixed on the floor.

"There is a seat this way, lady," the waiter said in a polite but business like manner.

Bena followed him obediently.

dukas: small, native shops.

"What can I do for you, lady?" the waiter asked. She hesitated. Her fingers found the tablecloth and she began playing with it. After a time, she looked up. The waiter was patiently waiting for an answer.

Reluctantly she said, "I . . . I . . . wanted to see somebody."

"Do you know him?"

"I was expecting him to meet me at the bus," she said softly.

"Do you know where he stays?"

"I am a stranger here," she said innocently, without looking at the waiter, "but he works on the railways," she added.

"Then go to the railway headquarters and ask for him there. The place is near. Once out, walk on straight right," advised the waiter.

Bena rose, collected her bundle and tucked it under her left armpit. For the first time, she heard the noise the people were making. Laughter. Music. It was all unusual to her. She threw a glance at the waiter and said politely, "Thank you, sir."

She went out. Almost running. The waiter stood looking at her until she disappeared. Then he shook his head and went about this business. Bena followed the waiter's advice. A train of images passed through her mind. The crowd that pushed around her, without any apologies, did not exist. She felt bitter at heart. Beads of sweat that had collected on her forehead reminded her of tears, and her eyes filled. She let the tears flow freely as if they alone could heal the ache in her heart. Hatred burned within her. Was it her fault that she had not liked Bako? Her father had chosen him for her because Bako came from a rich family. How could he be her husband? A coward. A man who had wept at his initiation ceremony. A man who could not stand up to any challenge. The other women would taunt her at having married a coward.

"Bako a husband indeed!" she whispered to herself.

While she was debating in her mind and wondering whether she would find Gatimu in the railway headquarters, a soft hand touched her shoulders. Without looking back to see who had touched her, she shouted with joy, "Gatimu, my love." Sarah was surprised at this, but happy to see Bena. The two girls looked at each other without speaking. Sarah grasped Bena's hand and shook it hard.

"Bena, so you are in town!" Sarah said happily.

"Oh, I just arrived a moment ago."

"It is a surprise. You must have come for something special?"

At this, Bena looked down shyly; wiped her face with her bare hand, then changed her bundle to her other arm.

"Bena, dear, you must be tired and hungry. Let's go to that hotel across the street," Sarah said encouragingly, leading Bena.

Bena followed obediently.

"What will you have?"

"Something cold," Bena answered.

They were brought two *Fantas*° and some cakes.

"How is everyone at home?" Sarah asked, pouring herself a drink.

"Fine," Bena said.

"Sarah, I came to this town to look for—" She stopped, picked up her drink; put it down; took the cake, but when she was about to bite it, put that down too.

"Don't tell me you're looking for a job," Sarah said teasingly.

Bena tried to force out a smile.

Looking at Sarah pleadingly, Bena asked, "Tell me, where is Gatimu?"

"Surely you didn't make the whole journey to ask that," Sarah answered innocently. Bena's moment of embarrassment and tension, a moment of hope and desire had come. Her desire to know where her secret lover was, was mounting.

"Where is he?"

"Oh, just around."

"You mean in town? Here?"

"Oh no, he left with his wife some weeks ago for Tabora."

The glass Bena was holding fell and broke in pieces. Her head dropped down loosely. Her fingers were trembling. She stood up to pick up the pieces of glass. "I will do it, lady," the waiter assured her. She covered her face with her hands. Sobbingly she told Sarah, "I was to marry him very soon."

Fanta: the brand name of a soda pop common across Africa.

Sarah felt confused. So as not to cause any embarrassment she said, "Oh, I see!"

The waiter came. Sarah paid. She took Bena's hand politely and said, "Let's go home and have a rest. Don't make this the end of the world." Sarah hailed a taxi. It stopped. They moved towards slowly, Sarah carrying Bena's bundle. "Nyamongo quarters, please," Sarah told the taximan.

In the car, Bena felt the stabbing in her heart more severely. Her blood went cold. She could not convince herself that she was not going to Gatimu's home. She remembered the day Gatimu had told her, "I am yours and you are mine." Gatimu had grown fond of calling her Nancy. She now remembered the words he had said to her that night under a clear moon. The words came back to her. She could see Gatimu and herself leaning on a tree. Gatimu holding her tenderly and close to him. Her head on his wide shoulder. His voice sounding like distant music to her ears. The voice became louder and more real:

> "Nancy, Nancy, are you the angel of my dreams?
> Are you the beauty I see in the empty skies,
> The lass I see on the face of the moon?
> At night I sit and stare at the empty skies,
> The moon comes and the stars dance around her.
> The glow-worms sparkle her way,
> As the nightingales sing in her praise.
> And yet I am all alone.
> Fancy, Nancy, being the moon of my world:
> I'd be the nightingale to sing your praise,
> The glow-worm to sparkle your paths
> And the star to dance around you."

Slowly, the musical voice of Gatimu faded away. She strained hard to hear it but it trailed off. In that moment of darkness and loneliness, the words of her aged mother came back to her: "Bena, the city people are no good. You will only be happy in the village." Her mother had once told her so. *How true her prophecy!* Bena thought.

Did this mean that Bako was to marry her after all? No. Impossible. No one, nothing could shut her away from Gatimu for ever. There must be some hope. She must go to him. She must.

"Sarah, do you think he will love me, want me and need me while he has another woman?" Bena asked with a sob.

"Men are strange. Very strange," Sarah said in a whisper. Almost to herself.

FOUR

REACTIONS

The assertion of the values and virtues of one's group lies at the heart of the African cultural reaction. This reaction is, broadly considered, *négritude*—the reaction of Negro peoples to their experience with the European, and the praise of Negroness—and, more narrowly considered, *Africanism*—the self-assertion of Negro-Africans through the arts and literature, through alterations of habits of speech and dress, and through nationalistic and revolutionary independence movements.

Thomas has said that "in its original, explicit, form, *négritude* is at once the awareness of a traumatic situation and the reaction to that situation" and that the principal themes of *négritude* are to be oneself, "to affirm oneself *against* the Other, then *with* the Other: the rediscovery of one's past, one's culture, one's ancestors and one's language. . . ."[1]

Although most Negro-African protest, overt and covert, is negritudinous, it has become customary to refer to *négritude*, especially in its racial forms, as primarily an artistic and literary movement. Max Bilen has rightly said that

Contemporary African poetry is poetry for an Event since it celebrates, before anything else, the political emancipation of the Continent. But the action of its poets, with very few exceptions, is not limited to formulating revolt, violence or even expectations. Their creation is, in a particular way, essential and identifies itself with action as being and becoming, the sacred and the profane, the visible and the supernatural, mind and matter.[2]

Accordingly, literature of reaction varies greatly in kind, from that which forthrightly opposes the absurdities of colonialism and mission teachings—for example, Imoukhude's poem on monogyny —to literature which portrays the corruption of the African and African traditions because of contact with the Europeans, and literature which expresses definable *négritude,* class conflict, or nationalism.

Nationalistic writing does not appear in the same proportion as writing on other major themes. It tends to be produced by exceptionally oppressed peoples or by peoples who traditionally have been warlike, strongly group-conscious, and at the same time literary. More often one encounters the themes of culture loss, of the search for the African image, and even of *négritude* in the literature of most tribal, formerly colonial Africa. But nationalistic writing does appear in such areas as South Africa and the Somali Republic. The Somali have always known who they were, and perhaps it is too late for any real restoration of traditional ways or traditional images in the white-ruled land of *apartheid.* Non-white South African writers do, however, argue against *apartheid* and the racism which Bantu-speaking Africans and Cape Colored alike experience at the hands of the Afrikaner government. Balandier's remarks on this situation are apropos, that

Colonial African societies are distinguished by the color-bar situation . . . the world problem of minorities becomes translated into tropical terms . . . colonialized groups, having a racial base, are a dominated majority.[3]

But it is not everywhere the same, for although one encounters a plethora of protest writings about race problems in South Africa, the Somali seem blithely unconcerned with matters of race. The fact of the matter is that the black South African has experienced such racism *in extremis;* he is a member of an exceptionally oppressed group with indeed little hope for any alleviation of the situation; and he accordingly responds more violently than most Africans. The Somali respond violently in their literature because in fact they were (and are) warlike and they are strongly group-conscious, but they did not experience racistic oppression at all comparable with that of South Africa, Angola, or Mozambique, or even, for that matter, the Congo. Somali poetry has been closely allied with the rise of Somali nationalism and the Somali independence movements since before the Somali were ever conquered by the Europeans. Harnessing literature to the theme of Somali unification is therefore a natural development, as Colin Legum has argued.[4]

Aside from racial conflict, the literature of reaction was greatly influenced by the desire to gain political independence from Europe and to gain cultural freedom from the destructive Europeanism forced upon the African by the colonialist and the missionary. From the time when nationalist independence parties began to form in Angola (around 1953), nationalist and literary activities began to intermingle. The younger authors concentrated on describing the social disorder under colonialism, the consequences of detribalization, and the vicissitudes of the recruitment of labor. In these writings, said Mario de Andrade, "a common attitude can be detected: the desire to assume the condition of the native. . . . There is in these literary creations a conscious effort of identification, more than a movement of solidarity with Negroes in other parts of the world."[5]

In contrast with the more nationalistic and Africanistic reaction, *négritude*—Meloné has argued—furnishes a response of the Negro world in its anguished search for its own image; it is the language of Negro-African conscience.[6] This is often the case, although it is not always obvious in the works of literature. As a rule, *négritude* is assertion, including the complaint that the true or real Africa has been lost; it is partly a search for an image, as Chapter Two of this text indicates; and it is the voice of Negro-African conscience and values. It is, simply, the assertion of the positive values of being Negro and African. People can quite easily reach the limit of their patience when they are subject to closely related groups, as Faarah Nuur's "Limits of Submission" indicates. How much more humiliating, then, is that situation where the African on his own soil is subject to the foreigner. The Nigerian novelist Chinua Achebe summed up this situation when he said:

. . . no thinking African can escape the pain of the wound in our soul. You have all heard of the African personality, of African democracy, of the African way to socialism, of negritude, and so on. They are all props we have fashioned at different times to help us get on our feet again. Once we are up we shall not need any of them any more. But for the moment it is in the nature of things that we may need to counter racism with what Jean-Paul Sartre has called an anti-racist racism, to announce not just that we are as good as the next man but that we are better.[7]

Tshakatumba

(Republic of the Congo)

PRIERE SANS ECHO[8]

Pourquoi cette surdité
pourquoi ce morne silence
aux pater noster machinals
de ma race moulée
dans l'alliage de la souffrance
souffrance vieille comme le monde
O Dieu à la barbe grise
grinçant des dents de mort
du nègre surnommé païen.

Dieu de Moïse m'entends-tu
pourquoi l'extermination
des premiers-nés mâles du pays
des Raïs
Nil blanc Nil ensanglanté
Zambèze maté mais agaçant
Sourdes oreilles yeux aveugles
aux Wallace qui de leurs molosses
molosses dressées me traquent
jettent boyaux tripes au soleil
soleil à la senteur de narcotique
dans les becs des charognards
boyaux tripes disparaissent

PRAYER WITHOUT ECHO

Why this deafness
why this dismal silence
at the mechanical Our Fathers
of my race formed
with the alloy of suffering
suffering as old as the world
O gray-bearded God
grinding in death the teeth
of the Negro called pagan.

God of Moses do you hear me
why the extermination
of the first-born males of the land
of the Sun-gods
White Nile bloody Nile
Zambezi subjugated but restless
Ears deaf eyes blind
to the Wallaces° who with their mastiffs
trained mastiffs hunt me
throw guts and bowels to the sun
sun with the smell of narcotics
into the mouths of scavengers
guts and bowels disappear

Wallaces: Former Governor George Wallace of Alabama is considered a typical white supremacist.

Vers un Dieu qui ne s'apitoie
des miserere d'une race
montent sans écho en plein midi
midi des Tropiques pauvres hommes
votre émancipation réside en vous-même
car les spirituals fruits éclos
des tristes labeurs ne purent
émouvoir ni toi ni tes puritains
et je dis à mes congénères
que la rédemption de la race timorée
niche en elle-même
Que de plumes dénoncèrent les brimades
que des voix s'élèveront pur écho
des temples noirs du monde noir
que d'enfants meurent
nourrissant l'espoir d'un jour meilleur
tissant le drapeau de la délivrance
délivrance de la race vendue
à ton su à ta vue en ton nom.

Toward a God who is not moved to pity
by the *misereres*° of a race
they rise up without echo at high noon
noon of the tropics poor men
your emancipation depends upon yourselves
for the spirituals, fruits born
of sorrowful labors, could not
move either thee or thy puritans
and I say to my own kind
that the redemption of the fearful race
resides in itself
How many pens denounced the tormenting
how many voices will raise up a pure echo
from the black temples of the black world
how many children die
nourishing the hope of a better day
weaving the flag of deliverance
deliverance of the betrayed race
with thy knowledge, in thy sight, in thy name!

---

misereres: prayers. Reference is to the *Miserere,* the 51st Psalm of David.
Verses 18–19 are apropos here: "For you" are not pleased with sacrifices;
should I offer a holocaust, you would not accept it. My sacrifice, O God, is
a contrite spirit; a heart contrite and humbled, O God, you will not spurn."

Tchicaya U Tam'si
(Congo)

from AU SOMMAIRE D'UNE PASSION[9]

Nous étions gens de nuit
nous eûmes le destin que nous eûmes
congénitalement

Et moi
J'oublie d'être nègre pour pardonner
Je ne verrai plus mon sang sur leurs mains
c'est juré

Le monologue d'une vertèbre
(c'était déjà la mienne, jadis)
Le monologue d'une vertèbre
ne fait pas délirer la chrétienté
Qui a tort d'être fourbe
la vertèbre la chrétienté moi-même

La farce continue à la prochaine mort
qu'on me brûle mon épine dorsale
Assez de scandale sur ma vie

from TOWARD AN ABSTRACT
OF A PASSION

We were people of the night°
we had the destiny which we possessed
congenitally

And me
I forget about being Negro in order to forgive
I will not see any more of my blood on their hands
it is promised

The soliloquoy of a vertebra
(it was indeed my own, formerly)
The soliloquoy of a vertebra
does not madden Christendom
Which is wrong by being deceitful
the vertebra Christendom myself

The farce continues to the next death
let them burn my spine
Enough disgrace about my life

We were people of the night: reference to one common stereotype about
Africans. Aimé Césaire, one of the founders of the French group of *Négritude*
poets, wrote:
    Ceux qui n'ont inventé ni la poudre ni la boussole,
    Ceux qui n'ont jamais su dompter ni la vapeur, ni l'électricité,
    Ceux qui n'ont exploré ni les mers ni le ciel,
    Mais ils savent en ses moindres recoins le pays de souffrance. (10)
T. Meloné in "New Voices of African Poetry in French," said that "Tchicaya
is in no way ashamed of his Negroness. On the contrary, he totally assumes
it, drains to the dregs the cup of the sufferings of the Congolese people." (11)

Je ne verrai plus mon sang sur leurs mains
J'oublie d'être nègre pour pardonner cela au monde
C'est dit qu'on me laisse la paix d'être Congolais

Bernard Dadié

(Ivory Coast)

AUX POETES[12]

Pêcheurs d'aurores
briseurs de çhaînes
dans la nuit,
Moissonneurs d'étoiles
Vieux paladins, courant le monde,

Ma terre geint de tous les murmures
Mon ciel gronde de tous les cris étouffés.

J'ai mal aux angles
Dans ma cage d'acier
Dans mon silence d'orage.

Pêcheurs d'aurores
Moissonneurs d'étoiles
Faites le Jour autour de moi,
le jour autour des miens.

I will not see any more of my blood on their hands
I forget about being Negro in order to forgive the
world for that
That's all. Let them leave me to be Congolese in peace.

TO THE POETS

Fishermen of the dawn
breakers of chains
in the night,
Harvesters of stars
Old paladins, roaming the world,

My earth moans from all the murmuring
My heaven rumbles from all the crooked cries.

I am sick of the corners
In my steel cage
in my tumultuous silence.

Fishermen of the dawn
Harvesters of stars
Make it Day around me,
day around all of my brothers.

George Awoonor-Williams

(Ghana)

THE YEARS BEHIND[13]

Age they say cannot wither the summer smiles
Nor will the trappings of our working clothes
Change into the glamour of high office.
Twenty-eight seasons have passed
And fleshy flushes of youth are receding
Before the residuary worm's dominion
In the house of the fire-god.°
On the sacred stone with the neglected embers
The cock offering has fluttered and gone;
The palm oil on the stone gods has turned green,
And the god looks on, concerned and forgotten,
And the moon marks are stamped deep
On the thunder's voice at storm time.°

---

fire-god: the poet's self, insofar as man is the user and controller of fire. This is probably ironic.

sacred stone . . . storm time: reference to the sense of loss of traditional worship. The old gods are not dead (*concerned*), even though man has "forgotten" them temporarily.

The tide of the river beckons the lost souls
That are still lost at the turbulent estuary.
My life's song falls low among alien peoples
Whose songs are mingled with mine,
And the tuneful-reverberate is reborn—
Reborn on the tabernacle of my father's temple.°
Sew the old days for me, my fathers:
Sew them that I may wear them
For the feast that is coming,
The feast of the new season that is coming.

the tuneful-reverberate . . . my father's temple: The poet is a product of both Africa and Europe, the former by birth and childhood training, the latter by education, and he reflects both. As a poet, a speaker, he is the "reverberate" or echo "reborn" to temporarily inhabit this body or "tabernacle"; the "father's temple," the body, which is at present perhaps the only apparent remnant of the traditional past, will reassert its traditionalism and, presumably, the soul itself will steadily conform to the traditionalistic "form" of the body.

Sembène Ousmane

(Senegal)

NOSTALGIE[14]

Diouana
Notre Soeur
Née des rives de notre Casamance
S'en va l'eau de notre fleuve Roi
Vers d'autres horizons
Et la barre tonnante harcèle les flancs de notre Afrique.

Diouana
Notre Soeur
Sur la barre ne tanguent plus les négriers
L'épouvante, le désespoir, la course éperdue
Les cris, les hurlements se sont tus
Dans nos mémoires résonnent les échos
Diouana
La barre demeure
Les siècles se sont ajoutés aux siècles
Les chaînes sont brisées
Les carcans dévorés par les termites
Sur les flancs de notre Mère
Afrique
Se dressent les maisons d'esclaves
(Ces maisons sont des monuments à notre histoire)

NOSTALGIA°

Diouana
Our Sister
Born on the banks of our Casamance°
Away goes the water of our river King
Toward other horizons,
And the thundering tidal bore lashes the flanks of our Africa.

Diouana
Our Sister
The slave-ships no longer pitch at the reef
The terror, the despair, the bewildering raid
The cries, the screaming are hushed
In our memories the echoes resound
Diouana,
The reef remains.
Centuries are added to centuries
The chains are broken
The pillories devoured by termites
On the flanks of our Mother
Africa
Stand the slave-houses
(These houses are monuments to our history)

Nostalgia: the story *La Noire de* . . . , which this poem supplements, is about Diouana, a Senegalese maid-servant to a French family. She is taken away from Senegal, is subjected constantly to racism and exploitation, and in despair she finally kills herself. The story closes with the lines: "Le lendemain, les quotidiens, publièrent en quatrième page, colonne six, à peine visible: 'A Antibes, une Noire nostalgique se tranche la gorge.'"

Casamance: the river (and the region) in Senegal between Gambia and Guinea.

Diouana fière Africaine
Emportes-tu dans ta tombe
Les rayons dorés de notre soleil couchant
La danse des épis de fonio
La valse des boutures du riz

Diouana
Notre Soeur
Déesse de la nuit
Le parfum de notre brousse
Nos nuits de réjouissances
Notre rude misérable vie
Sont préférables au servage
Nostalgie de la Patrie
Nostalgie de la liberté
Diouana
Rayon de nos aubes prochaines
Tu es victime comme nos ancêtres
Du troc
Tu meurs de l'implantation
Tels les cocotiers et les bananiers
Meublant les rives d'Antibes
Ces arbres implantés et stériles.

Diouana
Notre Soeur
Clarté des jours à venir
Un jour—un jour très prochain—
Nous dirons
Ces forêts
Ces champs
Ces fleuves
Cette terre
Nos chairs
Nos os
Sont à nous
Effigie de Notre Mère l'Afrique

Diouana, proud African woman
Do you carry into the tomb
The golden rays of our setting sun
The dance of the ears of new corn
The waltz of the rice-cuttings

Diouana
Our Sister
Goddess of the night
The perfume of our forest
Our nights of rejoicing
Our rude and miserable life
Are preferable to servitude
Nostalgia for the homeland
Nostalgia for liberty
Diouana
Light of our coming dawns
You are a victim, like our ancestors
Of barter
You die from transplanting
Like the cocoa and banana trees
Decorating the sidewalks in Antibes
Those transplanted and sterile trees.

Diouana
Our Sister
Splendor of the mornings to come
One day—a day very soon—
We will say:
These forests
These fields
These rivers
This earth
Our flesh
Our bones
Belong to us
Image of Our Mother Africa

Nous gémissons sur ton corps vendu
Tu es notre
Mère
Diouana.

Ouologuem Yambo
(Mali)

1901[15]

Les gens me croient cannibale mais vous savez ce que les gens
disent

Les gens me voient les gencives rouges mais qui les a blanches
Vivent les tomates

Les gens disent qu'il vient beaucoup moins de touristes main-
tenant
Mais vous savez nous ne sommes pas en Amérique et les gens
sont
Tous des fauchés

Les gens croient que c'est ma faute et qu'ils ont peur de mes
dents
Mais voyez
Mes dents sont blanches et pas rouges je n'ai mangé personne

Les gens sont méchants et disent que je bouffe les touristes cuits
Ou grillés peut-être
Cuits ou grillés ai-je demandé
Ils se sont tus et ont regardé avec inquiétude mes gencives
Vivent les tomates

We grieve over your bartered body
You are our
Mother
Diouana.

1901

People believe I'm a cannibal but you know what people say

People stare at my red gums but whoever has white ones
Long live tomatoes

People say that far fewer tourists come nowadays
But you know we are not in America and the people are
All dead broke

People believe that it is my fault and that they fear my teeth
But see
My teeth are white and not red I have not eaten anyone

People are malicious and say that I devour tourists boiled
Or perhaps roasted.
Boiled or roasted I asked
They were silent and looked nervously at my gums
Long live tomatoes

Tout le monde sait qu'un pays agricole fait de l'agriculture
Vivent les légumes

Tout le monde soutient que les légumes
Ça ne nourrit pas son cultivateur
Et que je suis costaud pour un sous-développé
Misérable vermine vivant de touristes
A bas mes dents

Des gens m'ont soudain tous entouré
Ligoté
Jeté terrassé
Aux pieds de la justice

Cannibale ou pas cannibale
Répondez

Ha vous vous croyez malin
Et faites le fier
On va voir çà moi je vous réglerai votre compte
Quel est votre dernier mot
Pauvre condamné à mort

Je hurlais vivent les tomates

Les gens sont méchants et les femmes curieuses vous savez
Il s'en trouva une dans le cercle curieux
Qui de sa voix de crécelle au gargouillis de casserole percée
Glapit
Ouvrez-lui le ventre
Je suis sûre que père y est encore

Les couteaux faisant défaut
Ce qui s'explique chez des végétariens
On se saisit d'une lame Gillette
Et patiemment

Everybody knows that an agricultural country practices agriculture
Long live vegetables

Everybody maintains that vegetables
Do not nourish their cultivator
And that I'm a big strapping fellow for someone from an under-
developed country
Miserable vermin living on tourists
Down with my teeth

Some people suddenly surrounded me
Tied me up
Threw me to the ground
At the feet of the judge

Cannibal or not cannibal
Answer

Ha you think you're a sly one
And you act proud
We'll see about that I'll take care of you
Do you have any last words
Wretch condemned to death

I yelled long live tomatoes

People are malicious and women curious you know
There was one in the curious circle
Who in a rasping voice like the gargling of a leaky saucepan
Screeched
Open up his belly
I'm sure Father's still in there

Since there were no knives
Which is understandable among vegetarians
Somebody picked up a Gillette blade
And patiently

Crisss
Crassss
Floccc
On m'ouvrit le ventre

Une plantation de tomates y fleurissait
Irriguée par les ruisseaux de vin de palme
Vivent les tomates.

Agostinho Neto
(Angola)

ASPIRATION[16]

    Plus fort mon chant douloureux
    et ma tristesse
    sur le Congo, en Georgie, sur les Amazones

    Plus fort
    mon rêve de danse noire
    dans les nuits de pleine lune

    Plus fort mes bras
    plus fort mes yeux
    plus fort mes cris

    Plus fort le dos fouetté
    le cœur abandonné
    l'âme toute à sa foi
    plus fort le doute

Crissss
Crossss
Flappp
They cut open my belly

A tomato plantation was flourishing there
Irrigated by rivers of palm wine
Long live tomatoes

ASPIRATION

Stronger my mournful song
and my sadness
on the Congo, in Georgia, on the Amazon

Stronger
my dream of black dancing
on the nights when the moon is full

Stronger my arms
stronger my eyes
stronger my cries

Stronger the whipped back
the forsaken heart
the soul alone in its faith
stronger the uncertainty

Et sur mes chants
sur mes rêves
sur mes yeux
sur mes cris
sur mon Univers isolé
le temps suspendu

Plus fort mon esprit
plus fort le quissange
la marimba
la guitare
le saxophone
plus fort mes rythmes de rituel orgiaque

plus fort ma vie
en offrande à la vie
plus fort mon désir

Plus fort mon rêve
mon cri
mon bras
pour soutenir ma volonté

Et dans les cases
dans les maisons
dans les banlieues des cités
au-delà de la zone
dans les recoins obscurs des maisons bourgeoises
où les nègres murmurent: plus fort

O mon désir
deviens force
pour soulever les consciences désespérées.

And over my songs
over my dreams
over my eyes
over my cries
over my isolated World
time suspended

Stronger my spirit
stronger the quissange°
the marimba
the guitar
the saxophone
stronger my rhythms of orgiastic ritual

Stronger my life
as an offering to life
stronger my desire

Stronger my dream
my cry
my arm
to sustain my will

And inside the cabins
inside the houses
in the suburbs of the cities
beyond the zone
in the dark corners of the middle class homes
where the Negroes whisper: stronger

O my desire
become a force
to lift up beings in despair.

quissange: a musical instrument common to many African cultures, consisting of a hollowed half of a gourd covered on the outside with a sounding board with a number of long iron tines which are plucked to produce melody.

Leopold Sédar Senghor

(Senegal)

PRIERE AUX MASQUES[17]

Masques! O Masques!
Masque noir masque rouge, vous masques blanc-et-noir
Masques aux quatre points d'où souffle l'Esprit
Je vous salue dans le silence!
Et pas toi le dernier, Ancêtre à tête de lion
Vous gardez ce lieu forclos à tout rire de femme, à tout sourire
    qui se fane
Vous distillez cet air d'éternité où je respire l'air de mes Pères.
Masques aux visages sans masque, dépouillés de toute fossette
    comme de toute ride
Qui avez composé ce portrait, ce visage mien penché sur l'autel
    de papier blanc
A votre image, écoutez-moi!
Voici que meurt l'Afrique des empires—c'est l'agonie d'une prin-
    cesse pitoyable
Et aussi l'Europe à qui nous sommes liés par le nombril.
Fixez vos yeux immuables sur vos enfants que l'on commande
Qui donnent leur vie comme le pauvre son dernier vêtement.
Que nous répondions présents à la renaissance du Monde

PRAYER TO THE MASKS

Masks! O Masks!
Black mask red mask, you black and white masks°
Masks with the four points from which the Spirit blows
I greet you in the silence!
And not you the last, lion-headed Ancestor°
You guard this place forbidden to all laughter of woman, to every
  smile that fades
You give forth this air of eternity wherein I breathe the breath
  of my Fathers.
Masks with maskless faces, bereft of every dimple as of every
  wrinkle
Who have fashioned this image, this face of mine leaning over
  the altar of white paper
In your image, hear me!
Behold, Africa of the empires is dying—it is the agony of a piti-
  able princess
And also Europe to whom we are bound by the navel.°
Fix your immutable eyes upon your children who are commanded
Who give their lives like the poor man his last garment.°
May we answer Present at the rebirth of the World

Black mask . . . white masks: the mask is the symbol for the returned
ancestor or the incarnated supernatural being (usually a tutelary deity) who
ritually and regularly revisits the living, or returns on occasions critical to
the life of the people. It is a force of social control and a reassurance that
the living are protected by the gods and the ancestors.
  lion-headed Ancestor: reference to the totem of the patronymic group.
  And also Europe . . . by the navel: reference to Africa's contact with
Europe, resulting in acculturation of the African, but suggesting a necessary
two-way influence between Europe and Africa.
  Who give . . . last garment: that is, sacrificing the last vestige of comfort
and decency, apparently giving up the last sign of dignity; but through loss,
the African lives are made holy.

Ainsi le levain qui est nécessaire à la farine blanche.
Car qui apprendrait le rythme au monde défunt des machines
   et des canons?
Qui pousserait le cri de joie pour réveiller morts et orphelins à
   l'aurore?
Dites, qui rendrait la mémoire de vie à l'homme aux espoirs
   éventrés?
Ils nous disent les hommes du coton du café de l'huile
Ils nous disent les hommes de la mort.
Nous sommes les hommes de la danse, dont les pieds reprennent
   vigueur en frappant le sol dur.

Tsegaye Gabre Medhen
(Ethiopia)

HOME-COMING SON[18]

Look where you walk, unholy stranger—°
this is the land of the eighth harmony
in the rainbow: Black.
It is the dark side of the moon
brought to light;
this is the canvas of God's master stroke.

Out, out of your foreign outfit, unholy stranger—
feel part of the great work of art.
Walk in peace, walk alone, walk tall,
walk free, walk naked.
Let the feelers of your motherland
caress your bare feet,
let Her breath kiss your naked body.

Look where you walk, unholy stranger: The returning "son" is a "stranger"
because he has been altered by contact with Europe and the West, and
possibly has lost too many of his traditional values.

As the leaven which is necessary to the white flour.°
For who would teach rhythm to the dead world of machines and
of cannons?
Who would raise the cry of joy to awaken the dead and the
orphans at dawn?
Speak, who would restore the memory of life to the man with
gutted hopes?
They call us the men of cotton, of coffee, of oil
They call us the men of death.°
We are the men of dance, whose feet regain vigor in striking
the hard earth.

But watch, watch where you walk, forgotten stranger—
this is the very depth of your roots: Black.
Where the tom-toms of your fathers vibrated
in the fearful silence of the valleys,
shook in the colossus bodies of the mountains,
hummed in the deep chests of the jungles.
Walk proud.
Watch, listen to the calls of the ancestral spirits, prodigal son—
to the call of the long-awaiting soil.
They welcome you home, home. In the song of birds
you hear your suspended family name,
the winds whisper the golden names of your tribal warriors,
the fresh breeze blown into your nostrils
floats their bones turned to dust.
Walk tall. The spirits welcome
their lost-son-returned.

As the leaven . . . white flour: a common notion in *négritude,* that white
Europe—although technologically advanced—is not complete and cannot
"rise" without the abilities of Africans, including rhythm and the joy and
hope of optimism and love.
They call us the men of death: insofar as the color black is also the
European symbol for death. The ritual dance restores the link between
the living and the spiritually powerful dead, so powers unknown to Europe
are thus gained by the African.

Watch, and out of your foreign outfit, brother,
feel part of the work of art.
Walk in laughter, walk in rhythm, walk tall,
walk free, walk naked.
Let the roots of your motherland caress your body,
let the naked skin absorb the home-sun and shine ebony.

Francis E. K. Parkes
(Ghana)

AFRICAN HEAVEN[19]

> Give me black souls,
> Let them be black
> Or chocolate brown
> Or make them the
> Color of dust—
> Dustlike,
> Browner than sand,
> But if you can
> Please keep them black,
> Black°
> Give me some drums;
> Let them be three
> Or maybe four
> And make them black—
> Dirty and black:°

Give me black souls . . . Black: One of the most common and obvious expressions of *négritude* is the emphasis upon the Negro's color as beautiful, to counteract the European prejudice against Negro Africans. Reference here also is to the traditional European color symbolism: good souls, angels, God, and other "good" things were white, like Europeans, whereas evil things and the Devil were black, like Africans.

dirty and black: from the caked blood of animal sacrifices offered to the ceremonial drums.

Of wood,
And dried sheepskin,
But if you will
Just make them peal,
Peal.

Peal loud,
Mutter.
Loud,
Louder yet;
Then soft,
Softer still
Let the drums peal.
Let the calabash
Entwined with beads
With blue Aggrey beads°
Resound, wildly
Discordant,
Calmly
Melodious.
Let the calabash resound
In tune with the drums.
Mingle with these sounds
The clang
Of wood on tin:
Kententsekenken
Ken-tse ken ken ken:
Do give me voices
Ordinary
Ghost voices
Voices of women
And the bass
Of men.

Aggrey beads: Akan, *bodom.* Beads, usually blood-red, sometimes blue, made of glass sometimes mixed with gold dust. The *akori* beads as such were usually blue, with greenish translucence. (20)

Let there be dancers,
Broad-shouldered Negroes
Stamping the ground
With naked feet
And half-covered
Women
Swaying, to and fro,
In perfect
Rhythm
To *"Tom shikishiki"*
And *"ken,"*
And voices of ghosts
Singing,
Singing!
Let there be
A setting sun above,
Green palms
Around,
A slaughtered fowl°
And plenty of
Yams.

And dear Lord,
If the place be
Not too full,
Please
Admit spectators.
They may be
White or
Black.

Admit spectators
That they may
See:
The bleeding fowl,

---

slaughtered fowl: that is, a sacrificial offering.

And yams,
And palms
And dancing ghosts.°
Odomankoma,°
Do admit spectators
That they may
Hear:
Our native songs,
The clang of wood on tin
The tune of beads
And the pealing drums.

Twerampon,° please, please
Admit
Spectators!
That they may
Bask
In the balmy rays
Of the
Evening Sun,
In our lovely
African heaven!

---

dancing ghosts: dancers wearing masks, representing spirits or ancestors.
Odomankoma (*Odumankoma,* a Creator—*oboadee*): along with Nyame
and Nyankopon forms a triad, Odumankoma representing consciousness
and the visible world; "Lord."
Twerampon: (pronounced tchwair-ahm'-pone "Lord."

Frank Aig-Imoukhuede
(Nigeria)

ONE WIFE FOR ONE MAN°

I done try go church, I done go for court°
Dem all day talk about di "new culture":
Dem talk about "equality," dem mention "divorce"
Dem holler am so-tay my ear nearly cut;°
     One wife be for one man.

My fader before my fader get him wife borku.°
E no' get equality palaver; he live well
For he be oga° for im own house.
But dat time done pass before white man come
Wit 'im
     One wife for one man.

One Wife for One Man: One of the most persistent misionary teachings concerned the moral superiority of monogyny—one of the more objectionable teachings to the traditional African. The language of this poem is pidgin English, a corruption of English used as a trade language by many Guinea Coast Africans, especially those with little education. Implied in its use is the idea that even the ignorant or unlearned African knows that monogyny is absurd. (21)

I done try . . . for court: The link between mission activity and European colonialism is suggested here, setting the tone of the entire poem: missionary teaching is not "universal" Christianity, but transplanted Europeanism barely disguised.

Dem holler . . . nearly cut: that is, they shout so much that my eardrums almost burst.

borku: many. His father's father was polygynous. Here the poet refers to the sanction of traditionalism and respect for ancestors to support his own opposition to monogyny.

oga: lord. That a man be master of his own house is, of course, understood as proper in patrilineal societies—that is, those in which inheritance, including name, is handed down in the line of the males.

Tell me how una° woman no go make yanga°
Wen 'e know say na 'im only dey.°
Suppose say—make God no 'gree— 'e no born at all?°
A'tell you dat man bin dey crazy wey start
    One wife for one man.

Jus' tell me how one wife fit do one man;
How go fit stay all time for him house
For time when belleh done kommot?°
How many pickin',° self, one woman fit born
    Wen one wife be for one man?

Suppose, self, say na so-so woman your wife dey born
Suppose your wife sabe book, no' sabe make chop;°
Den, how you go tell man make 'e no' go out
Sake of dis divorce? Bo, dis culture na waya O!°
    Wen one wife be for one man.

una: your
make yanga: be difficult or shrewish.
Wen . . . only dey: that is, when she knows that she is the only one you can have.
Suppose say . . . 'e no born at all: that is, suppose that—Let God not agree with it!—she never bears any children at all?
How go fit . . . done kommot: that is, how can the wife stay in a man's house during the time when she is pregnant—how can she give sexual satisfaction to him?
pickin': children.
Suppose, self, . . . make chop: that is, perhaps your wife was born badly, is literate but cannot cook. Compare Mista Courifer's argument when Tomas, Jr., wants to get married.
Bo, dis culture na waya O: that is, that kind of culture cannot work.

David Diop

(Senegal)

DEFI A LA FORCE[22]

> Toi qui plies toi qui pleures
> Toi qui meurs un jour comme ça sans savoir pourquoi
> Toi qui luttes qui veilles pour le repos de l'Autre
> Toi qui ne regardes plus avec le rire dans les yeux
> Toi mon frère au visage de peur et d'angoisse
> > Relève-toi et crie: NON!

DEFIANCE AGAINST FORCE

You who bow you who mourn
You who die one day like that without knowing why
You who struggle, who sit up and watch so the Other° can rest
You who no longer look with laughter in your eyes
You my brother with the face of fear and anguish
> Rise up and shout: NO!

the Other: the white man.

Faarah Nuur

(Somali Republic)

THE LIMITS OF SUBMISSION°

Over and over again to people°
I show abundant kindness.

If they are not satisfied,
I spread out bedding for them
And invite them to sleep.

If they are still not satisfied,
The milk of the camel whose name is Suub°
I milk three times for them,
And tell them to drink it up.

If they are still not satisfied,
The homestead's ram
And the fat he-goat I kill for them.

If they are still not satisfied,
The plate from Aden
I fill with ghee° for them.

If they are still not satisfied,
A beautiful girl
And her bridal house I offer them.

The Limits of Submission: "This poem describes how the poet's clan had
for long lived in submission to a stronger group, but were driven in the
end to rebel and to assert their independence." (23) Nuur's clan was the Arab
Clan (not *'Arab*), bound to the 'Iidegale Clan.
  people: the 'Iidegale Clan members.
  Suub: a milk camel.
  ghee: drawn butter, *sehen*, the liquid butter remaining when goat or
camel butter is melted, boiled, and strained. *Ghee* is a rich delicacy.

If they are still not satisfied,
I select livestock also
And add them to the tribute.°

If they are still not satisfied,
"Oh, brother-in-law, O Sultan, O King!"—°
These salutations I lavish upon them.

If they are still not satisfied,
At the time of early morning prayers I prepare
The dark grey horse with black tendons,
And with the words "Praise to the Prophet" I take
The iron-shafted spear
And drive it through their ribs
So that their lungs spew out.
Then they are satisfied!

ON THE PARTITIONING OF SOMALIA
BY THE EUROPEANS°

The English, Ethiopians, and Italians are squabbling;
The country is snatched and divided by whoever is stronger;
The country is sold piece by piece without our knowledge.
And for me, all this is the teeth of the last days of the world.

tribute: the regular offerings of material goods and services made by a subject group to a dominant, conquering group.
Oh, brother-in-law, O Sultan, O King!: indicates praise. Betrothal, the first stage in the marriage arrangement, is effected by the presentation of the *gabbati* (gifts consisting of a spear, shield, horse, and *tusbah,* the 99-bead rosary) by the suitor to his betrothed's brother. (24)
On the Partitioning of Somalia by the Europeans: After the Berlin Conference of 1884–1885, the European scramble for African colonies began in earnest. Beginning about 1890, Somaliland was partitioned, although not until after 1920 was it effectively controlled by the Europeans and Ethiopians. (25)

Seek Ahmad Gabion

(Somali Republic)

PROPHECY°

Before the end of the world the Somalis shall be divided in three:
One will live in a palace, surrounded by his guards;
One will continue to live in the bush, drawing sustenance from
   the sale of milk, which he will carry to the town in his goat-
   skin bag;
And one will die in the dusty street, crying out, "Somalia!"

Mahammad 'Abdille Hasan

(Somali Republic)

THE DEATH OF RICHARD
CORFIELD°

You have died, Corfield, and are no longer in this world:
A merciless journey was your portion.
When, Hell-destined, you set out for the Other World.°
Those who have gone to Heaven will question you, if God be
   willing;

Prophecy: The poem was composed ca. 1903 at Itala. (26)
The Death of Richard Corfield: The Englishman Richard Corfield commanded a camel detachment in Somaliland as part of the British Government's coastal penetration between 1910 and 1912. Against orders, Corfield
fought Mahammad's men and, on 9 August 1913, was surrounded and
killed by a bullet in the head. (27)
the Other World: that is, death.

When you see the companions of the faithful and the jewels
   of Heaven,
Answer them how God tried you.

Say to them: "From that day to this the Dervishes° never ceased
   their assaults upon us;
The British were broken, the noise of battle engulfed us;
With fervour and faith the Dervishes attacked us."
Say: "They attacked us at mid-morning."
Say: "Yesterday in the holy war° a bullet from one of their old
   rifles struck me.
And the bullet struck me in the arm."
Say: "In fury they fell upon us."
Report how savagely their swords tore you,
Show these past generations° in how many places the daggers
   were plunged.
Say: *"Friend,* I called, *have compassion and spare me!"*
Say: "As I looked fearfully from side to side my heart was
   plucked from its sheath."°
Say: "My eyes stiffened as I watched with horror;
The mercy I implored was not granted."
Say: "Striking with spear-butts at my mouth they silenced my
   soft words;
My ears, straining for deliverance, found nothing;
The risk I took, the mistake I made, cost my life."
Say: "Like the war leaders of old, I cherished great plans for
   victory."

Dervishes: followers of Mahammad, the poet (1864–1920) and leader of
the Saalihiya Islamic Order, which was bitterly opposed to Christian missionary and colonialist activities in the Horn of Africa.
   holy war: jihad, the holy war, was important to many Islamized peoples,
who believed that death incurred during a *jihad* would cause the Muslim
to be lifted immediately to Heaven.
   these past generations: that is, of ancestors.
   my heart was plucked from its sheath: that is, my heart leaped into my
throat, from fear.

Say: "The schemes the djinns° planted in me brought my ruin."
Say: "When pain racked me everywhere,
Men lay sleepless at my shrieking."
Say: "Great shouts acclaimed the departing of my soul."
Say: "Beasts of prey have eaten my flesh and torn it apart for
meat."
Say: "The sound of swallowing the flesh and the fat comes from
the hyena."
Say: "The crows plucked out my veins and tendons."
Say: "If stubborn denials are to be abandoned, then my clans-
men were defeated."°
In the last stand of resistance there is always great slaughter.
Say: "The Dervishes are like the advancing thunderbolts of a
storm, rumbling and roaring."[28]

Ali Abdullah Gureh

(Somali Republic)

TO ARMS!°

The British have forcibly taken our land!
They have murdered our women and children!
Rise up, all you Somalis, rise up together,
Take up your arms for battle
To recover the land and restore our people!

Rise, take up your arms to do battle,
Free our people and recover our sacred land!

djinn: a supernatural being, usually diabolical, which can take animal or
human form and influence human beings.
If stubborn denials . . . clansmen were defeated: that is, the British were
defeated by the Dervishes, despite British attempts to deny the fact.
To Arms!: This poem is a result of the recent clash between the Somalis
and Kenya in 1962–1963. (29)

Tighten your belts and adjust your cloth!
Prepare to recover your missing clansmen,
And restore our land from the enemy's grasp!
Never sleep nor rest until they° are with us!
Somalis, take up your arms and recover our kin!

Rise, take up your arms to do battle,
Free our people and recover our sacred land!

Do not sit back or relax for a minute:
Stand by with your arms, always prepared
To go to the battle and sacrifice self
To free our brothers and our stolen land!

they: The reference here and in other passages to the Somali tribesmen
who were separated from the main group of the Somali Republic near the
border of Kenya. Kenya's Northern Frontier District contains many Somali,
who naturally feel stronger ties with the Somali Republic than with Kenya.

James T. Ngugi

(Kenya)

THE MARTYR°

When Mr and Mrs Garstone were murdered in their home by un-known gangsters, there was a lot of talk about it. It was all in the front page of the daily papers and figured importantly in the Radio Newsreel. Perhaps this was so because they were the first European settlers to be killed in the increased wave of violence that had spread all over the country. The violence was said to have political motives. And wherever you went, in the market-places, in the Indian bazaars, in a remote African *duka,*° you were bound to hear something about the murder. There were a variety of accounts and interpretations.

Nowhere was the matter more thoroughly discussed than in a remote, lonely house built on a hill, which belonged, quite ap-propriately, to Mrs Hill, whose husband, an old veteran settler of the pioneering period, had died the previous year after an attack of malaria, while on a visit to Uganda. Her only son and daughter were now getting their education at "Home"—home being an-other name for England. Being one of the earliest settlers and owning a lot of land° with big tea plantations sprawling right

---

The Martyr: This story is set in Kenya during the Mau Mau Emergency. On October 21, 1952, a State of Emergency was declared after the first attacks on European settlers. During the Emergency, a total of thirty-two white civilians were killed. Mau Mau (referring to the oath of unity, from initials of a political organization—Mombi African Union—or from *umauma,* "Get out!" or from *mau-mau,* "eating quickly," or from *muuma,* "oath") was a nationalistic revolutionary movement chiefly among the Gikuyu because of the European settlers' alienation of their land. (30)

duka: shop.

owning a lot of land: the Europeans felt they owned the land, which they considered a commodity, whereas the Gikuyu considered the Euro-peans to be only temporary users of and interlopers upon the land. That the Europeans did not feel tied to the land is suggested by the attitude toward "Home," which is England, not Kenya.

across the country, she was much respected by the others if not liked by all.

For some did not like what they considered her too "liberal" attitude to the "natives." When Mrs Smiles and Mrs Hardy came into her house two days later to discuss the murder, they wore a look of sad triumph,—sad because Europeans (not just Mr and Mrs Garstone) had been killed, and of triumph, because the essential depravity and ingratitude of the natives had been demonstrated beyond all doubt. No longer could Mrs Hill maintain that natives could be civilized if only they were handled in the right manner.

Mrs Smiles was a lean, middle-aged woman whose tough, determined nose and tight lips reminded one so vividly of a missionary. In a sense she was. Convinced that she and her kind formed an oasis of civilization in a wild country of savage people, she considered it almost her calling to keep on reminding the natives and anyone else of the fact, by her gait, talk and general bearing.

Mrs Hardy was of Boer descent and had early migrated into the country from South Africa. Having no opinions of her own about anything, she mostly found herself agreeing with any views that most approximated those of her husband and her race. For instance, on this day, she found herself in agreement with whatever Mrs Smiles said. Mrs Hill stuck to her guns and maintained, as indeed she had always done, that the natives were obedient at heart and *all* you needed was to treat them kindly.°

"That's all they need. *Treat them kindly.* They will take kindly to you. Look at my 'boys.' They all love me. They would do anything I ask them to!" That was her philosophy and it was shared by quite a number of the liberal, progressive type. Mrs Hill had done some liberal things to her "boys." Not only had she built

Mrs. Hardy was of Boer descent . . . treat them kindly: The author has introduced three types of the white settler: the patronizing white liberal who thinks of Africans as children, the self-commiserating missionary type convinced of her complete cultural superiority over Africans, and the racist. Because racism underlies the other two attitudes, Mrs. Hardy need say nothing.

some brick quarters (*brick*, mind you) but had also put up a school for the children. It did not matter if the school had not enough teachers or if the children learnt only half a day and worked in the plantations for the other half; it was more than most other settlers had the courage to do!

"It is horrible. Oh, a horrible act," declared Mrs Smiles rather vehemently. Mrs Hardy agreed. Mrs Hill remained neutral.

"How could they do it? We've brought 'em civilization. We stopped slavery and tribal wars. Were they not all leading savage miserable lives?" Mrs Smiles spoke with all her powers of oratory. Then she concluded with a sad shake of her head. "But I've always said they'll never be civilized, simply can't take it."

"We should show tolerance," suggested Mrs Hill. Her tone spoke more of the missionary than Mrs Smiles's looks.

"Tolerant! Tolerant! How long shall we continue being tolerant? Who could have been more tolerant than the Garstones? Who more kind? And to think of all the squatters° they maintained!"

"Well, it isn't the squatters who—"

"Who did? Who did?"

"They should all be hanged!" suggested Mrs Hardy. There was conviction in her voice.

"And to think they were actually called from bed by their houseboy!"

"Indeed?"

"Yes. It was their houseboy who knocked at their door and urgently asked them to open. Said some people were after him—"

"Perhaps there—"

"No! It was all planned. All a trick. As soon as the door was opened, the gang rushed in. It's all in the paper."

Mrs Hill looked away rather guiltily. She had not read her paper.

---

squatters: resident African farm laborers who are sharecroppers or, more commonly, who have rights of cultivation and grazing on some portions of land alienated by Europeans. Because the Gikuyu considered the land to be their own, the use of the word "squatter" is highly ironic. (31)

It was time for tea. She excused herself and went near the door and called out in a kind, shrill voice,

"Njoroge! Njoroge!"

Njoroge was her houseboy. He was a tall, broad-shouldered person nearing middle age. He had been in the Hills' service for more than ten years. He wore green trousers, with a red cloth-band round the waist and a red fez on the head. He now appeared at the door and raised his eyebrows in inquiry—an action which with him accompanied the words "Yes, Memsahib?" or "Ndio, Bwana."

"Leta chai."°

"Ndio, Memsahib!"° and he vanished back after casting a quick glance round all the Memsahibs there assembled. The conversation which had been interrupted by Njoroge's appearance was now resumed.

"They look so innocent," said Mrs Hardy.

"Yes. Quite the innocent flower but the serpent under it." Mrs Smiles was acquainted with Shakespeare.

"Been with me for ten years or so. Very faithful. Likes me very much." Mrs Hill was defending her boy.

"All the same I don't like him. I don't like his face."

"The same with me."

Tea was brought. They drank, still chatting about the death, the government's policy, and the political demagogues who were undesirable elements in this otherwise beautiful country. But Mrs Hill, with a great conviction that almost carried the point through, maintained that these semi-illiterate demagogues° who went to Britain and thought they had education did not know the true aspirations of their people. You could still win your boys by being kind to them.

Nevertheless, when Mrs Smiles and Mrs Hardy had gone, she

Leta chai: "Bring tea."
Ndio, Memsahib: "Yes, Madame."
demagogues: a popular European colonialist term for African nationalists. The nationalists and independence leaders were almost universally stigmatized as self-seekers. Nationalists suggested in this passage include, especially, Jomo Kenyatta, who apparently was the ultimate organizer of Mau Mau and who later led Kenya to independence from Great Britain.

brooded over that murder and the conversation. She felt uneasy and for the first time noticed that she lived a bit too far from any help in case of an attack. The knowledge that she had a pistol was a comfort.

Supper was over. That ended Njoroge's day. He stepped out of the light into the countless shadows and then vanished into the darkness. He was following the footpath from Mrs Hill's house to the workers' quarters down the hill. He tried to whistle to dispel the silence and loneliness that hung around him. He could not. Instead he heard the owl cry.

He stopped, stood stock-still. Below, he could perceive nothing. But behind him, the immense silhouette of Memsahib's house— large, imposing—could be seen. He looked back intently, angrily. In his anger, he suddenly thought he was growing old.

"You. You. I've lived with you so long. And you've reduced me to this! In my own land! What have I got from you in return?" Njoroge wanted to shout to the house all this and many other things that had long accumulated in his heart. The house would not respond. He felt foolish and moved on.

Again the owl cried. Twice!

"A warning to her," Njoroge thought. And again his whole soul rose in anger—anger against all those with a white skin, all those foreign elements that had displaced the true sons of the land from their God-given place. Had God not promised Gekoyo° that he would give all the land to the father of the tribe—he and his posterity? Now all the land had been taken away.

He remembered his father as he always did when these moments of anger and bitterness possessed him. He had died in the struggle—the struggle to rebuild the destroyed shrines. That was at the famous Nairobi Massacre° when police fired on a people peacefully demonstrating for their right. His father was among the people who died. Since then Njoroge had had to strug-

Gekoyo: mythical ancestor of the Gikuyu people.
Nairobi Massacre: Three Africans were killed in the Nairobi Riot in March, 1922, when Harry Thuku, leader of the Young Kikuyu Association, was arrested for leading opposition against further alienation of Gikuyu land, the pass-card (*kipande*) for employment, and increases in taxation.

gle for a living—seeking employment here and there on European farms. He had met many types—some harsh, some kind, but all dominating, giving him just what salary they thought fit for him. Then he had come to be employed by the Hills. It was a strange coincidence that he had come here. A big portion of the land now occupied by Mrs Hill was the land his father had always shown him as belonging to the family.° They had found the land occupied when his father and some of the others had temporarily retired to Muranga° owing to famine. They had come back and *Ng'o!*° the land was gone.

"Do you see that fig tree? Remember that land is yours. Be patient. Watch these Europeans. They will go and then you can claim the land."

He was then small. After his father's death, Njoroge had forgotten all about this injunction. But when he coincidentally came here and saw the tree, he had remembered. He knew it all—all by heart. He knew where every boundary went through.

Njoroge had never liked Mrs Hill. He had always resented her complacency in thinking she had done so much for the workers. He had worked with cruel types like Mrs Smiles and Mrs Hardy. But he always knew where he stood with such. But Mrs Hill! Her liberalism was almost smothering. Njoroge hated all settlers. He hated above all what he thought was their hypocrisy and self-satisfaction. He knew that Mrs Hill was no exception. She was like all the others, only she loved paternalism. It convinced her she was better than the others. But she was worse. You did not know exactly where you stood with her.

All of a sudden, Njoroge shouted, "I hate them! I hate them!" Then a grim satisfaction came over him. Tonight, anyway, Mrs Hill would die—pay for her own smug liberalism or paternalism and pay for all the sins of her settlers' race. It would be one settler less.

---

family: this reference is to the extended family, *mbari,* who have joint rights in an area of land, *githaka,* throughout which the homesteads of elementary families are situated. A *githaka* area and its inhabitants is called *itura.*

Muranga: the place, near Fort Hall, where the Gikuyu originated and from which they spread. Actually, *Mukurwe wa nyagathanga.* (32)

Ng'o!: exclamation of surprise.

He came to his own room. All the other rooms belonging to the other workers had stopped smoking. The lights had even gone out in many of them. Perhaps, some were already asleep or gone to the Native Reserve° to drink beer. He lit the lantern and sat on the bed. It was a very small room. Sitting on the bed one could almost touch all the corners of the room if one stretched the arms afar. Yet it was here, *here*, that he with two wives and a number of children had to live, had in fact lived for more than five years. So crammed! Yet Mrs Hill thought that she had done enough by just having the houses built with brick.

"*Mzun sana*, eh?" (very good, eh?) she was very fond of asking. And whenever she had visitors she brought them to the edge of the hill and pointed at the houses.

Again Njoroge smiled grimly to think how Mrs Hill would pay for all this self-congratulatory piety. He also knew that he had an axe to grind. He had to avenge the death of his father and strike a blow for the occupied family land. It was a foresight on his part to have taken his wives and children back to the Reserve. They might else have been in the way and in any case he did not want to bring trouble to them should he be forced to run away after the act.

The other *Ihii*° (Freedom Boys) would come at any time now. He would lead them to the house. Treacherous—yes! But how necessary.

The cry of the owl, this time louder than ever, reached his ears. That was a bad omen. It always portended death—death for Mrs Hill. He thought of her. He remembered her. He had lived with Memsahib and Bwana for more than ten years. He knew that she had loved her husband. Of that he was sure. She almost died of grief when she had learnt of his death. In that moment her set-tlerism had been shorn off. In that naked moment, Njoroge had been able to pity her. Then the children! He had known them. He had seen them grow up like any other children. Almost like his

---

Native Reserve: After the colonization of the Kenya Highlands, the English colonial government moved the Gikuyu into the Kikuyu Native Land Unit, an area of approximately 15,000 square miles.

Ihii: boys just before initiation, before coming-of-age ceremonies; by extension, warriors, or youths with a common cause.

own. They loved their parents and Mrs Hill had always been so tender with them, so loving. He thought of them in England, wherever that was, fatherless and motherless.

And then he realized, all too suddenly, that he could not do it. He could not tell how, but Mrs Hill had suddenly crystallized into a woman, a wife, somebody like Njen or Wambuu, and above all, a mother. He could not kill a woman. He could not kill a mother. He hated himself for this change. He felt agitated. He tried hard to put himself in the other condition, his former self, and see her as just a settler. As a settler, it was all easy. For Njoroge hated settlers and all Europeans. If only he could see her like this (as one among many white men or settlers) then he could do it. Without scruples. But he could not bring back the other self. Not now, anyway. You see, he had never thought of her in these terms. Never! Never! Until today. And yet he knew she was the same, and would be the same tomorrow—a patronizing, complacent woman. It was then that he knew that he was a divided man and perhaps would ever remain like that. For now it even seemed an impossible thing to snap just like that ten years of relationship, even though to him they had been years of pain and shame. He prayed and wished there had never been injustices. Then there would never have been this rift—the rift between white and black. Then he would never have been put in this painful situation.

What was he to do now? Would he betray the "Boys"? He sat there, irresolute, unable to decide on a course of action. If only he had not thought of her in human terms! That he hated settlers was quite clear in his mind. But to kill a mother of two seemed too painful a task for him to do in a free frame of mind.

He went out.

Darkness still covered him and he could see nothing clearly. The stars above seemed to be anxiously awaiting Njoroge's decision. Then, as if their cold stare was compelling him, he began to walk, walk back to Mrs Hill's house. He had decided to save her. Then probably he would go to the forest.° There, he would for-

---

forest: the *batuni* oath was administered and the base of Mau Mau activities were centered in the forests about Mt. Kenya. (33)

ever fight with a freer conscience. That seemed excellent. It would also serve as a propitiation for his betrayal of the other "Boys."

There was no time to lose. It was already late and the "Boys" might come any time. So he ran with one purpose—to save the woman. At the road he heard footsteps. He stepped into the bush and lay still. He was certain that those were the "Boys." He waited breathlessly for the footsteps to die. Again he hated himself for this betrayal. But how could he fail to hearken to this voice—the true Voice that speaks to all men and women of all races and all times. He ran on when the footsteps had died. It was necessary to run for, if the "Boys" discovered his betrayal, he would surely meet death. But then he did not mind that. He only wanted to finish this other task first.

At last, sweating and panting, he reached Mrs Hill's house and knocked at the door, crying, "Memsahib! Memsahib!"

Mrs Hill had not yet gone to bed. She had sat up, a multitude of thoughts crossing her mind. Ever since that afternoon's conversation with the other women, she had felt more and more uneasy. When Njoroge went and she was left alone she had gone to her safe and taken out her pistol, with which she was now toying. It was better to be prepared. It was unfortunate that her husband had died. He might have kept her company.

She sighed over and over again as she remembered her pioneering days. She and her husband and others had tamed the wilderness of this country and had developed a whole mass of unoccupied land.° People like Njoroge now lived contented without a single worry about tribal wars. They had a lot to thank the European for.

Yet she did not like those politicians who came to corrupt the otherwise obedient and hard-working men, especially when treated kindly. She did not like this murder of the Garstones. No! She did not like it. And when she remembered the fact that she

---

She and her husband . . . unoccupied land: a common rationalization used by white settlers. The Gikuyu argue that the Europeans agreed upon a *mohoi* settlement, acquiring cultivation rights on the land, but not ownership of the land. (34)

was really alone, she thought it might be better for her to move down to Nairobi or Kinangop and stay with friends for a while.

But what would she do with her boys? Leave them there? She wondered. She thought of Njoroge. A queer boy. Had he many wives? Had he a large family? It was surprising even to her to find that she had lived with him so long, yet had never thought of these things. It was a shock to her. It was the first time she had ever thought of him as a man with a family. She had always seen him as a servant. Even now it seemed ridiculous to think of her houseboy as a father with a family. She sighed. This was an omission, something to be righted in future.

And then she heard a knock on the front door and a voice calling out, "Memsahib! Memsahib!"

It was Njoroge's voice. Her houseboy. Sweat appeared all over her face. She could not even hear what the boy was saying, for all the circumstances of the Garstones' death came to her. This was her end. The end of the road. So Njoroge had led them here! She trembled and felt weak.

But all of a sudden, strength came back to her. She knew she was alone. She knew they would break in. No! She would die bravely. Holding her pistol more firmly in her hand, she opened the door and quickly fired. Then a nausea came to her. She had killed a man for the first time. She felt weak and fell down, crying, "Come and kill me!" She did not know that she had in fact killed her saviour. Njoroge was dead.

On the following day, it was all in the papers. That a single woman could fight a gang fifty strong was bravery unknown. And to think she had killed one, too!

Mrs Smiles and Mrs Hardy were especially profuse in their congratulations.

"We told you they're all bad."

"They are all bad," agreed Mrs Hardy. Mrs Hill kept quiet. The whole circumstance of Njoroge's death still worried her. The more she thought about it, the more of a puzzle it was to her. She gazed still into space. Then she let out a slow enigmatic sigh.

"I don't know," she said. "Oh! I think I *didn't* understand Njoroge."

"Don't know?"

"Yes, that's it. Inscrutable." Mrs Smiles was triumphant. "All of them should be whipped."

"All of them should be whipped," agreed Mrs Hardy.

Perhaps none would ever know that Njoroge was a martyr. Nor would anyone ever know that Mrs Hill felt remorse.

Richard Rive
(South Africa)

THE BENCH[35]

"We form an integral part of a complex society, a society complex in that a vast proportion of the population are denied the very basic privileges of existence, a society that condemns a man to an inferior position because he has the misfortune to be born black, a society that can only retain its precarious social and economic position at the expense of an enormous oppressed proletariat!"°

Karlie's eyes shone as he watched the speaker. Those were great words, he thought, great words and true. The speaker paused for a moment and sipped some water from a glass. Karlie sweated. The hot October sun beat down mercilessly on the gathering. The trees on the Grand Parade afforded very little shelter and his handkerchief was already soaked where he had placed it between

We form an integral part . . . an enormous oppressed proletariat: References are to the Union of South Africa and the system of segregation of races known as *apartheid* or "separate development." Three million European settlers control the country and constitute its privileged class, as distinct from the subject populations of 450,000 Asians (mostly Indians), 1,400,000 Cape Colored, or people of mixed ancestry (including Karlie, the main character of this story), and especially 9,600,000 native Africans, referred to usually as *Bantu*.

his neck and shirt collar. Karlie stared round him at the sea of faces. Every shade of colour was represented, from shiny ebony to the one or two whites in the crowd. He stared at the two detectives who were busily making shorthand notes of the speeches, and then turned to stare back at the speaker.

"It is up to us to challenge the rights of any groups who wilfully and deliberately condemn a fellow group to a servile position. We must challenge the rights of any people who see fit to segregate human beings solely on grounds of pigmentation. Your children are denied the rights which are theirs by birth. They are segregated socially, economically. . . ."

Ah, thought Karlie, that man knows what he is speaking about. He says I am as good as any other man, even a white man. That needs much thinking. I wonder if he thinks I have the right to go into any bioscope° or eat in any restaurant, or that my children can go to any school? These are dangerous ideas and need much thinking; I wonder what Ou Klaas would say to this. Ou Klaas said God made the white man and the black man separately and the one must always be *"baas"*° and the other *"jong."*° But this man says different things and somehow they seem true.

Karlie's brow was knitted as he thought. On the platform were many speakers, both white and black, and they were behaving as if there were no difference of colour between them. There was a white woman in a blue dress offereing a cigarette to Nxeli. That could never happen at Bietjiesvlei. Old Lategan at the store would have fainted if his Annatjie had offered Witbooi a cigarette. And Annatjie had no such pretty dress. These were new things, and he, Karlie, had to be careful before he accepted them. But why shouldn't he accept them? He was not coloured any more, he was a human being. The speaker had said so. He re-

---

bioscope: cinema, movie.
baas: "master," "boss"
jong: "boy." The doctrine of *apartheid* has been and still is not only enforced by Government, but taught by most schools and emphasized as right and moral by the majority of Christian ministers, especially those who are *Afrikaners,* of Dutch descent.

membered seeing pictures in the newspaper of people who defied
laws which relegated them to a particular class, and those people were smiling as they went to prison. This was a strange world.

The speaker continued and Karlie listened intently. His speech
was obviously carefully prepared and he spoke slowly, choosing
his words. This is a great man, Karlie thought.

The last speaker was the white lady in the blue dress, who
asked them to challenge any discriminatory laws or measures in
every possible manner. Why should she speak like that? thought
Karlie. She could go to the best bioscopes, and swim at the best
beaches. Why, she was even more beautiful than Annatjie Lategan. They had warned him in Bietjiesvlei about coming to the city.
He had seen the *Skollies°* in District Six and knew what to expect there. Hanover Street held no terrors for him. But no one had
told him about this. This was new, this set one's mind thinking,
yet he felt it was true. She said one should challenge. He would
challenge. He Karlie, would astound old Lategan and Balie at the
dairy farm. They could do what they liked to him after that. He
would smile like those people in the newspaper.

The meeting was almost over when Karlie threaded his way
through the crowd. The words of the speakers were still milling
through his head. It could never happen in Bietjiesvlei, he
thought, or could it? The sudden screech of a car pulling to a hurried stop whirled him back to his senses. A white head was angrily
thrust through the window. "Look where you're going, you black
bastard!"

Karlie stared dazedly at him. Surely this white man had never
heard what the speakers had said. He could never have seen the
white woman offering Nxeli a cigarette. Karlie could never imagine the white lady shouting those words at him. It would be best
to catch a train and think these things over.

He saw the station in a new light. Here was a mass of human
beings, some black, some white, and some brown like himself.
Here they mixed with one another, yet each mistrusted the other
with an unnatural fear. Each treated the other with suspicion,

Skollies: thugs, ruffians.

each moved in a narrow, haunted pattern of its own manufacture. One must challenge these things the speaker had said . . . in one's own way. Yet how in one's own way? How was one to challenge? Slowly it dawned upon him. Here was his chance, *the bench.* The railway bench with the legend "Europeans Only" neatly painted on it in white. For one moment it symbolized all the misery of the plural South African society. Here was a challenge to his rights as a man. There it stood, a perfectly ordinary wooden railway bench, like hundreds of thousands of others in South Africa. His challenge. That bench, now, had concentrated in it all the evils of a system he could not understand. It was the obstacle between himself and humanity. If he sat on it he was a man. If he was afraid he denied himself membership as a human in a human society. He almost had visions of righting the pernicious system if only he sat on that bench. Here was his chance. He, Karlie, would challenge.

He seemed perfectly calm when he sat down on the bench, but inside his heart was thumping wildly. Two conflicting ideas now throbbed through him. The one said, "I have no right to sit on this bench"; the other said, "Why have I no right to sit on this bench?" The one voice spoke of the past, of the servile position he had occupied on the farms, of his father and his father's father who were born black, lived like blacks and died like oxen. The other voice spoke of the future and said, "Karlie, you are a man. You have dared what your father would not have dared. You will die like a man!"

Karlie took out a cigarette and smoked. Nobody seemed to notice his sitting there. This was an anti-climax. The world still pursued its monotonous way. No voice shouted "Karlie has conquered!" He was a normal human being sitting on a bench in a busy station, smoking a cigarette. Or was this his victory, the fact that he was a normal human being? A well-dressed white woman walked down the platform. Would she sit on the bench, Karlie wondered. And then that gnawing voice, "You should stand and let the white woman sit." Karlie narrowed his eyes and gripped tighter at his cigarette. She swept past him without the slightest twitch of an eyelid and walked on down the platform. Was she afraid to challenge, to challenge his right to be human? Karlie now felt tired. A third conflicting emotion was now creeping in, a compensatory emotion which said, "You do not sit on this bench to challenge, you sit there because you are tired. You are tired; therefore you sit." He would not move, because he was tired, or was it because he wanted to sit where he liked?

People were now pouring out of a train that had pulled into the station. There were so many people pushing and jostling one another that nobody noticed him. This was his train. It would be quite easy to step into the train and ride off home, but that would be giving in, suffering defeat, refusing the challenge, in fact admitting that he was not a human being. He sat on. Lazily he blew the cigarette smoke into the air, thinking . . . his mind was far from the meeting and the bench, he was thinking of Bietjiesvlei and Ou Klaas, how he had insisted that Karlie should come to Cape Town. Ou Klaas could look so quizzically at one and suck at his pipe. He was wise to know and knew much. He had said one must go to Cape Town and learn the ways of the world. He would spit and wink slyly when he spoke of District Six and the women he knew in Hanover Street. Ou Klaas knew everything. He said God made us white or black and we must therefore keep our places.

"Get off this seat!"

Karlie did not hear the gruff voice. Ou Klaas would be on the land now, waiting for his tot of cheap wine.

"I said get off the bench, you swine!"

Karlie suddenly whipped back to reality. For a moment he was going to jump up, then he remembered who he was and why he was sitting there. Suddenly he felt very tired. He looked up slowly into a very red face that stared down at him.

"Get up! I said. There are benches down there for you!"

Karlie stared up and said nothing. He stared up into very sharp, cold gray eyes.

"Can't you hear me speaking to you, you black swine!"

Slowly and deliberately Karlie puffed at his cigarette. So this was his test. They both stared at each other, challenged with the eyes, like two boxers, each knowing that they must eventually trade blows yet each afraid to strike first.

"Must I dirty my hands on scum like you?"

Karlie said nothing. To speak would be to break the spell, the supremacy he felt he was slowly gaining. An uneasy silence. Then,

"I will call a policeman rather than kick a Hotnot° like you! You can't even open your black jaw when a white man speaks to you!"

Karlie saw the weakness. The white youth was afraid to take action himself. He Karlie, had won the first round of the bench dispute!

A crowd now collected. "Afrika!" shouted one joker. Karlie ignored the remark. People were now milling around, staring at the unusual sight of a black man sitting on a white man's bench. Karlie merely puffed on.

"Look at the black ape! That's the worst of giving these Kaffirs° too much rope!"

"I can't understand it, they have their own benches!"

"Don't get up, you have every right to sit there!"

"He'll get hell when a policeman comes!"

"Mind you, I can't see why they shouldn't sit where they please!"

"I've said before, I've had a native servant, and a more impertinent . . ."

Karlie sat and heard nothing. Irresolution had now turned to determination. Under no condition was he going to rise. They could do what they liked.

"So this is the fellow. Hey, get up there! Can't you read?" The policeman was towering over him. Karlie could see the crest on his buttons and the thin wrinkles on his neck. "What is your name and address?"

Karlie still maintained his obstinate silence. It took the policeman rather unawares. The crowd was growing every minute.

"You have no right to speak to this man in such a manner!" It was the white lady in the blue dress.

Hotnot: Hottentot, member of the group of peoples aboriginally settled in the Cape area of South Africa.

Kaffir: term of contempt used by Europeans against Africans. From Arabic, *kufr,* "pagan."

"Mind your own business! I'll ask your help when I need it. It is people like you who make Kaffirs think they're as good as white people!" Then, addressing Karlie, "Get up, you!"

"I insist that you treat him with proper respect!"

The policeman turned red. "This . . . this . . . " He was at a loss for words.

"Kick up the Hotnot if he won't get up!" shouted a spectator.

Rudely a white man laid hands on Karlie. "Get up, you bloody bastard!"

Karlie turned to resist, to cling to the bench, his bench. There were more than one man now pulling at him. He hit out wildly and then felt a dull pain as somebody rammed a fist into his face. He was now bleeding and wild-eyed. He would fight for it. The constable clapped a pair of handcuffs round Karlie's wrists and tried to clear a way through the crowds. Karlie was still struggling. A blow or two landed on him. Suddenly he relaxed and slowly struggled to his feet. It was useless fighting any longer. Now it was his turn to smile. He had challenged and won. Who cared at the result?

"Come on, you swine!" said the policeman, forcing Karlie through the crowd.

"Certainly," said Karlie for the first time, and stared at the policeman with the arrogance of one who dared to sit on a "European" bench.

Readings, Topics, and Questions For Further Study

One: Traditions

Oriki for Lagunju

1. Carefully check *Odu, A Journal of Yoruba, Edo, and Related Studies* (Ibadan, Nigeria: Ministry of Education, and University of Ibadan); U. Beier and B. Gbadamosi, *Yoruba Poetry*, A Special Publication of *Black Orpheus* (1959); *Nigeria Magazine*, Literary Supplement; P. Verger, *Notes sur le culte des orisha et vodoun* (Dakar, Senegal: Institut Français d'Afrique Noire, 1957).

2. Bakare Gbadamosi has said that "Every Yoruba has his own *oriki* which he accumulates in the course of his life" (*Yoruba Poetry*, p. 12). Apply this to Lagunju and, by study of his *oriki*, write a character sketch of him as a person and as a monarch. Which of his personality traits are most noteworthy? How do they compare with the traits of the ideal monarch among Yoruba peoples in general?

3. The epithet is a fairly common device in European and African epic poetry (for example, the horse-taming Trojans, resourceful Odysseus, Liyongo the Spear-Lord); *oriki*, of course, are almost exclusively epithets. What is the role of the epithet in one section of a European epic which you have studied? Does it serve as a praise-name, a memory device, or both? How does it function in relation to other mnemonic devices in the epic? What do the

epithets for a particular hero suggest of his major character traits and of the virtues sanctioned by the society?

4. Lagunju is praised for his strength and power, yet he is criticized for the particular use he makes of his powers. Can you discover any moral judgments consistently implied by this criticism? Does it indicate the same as the European saying that "power corrupts, and absolute power corrupts absolutely"? Why or why not?

5. What is satire as defined normally in relation to European literature? How does this definition apply to the song created to criticize Lagunju?

The Epic of Liyongo

1. How is "epic" defined according to European traditions? Consider carefully the *Iliad, Odyssey,* and *Aeneid.* To what extent is this *utendi* about Liyongo similar, and how does it differ, from these works? Does it resemble the northern European heroic poems, such as the Saxon *Beowulf* or the German *Niebelungenlied?*

2. What is this epic about—that is, what is its subject matter? What are the assumptions and beliefs about the nature of the universe and mankind upon which this story is based? Through the outcome of the action, is there an implied theme, a predication of the subject matter as you might state it? Does the *utenzi* seem to be concerned with making a particular point, proving some particular case?

3. Why is Liyongo given the epithet "Spear-Lord"? Does this suggest his political power and influence, or solely his prowess, or both? Explain carefully, comparing and contrasting him with Daud Mringwari.

4. Write a character sketch of Liyongo based upon the facts presented in the text. How does he resemble and differ from Odysseus, Achilles, Beowulf, and other epic heroes?

5. We usually judge a character by what an author says of him, by what others say of him and how they act toward him, and by what he says and does. What do other characters in this *utendi* think and say about Liyongo? Consider carefully the attitudes of Daud Mringwari and the waGalla, the waDahalo, and Liyongo's own people when he is dying. How does Saada, the slave-girl, treat him? What appears to be his mother's attitude toward him when he is imprisoned, and much later, when he is dying?

6. To what extent are Liyongo's traits human and to what degree are they those of a god? Why can he be killed only with a copper dagger or needle? What does this contribute to your investigation into his human and divine qualities? Consider the special, limited vulnerability of Achilleus in ancient Achaean and Greek legend. Is Liyongo's limited vulnerability similar?

7. Assess all the virtues of Liyongo described in the *utendi*. Do any of these particularly conflict with serious prescriptions of Islam? (Check J. S. Trimingham, *Islam in East Africa*) What do the virtues, explicit and implicit, possibly suggest about the relative time-setting of the *utendi*—pre-Islamic or post-Islamic?

8. Research Topics:

(a) Why is the story of Liyongo retold at weddings among the Swahili? Why not at funerals or other ritual or ceremonious events? Check wedding customs among related Bantu-speaking peoples of East Africa and among the Somali, Amhara, Arabs, Yemeni, Omani, and Shirazi.

(b) The Composition of Lyric Poetry as an aspect of Manliness among the Bedouin Arabs, the Somali, and the Swahili *gungu* tourneys described in *Epic of Liyongo: A Study of Culture Diffusion*.

(c) The Riddle-Enigma as a Literary Form with Ceremonial and Ritual Significance in the *gungu* tourneys of *Epic of Liyongo* and Old World Story in General.

(d) Evidences of Shirazi and other Cultures in the Swahili *Utendi wa Liyongo Fumo*.

(e) The concepts of status and prestige as determinants of leadership abilities in *Utendi wa Liyongo Fumo*, and in Swahili Culture.

(f) Filial Piety in *Utendi wa Liyongo Fumo*.

(g) Trade Contacts of Swahili Peoples: *Utendi wa Liyongo Fumo* as a Source Document.

(h) The Slaying of Liyongo: Assertion of Patrilineal Descent and Denial of the Sister's Son as the Favored Individual.

(i) Liyongo at the Well: The Culture Hero as the Fear-Inspirer.

Le Pagne Noir

1. What is the subject matter of this story? Is the story about Aïwa and her cruel stepmother, and nothing beyond this? Is it about the "impossible quest"? Is it about the relationships between spirit-forces and human beings? What is the theme? What does the author predicate of the subject matter?

2. To what extent is the setting realistic, and to what extent a vague "never-never land"? Where does the shift occur in the story, and why at that point? Is the shift of setting functional to the story; is it appropriate to the theme?

3. What devices does Dadié use to aid the reader in "choosing sides" in this story? Is he favouring Aïwa unreasonably, or does she possess virtues which themselves make her worthy of admiration?

4. Aïwa prayed more than once for her mother to help her, and her mother finally did "answer" the prayers. What is suggested by this? Does it indicate that prayer, to be efficacious, must be repeated? To what extent does Aïwa, through prayer, have the ability to manipulate and control the supernatural?

5. What is ancestralism in West African religion? To what extent do the ancestors have power over the living? Consult G. Parrinder, *West African Religion,* P. Tempels, *Bantu Philosophy,* and other sources. How are traditional attitudes toward ancestral force supported or modified by the events of this tale?

6. Essay topics: The Cruel Stepmother as a Motif in European and African Folklore; The "Impossible Quest" as a Folktale Motif.

The Sacrificial Egg

1. What is the subject, and what is the theme of this story?

2. Like "Le Pagne Noir," this story concerns a problem of man and the supernatural. What, precisely, is the relationship between mankind and the supernatural as suggested here? What is implied about man's freedom of will by the events of the story?

3. By breaking the sacrificial egg, Julius suffered a loss, instead of the people who had originally made the sacrifice. To what extent does the human will, in relation to "good" or "evil" deeds, affect the spirits or gods? Is Julius punished because of any evil deed he

has committed? If so, what is it, and why is it "evil"? If not, precisely why is he made to suffer?

4. Does a gulf exist between "innocence" and "sophistication"? If so, what is it? Does this story suggest such a gulf? How? Why?

5. The word "sacrifice" refers to an act by which something is made sacred. To what extent does such a definition apply to the sacrificial egg which Julius crushed? Why should Julius be caused to suffer?

6. Ma and Janet were Christians—indeed, so was Julius, yet all three were made to suffer because of Julius' unfortunate act, and their suffering resulted from the act of an Igbo spirit. What does this suggest about the efficacy of Christianity in combatting the traditional spiritual powers? Consult W. Bascom and M. Herskovits, *Continuity and Change in African Cultures,* "Introduction," on "additive" rather than "substitutive" culture change among Africans. Does this story support Herskovits' argument, or is it contrary?

7. What is the significance of the author's setting the story in the big commercial town of Onitsha rather than in an isolated "bush" village far from anything European?

8. Essay and research topics: The Concept of the Mermaid in West Africa and Europe; Religion and Medicine—the Notion of God's Influence in Causing and Curing Disease in Christian Europe and in Igboland of Eastern Nigeria; God's "Providence" in Non-Christian Igbo Belief and in Achebe's "The Sacrificial Egg."

Two: Images of Africa

The Continent That Lies Within Us

1. In this poem several comparisons are made between Europe and Africa, and between varying perspectives of Africa. How does the African "exile's" attitude differ from that of the "been-to" or returned African? Is Africa beautiful and England ugly, or vice-versa, solely because of the location of the speaker at any given moment, or do the differences result from deeper experiences?

2. What are the differences between Africa of the cities and Africa of the "bush"—the "up-country" or "real" Africa? How does the poet resolve these differences?

Flute-Players

1. How does the imagery of contrasts function in this poem? Consider especially the groups:
    desert *versus* stream
    day *versus* moonlit night
    shinbone *versus* reed
    angry bull *versus* bird in flight
2. Does the poet suggest only a set of dualistic contrasts, or are the contrasting images resolved in a merging of forces? Does such a merging indicate that the contrasts are only apparent and short-lived, not real or permanent?
3. Consult: R. Boudry, *Jean-Joseph Rabearivelo et la mort* (Paris: Editions Présence Africaine, 1960); H. Casseville, "Poésie de Madagascar," *Revue de Madagascar*, XXVII (October, 1946–January, 1947), 3–8.

Night of Siné

1. In a review of Senghor's *Nocturnes*, Guy de Bosschere said that "the theme of the poet is sumptuously African. . . . This African touch and the living négritude vividly colour the expression which often reacts in quite an imponderable fashion." Evaluate this statement as it applies or fails to apply to "Night of Siné."
2. Trace the developing mood of peace and tranquility in this poem, the movement from weariness and awareness of earthly matters toward sleep and the visitation of ancestral spirits. How do Senghor's notions of the proper setting for such visitation compare with Clark's in "Night Rain" and Diop's in "To a Black Dancer"?

Totem

1. This poem expresses one aspect of négritude. Although the poet says he must "hide" his Guardian-Animal, does he actually succeed?
2. To what extent does he employ verbal irony in relation to his "secret"? Consider carefully such terms as "hide," "scandals," "naked pride," and "insolence."

3. Essay Topic: The Imagery of Racial Pride in Senghor's Poetry. Black Women and White in Senghor's Poetry.

Africa

1. What is implied by the poet's admission that he has never known Africa? Does he mean that *in no manner* has he known Africa? If so, what is the source of his assertions about Africa's travails? Is he suggesting that intuitive knowledge ("my eyes are full . . .") is superior to sensed awareness and reasoned conclusions?
2. What is meant by "the bitter taste of liberty" in relation to the new growth of Africa as symbolized by the "young and strong tree"?
3. How do the following images summarize the overall theme of this poem:
   black blood
   red lacerations
   white flowers

To a Black Dancer

1. Lines 1–10 describe the functions of the dancer as the bringer of joy, a symbol of sexual fertility and thus a force leading to the constant renewal of life. Lines 11–20 develop the function of the dancer as the dispeller of falsehood, the force of maturation, and the ultimate power of creativity.

   To what extent are such "claims" based upon Wolof and/or Cameroonian traditions? Are the points literally true, or are they only figuratively so? Why?

The Dancer

1. How does Adiko's poem differ essentially from Diop's "To a Black Dancer"? Is Diop's poem more rationalistic than Adiko's? Compare and contrast the two works especially with regard to the extent of "claims" made for the dance by each poet, the rhythmic quality of the verses, and the kinetic values of the imagery.

Night Rain

1. Does rain at night seem to have a mystical origin or meaning differing it from daytime rain? Why? Why is darkness associated symbolically with supernatural and preternatural matters?
2. How does the poet use diction and imagery to emphasize the possibly mystical values of the night rain? Consider particularly the following:
   drumming
   beads I could in prayer tell
   spell

Message to Mputu Antoinette . . .

1. Consult *African Forum*, I, No. 4 (Spring, 1966): special issue on Negro Creativity: The Writer, for helpful discussions of Negro-American poets of the West Indies and the United States.
2. What does the poet mean when he says that the African girl must "learn" Césaire and Senghor, the two poets most closely associated with *négritude?*
3. What appears to be the function of the poet's relating the girl to forest trees? Is this possibly related to "ancient goddess"? How?
4. Is there any contradiction between "gazelle" and "forest"? What is it? Is the poet's use of this juxtaposition justified, or does it indicate mere carelessness?

Ours

1. What does the author mean by the line, "Where all history ends?" Does this suggest a boast that Ethiopia is the eldest among nations? Is the boast valid? Compare the related images: "Deep-throated giant" and "mighty earth."
2. How do the boast-images relate to such lines as "Progress rotted," "peasants died," "of reviving intrigue / Like fangs of serpents," and "Symbolic / Of your decadence"? Does the relationship between the boast and the criticism suggest the subject matter of this poem? What is the poet talking about? What is his theme— that is, what does he say about his subject?

Anticipation

1. The action of this story is set, first, in the "state park" where the *Odwira* ceremony is staged and, next, in the Omanhene's palace. Why does the author devote so much attention at the beginning to her description of the people, their dress, and the ceremonies? Is she perhaps expressing pride in traditional Akan ceremony, or does the description help to establish a situation and a mood which will be relevant to the rest of the story? What is this mood?
2. What does the author suggest about the public character of the Omanhene? How is this contrasted with his private behavior?
3. What does marriage mean to the Omanhene? What is the relationship between man and wife(s)? Consider carefully his boredom with his forty wives, his belief that the dancing girl will be "totally different," his willingness to pay such a large amount of money as bride-wealth, and his ignorance of her name. What is the author suggesting about the nature of polygynous marriage? Does it reduce the woman to the level of a commodity? Is this a valid argument about traditional marriage in the Gold Coast (present-day Ghana)?
4. How does the author employ humor in this story? Upon what, specifically, is the incongruity based? Is it related to irony or satire? Is this humorous mood possibly more effective than direct criticism of polygynous marriage? Why, or why not?
5. Topic: Variations upon the Theme of African Marriage: African Women as Authors and Debaters

Three: The Middle Passage

Stanley Meets Mutesa

1. The poet develops the mood of a quest, a holy journey fraught with sufferings. To what extent is such a mood ironic in this poem, and to what extent is it possibly a correct interpretation of the events?
2. The land of Uganda is called "the promised land." What did it "promise," if anything, or to whom was it "promised"? What was

Stanley's main purpose in this expedition, and what were subordinate purposes? Was the expedition and the visit with Mutesa
purely initiated by Stanley and other Europeans, or did the African
king in fact wish to contact Europeans?

3. What is implied by the closing lines of the poem? Do they suggest that Mutesa and his councillors erred in admitting the white
man? Does the close of the poem suggest dramatic irony (that is,
that apparently simple actions can result in disaster)?

To Pre-Colonial Africa

1. In this poem the author indicates, like Rubadiri, that a kind of
myopia of judgment affected Africans in their original contacts
with whites. Stanzas 1–2 suggest the movement of the sea and
the interpretation of what was seen: for example, "hump-backed
divers" and "pearls." What is the function of the simile "mighty
canoes . . . whales"? Is this simply realistic description of long-
boats or surfboats off European ships, or does the diction suggest
that the "canoes" appeared much bigger than life? Why does the
poet make such an emphatic point?

2. What does the author mean by "our sight misled us" in Stanza
Three? Link this with the images "sun's glint . . . lightning" and
"gunfire . . . thunderbolt." What does this imply about the Africans
face to face with their conquerors?

3. How does Stanza Three function in relation to Stanza Four? Which
specific elements of these stanzas are analogous? Consider carefully the change from the "hide of leopard skin" to "print of false
lions." Does the closing stanza indicate the results of the earlier
described misinterpretations? Does the poet imply that misinter-
pretation itself was the weakness, that pre-colonial Africa had not
only misinterpreted the strangers but also itself?

Parachute, Homecoming, and The Blaze

1. Bascom and Herskovits have said that African cultural change is
chiefly additive rather than substitutive. Is this notion in any way
suggested by the closing stanza of "Parachute"? What does the
author mean by "awkward fall"? Is it true that the person changing is "always at the starting point"? Consider carefully the fact

that he might have been born in a rural village among illiterates, but becomes Europeanized, literate, "different." Does he make such a complete return to sources? Has he ever "gone away" from his beginnings? How does this resemble or differ from the closing stanza of "Homecoming" and from "The Blaze"?

2. Does "Homecoming" indicate that changes have occurred? What are these changes? Upon what aspects of change does Peters focus attention in "Parachute" and "Homecoming"? Is Ologoudou's emphasis in "The Blaze" directed toward an object similar to that in "Parachute" or "Homecoming"? What is the poet's conclusion in each of these poems?

A Plea for Mercy and *Piano and Drums*

1. Compare and contrast these two poems especially with regard to diction, imagery, and resulting mood and meaning.
2. What are the major personal traits of Brew's African vis-à-vis the European as compared with Okara's African?
3. Why does Brew develop a pastoral mood in his poem? Is this appropriate to his apparent intent? Does he indicate that the African possesses rebellious feelings or resentment of any sort? How does Okara's mood of mystic power differ from Brew's theme? According to Okara, is the mystic power available to Europeans? How does this contrast with Brew's idea that the African is a supplicant?
4. According to these poets, what has been the effect of the many contacts between Africans and Europeans?

Lustra

1. Perhaps more than any other West African poet of his age-group, Okigbo has been influenced by and is a direct imitator of European poets and thinkers. Romanus Egudu of the University of Nigeria has done a good paper tracing Okigbo's debt to Ezra Pound, and other scholars have seen T. S. Eliot, W. H. Auden, Dylan Thomas, and other European poets as sources of Okigbo's verse. There is, accordingly, in Okigbo's work a strange amalgamation of European and Nigerian Igbo symbolism.
2. What does the poet mean by his return to the "hills" and the "fountain"? What do "hills" suggest? Do they resemble "up-

country" or the "real" Africa of Nicol's "The Continent That Lies Within Us"?

3. What is the symbolic value of "fountain"? Is a fountain similar to a principle? How? Consider the poet's indication that from the hill he can "see." Does this suggest a relationship between return to sources and principles, and clearer vision?

4. How does this compare with the notions of a return to sources according to Nicol, Peters, and Ologoudou?

5. What does "cleansing" (i, St. 3) add to "fountain," "hilltop," and "whitewashed"? Is the poet possibly employing irony in his use of "cleansing" and "whitewashed"?

6. How does the word "ascent" in Part ii, St. 1, relate to Part i?

7. What is the function of the following terms in Part iii in relation to the imagery of Parts i and ii:
   unbruised
   dim light
   Lumen mundi
   fingers of chalk

8. Does the poet in Part iii "convert" Christianity, or use Christian terminology and imagery to express what is in essence a return to African traditional religion? What does the Christian terminology of Part iii suggest about the personality changes of the poet resulting from his European education and his wide knowledge of Europeans and their behavior?

New Life at Kyerefaso

1. What are the character traits of Foruwa? How does the author arouse reader sympathy for her?

2. In describing Foruwa's beauties, the author emphasizes her posture, her eyes, her walk, her speech, and her smile. How are these particular qualities functional in the story as it develops? Does her beauty intensify the later contrast between her man and the men of Kyerefaso? How?

3. Why do the village men feel that Foruwa is proud when she will not select one from among them? Does this suggest that they believe she is their social superior and will not marry because of her class? Is this true? What is her social class? Do they realize that her "pride" is not simply that of most beautiful girls?

4. Why does Foruwa refuse to dance at the harvest festivals? The Queen-Mother argues that the men of the *asafo* company want some change, so why do they still not satisfy her?

5. Does Foruwa object to polygyny? How is this related to the presumed desire of the men for change, and to sociocultural change itself? What is the author suggesting about the relationship between polygyny and social progress?

6. What is the literary function of the stranger's presence in the village? Does the author suggest, by means of his influence upon the other villagers, that the best social and cultural change comes from outside a community?

7. See J. C. De Graft Johnson, "The Fanti *Asafu*," *Africa*, V, No. 3 (July, 1932), 307–322. What are the relationships between *dokpwe* and *asafu*? Why are the men of Foruwa's village depicted simply as members of the *asafu*? What literary purpose is served by this?

The Devil at Yolahun Bridge

1. What are the major personal forces affecting Sanderson before he knows that Hughes, the African, is coming to visit his station? Do these affect his relationship with Hughes, and his choice of Hounslow as a third at dinner?

2. Why did Sanderson choose Hounslow rather than another English colonial officer or an educated African? Was the decision sound, or was it based upon a false definition of "African"?

3. Why does Sanderson introduce Olu Hughes to Momoh, the clerk? What does this reveal about Sanderson, and what does Hughes' reaction indicate about him? Would Sanderson have introduced an English engineer to the clerk?

4. Why does Sanderson attempt "to soften the atmosphere with a joke here and there"? Does this reveal anything further about his reaction to the situation in which he finds himself? Why doesn't Hughes laugh at the jokes? Has he no sense of humor? Does this behavior indicate that Sanderson doesn't really understand educated Africans?

5. Has the author created three *types* of person resident in Africa, or are the three characters believable as persons each in his own right?

6. What is suggested about Hounslow's "Africanism" in the references

to his black "missus"? Does the possession of a black concubine indicate that he is adapted to life in Africa, or is it more closely related to European exploitation of Africa and Africans?

7. Why does Hughes hesitate so long before replying to Hounslow's remark about Africans finding European "food and clothes not quite so easy to maintain as they thought"? What is revealed about the character of Hounslow and Sanderson through their interpretations of Hughes' hesitation?

8. Sanderson tells Hounslow that by the "eternal recruitment of the fittest alien . . . great nations and privileged classes survive." How does this resemble the theme of the creative stranger in *New Life at Kyerefaso*? How do the ideas differ? Is Sanderson correct, or is this a rationalization of the British colonial presence?

9. Why did Hounslow go to the Yolahun bridge? Do you think he would have gone there had he been sober? Does one essential difference between European settler and educated African arise from each man's interpretation of the spirit-antelope's appearance? What is it? Why did the author call the story "The *Devil* at Yolahun Bridge"? Was the spirit-antelope a "devil"?

10. To what does the closing image of the story refer? Who is the "proud" woman and what does she "vaguely" fear?

Mista Courifer

1. What is the main conflict situation in which Mr. Courifer finds himself in this story? A short story often concerns one critical moment in the life of the main character, the outcome of the crisis causing a change in the direction of the character's life. Does the conflict and its outcome have such a result in this story?

2. Why does Mr. Courifer remain silent at home? What does his silence reveal about his character? Why isn't his wife introduced as an active character in the story? Is his being henpecked at home artistically functional—does it bear any relationship to the major conflict of the story?

3. Why does Mr. Courifer wear black clothing? What does this suggest about the case of black Africans involved in attempted imitation of white Europeans? Does Mr. Courifer's occupation have any symbolic value relative to his imitation of the English? Do the chief subjects of Mr. Courifer's sermons symbolize any aspect of the relationship between African and colonialist?

4. In his novel *No Longer at Ease* Chinua Achebe says, "the second

generation of educated Nigerians had gone back to eating pounded yams or *garri* with their fingers for the good reason that it tasted better that way. Also for the even better reason that they were not as scared as the first generation of being called uncivilised." (p. 21) How does this apply to the situation of father and son central to the story *Mista Courifer?*

5. When Tomas, Jr., speaks to Keren-happuch about his job, he cites especially economic grievances. Is his problem solely or chiefly economic, or does he really have other reasons for his antagonism toward the English and Europeanization?

6. What is the narrative function of Mr. Buckmaster's visit to the Courifer household? Does this episode demonstrate the author's balanced view of Africans and Europeans, rather than an over-simplification based upon either *négritude* and anticolonialism or, on the other hand, sympathy with colonialism and the concept of the white man's burden?

7. Tomas, Jr. decides to return to African housing and attire, yet he says, "the next time I appear in chapel it will be as a Wolof." What does this reveal about the nature and completeness of his rebellion against Europeanism and, by extension, the nature of African culture change and reversion? Compare and contrast this with A. J. Shelton, "Rebushing or Ontological Recession: Jagua's Return to the Village," *Présence Africaine,* XLVI, No. 2 (July, 1963), pp. 64–77. Is reversion ever complete? Indeed, is culture change from African traditional behavior to European-type behavior ever complete?

8. Why was Mr. Courifer unable to preach any more after Tomas, Jr., demonstrated his return to African dress and behavior? What is the thematic value of this point?

Four: Reactions

Prayer Without Answer

1. What does the poet mean by his reference to "my race formed / with the alloy of suffering"? Does suffering necessarily cause a people, or an individual person, to improve in character or otherwise? Are all Negroes "formed" because of the suffering which Negro peoples have undergone?

2. Is God actually "not moved to pity," or is this the poet's means

of rejecting a Christian God and emphasizing a human-centered approach? Note carefully the poet's claim that "emancipation depends upon yourselves."

3. Summarize the ways in which this poem is *reaction* and the ways in which it is nonprotesting *assertion*. What is its central or strongest emphasis—upon protest-reaction or upon simple assertion of African values?

Toward an Abstract of a Passion

1. How does U Tam'si's claim that he forgets "about being Negro in order to forgive" related to Tshakatumba's suggestion that Africans are somehow purified by suffering? Does U Tam'si appear to manifest (or claim to manifest) moral superiority over whites *because* he has suffered Negroness?

2. Does the last line suggest that the African ought to concentrate upon the problems closest at hand—for example, being Congolese—rather than those less immediate and more abstract? If so, for what purpose?

3. What is the main point made in this poem? Is there a clearcut subject matter and theme? Is the poem mainly protest-reaction or assertion? In this respect, how is it different from or similar to Tshakatumba's "Prayer Without Answer"?

4. In an interview ("Tchicaya U Tam'si, poète Congolais," *Afrique*, No. 29 [1963], pp. 42–44), U Tam'si said, "I am opposed to all those false taboos which constrain a man and hinder his self-expression. To free himself, man must know everything, be aware of everything, yes, love everything." In which ways does his poem support these statements?

To the Poets

1. In an article titled "Bernard Dadié, ou l'écrivain engagé" (*Afrique*, No. 43 [1964], pp. 59–63), the poet was quoted as saying, "Present-day African poems must be a cry of encouragement to surmount our problems. Poets should not permit themselves to sing again and again about the sweetness of life while there truly exists real economic difficulties which must be resolved." Does his poem "Aux poètes" support these statements? If so, how?

2. Which function of poets and writers is suggested by the images in lines 1–3? Which "chains / in the night" do they break, and how? In what sense are they "fishermen" of the "dawn"? What do they catch? What is symbolized by "stars"?
3. In what sense are poets "old paladins," and how can they run the world? Are they still functioning properly (see lines 5–9)? What is the result of their silence? Can the poets change the world?

The Years Behind

1. Do lines 2–3 suggest a problem of social change resembling that of *Mista Courifer*? Is there any indication of a clash between expectations (*glamour . . . office*) and actualities (*trappings . . . clothes*)?
2. What possible irony underlies "fire-god" (line 7)? Is this possibly a symbol for poetry or artistic ability?
3. Is a parallel to this alleged lessening of ability created in lines 8–15? In which ways does the individual case represent the experience of the group, the loss of traditions in Africa? To what cause does the poet ascribe the losses of self and tradition?
4. What will cause the "feast of the new season"? Could it be the poets, as Dadié suggested? The politicians? Something else?

Nostalgia

1. Useful articles: "Entretien avec Sembène Ousmane, le docker noir," *Afrique,* No. 25 (June, 1963), pp. 47–49; "Sembène Ousmane, un artiste prolifique," *Afrique,* No. 54 (April, 1966), pp. 37–38—concerns a movie based on the story *La noire de . . . .*
2. Why does the poet address Diouana as "our sister"? Does this invite extension of sibling-type relationship beyond the borders of Africa itself? Does it imply a common fatherhood?
3. Does the reference to Negro slavery support such a concept of brotherhood of Negroes? Did the slave trade and slavery affect not only Negroes of the New World but also those of Africa? How?
4. How does Diouana as *sister* change into Diouana as *mother*? What is the significance of such a change? Do the attitudes of protectiveness aroused for one's *mother* differ from those aroused for one's *sister*? How?
5. Does the promise of forthcoming revolt and self-assertion follow sensibly from the arguments presented in the poem?

1901

1. By referring to "cannibal," the poet is reminding his readers of one of the several stereotypes which in the past have been directed against Africans. What is ironic about such a reference, especially as it might apply to the relationships between Europeans and Africans?
2. What is ironic about the reference to the growing scarcity of tourists? Would a nation like Mali attract many tourists? Why or why not? Would Mali benefit economically from those tourists who did visit it? Does the blame for economic underdevelopment rest upon the African because of stereotyped notions about his past?
3. What do the poet's references to tomatoes and vegetables, in relation to the suspicion that he is a cannibal, reveal about the food habits and, by extension, the state of economic development of the country?
4. What is suggested by the missing knives? Is the poet possibly referring to another stereotype, that "vegetarians"—that is, Africans—are thieves? Why or why not?
5. Tchicaya U Tam'si was quoted ("Tchicaya U Tam'si, poète Congolais," *Afrique*, No. 29 [December, 1963], pp. 42–44) as saying, "Surrealism among us Africans is actually realism." Does Yambo's poem appear to bear this out? How?

Aspiration

1. What is the source of the developing strength to which the poet refers throughout this poem?
2. Does this poem express *négritude* or Africanism? How does line 3 suggest your answer? How are these terms different from one another?
3. Is this poem a catalogue of Negro or Negro-African experiences? What are the categories which the poet includes? For example, lines 4–6 refer to African traditionalism. What are the references in other groups of related verses?

Prayer to Masks

1. Ruth Schachter Morgenthau has said ("African Socialism: Declaration of Ideological Independence," *Africa Report*, VIII, No. 5 [May, 1963], pp. 3–6) that "To some, like Senghor, the village is the source from which African society will be transformed: it is almost a mystical entity whose institutions must be preserved." Is this idea borne out by Senghor's poems "Prayer to Masks," "Totem," and "Nuit de Sinê"?

2. The first part of this poem (lines 1–10) consists of an apostrophe to masks, describing and commenting upon them in the course of calling for their attention. The second part of the poem (lines 11–22) consists of the poet's "message." What, precisely, is this message? How is it related to and how does it differ from the themes of Senghor's poems "Totem" and "Nuit de Sinê"? Consult G. W. Harley, *Masks as Agents of Social Control in Northern Liberia* (Cambridge: Harvard University Press, Peabody Museum Papers, XXXII, No. 2, 1950). Do masks have analogous functions in this poem? What is the meaning of the variation?

3. What is meant by "[you who] fashioned this image"? How did the ancestors—represented by masks—fashion the poet's face? Is the poet's face an *image*? Consult A. J. Shelton, "Le principe cyclique de la personnalité Africaine," *Présence Africaine*, XLV, No. 1 (March, 1963), pp. 98–104; "The Presence of the 'Withdrawn' High God in North Ibo Religious Belief and Worship," *Man*, XLV, No. 4 (January, 1965), pp. 15–18; and G. Parrinder's studies of West African religions. What is involved in West African notions of reincarnation? Is this what the poet is referring to by "image . . . in your own image"?

4. Check Aimé Césaire's "Cahier d'un retour au pays natal." What is Senghor's debt to Césaire's poem? Consult Gabriel Okara's "You Laughed and Laughed and Laughed." What is Okara's debt to Senghor? Do the closing lines express attitudes common to Negro protest and to a black mystique?

Home-Coming Son

1. In what respect can "harmony" be a color? What is harmony? Is "black" a "harmony," an absence of light, or something else?
2. How is the "eighth harmony" ("black") a "work of art" created by God? Is this idea related to *négritude*? How do lines 12–13 contribute to the mystique of Africanism and *négritude*?
3. In view of the fact that Medhen's people have been Christians for well over a thousand years, what validity have his images and arguments in Stanza four? Compare and contrast this stanza, especially, with Senghor's "Totem," "Nuit de Sinê," and other works, and with the poetry of the Nigerian Gabriel Okara.

African Heaven

1. Make a detailed survey of European and Christian color symbolism, especially of the various meanings of the colors white and black.
2. Why does the poet want drums which are "dirty" and black? Is the word "dirty" synonymous (for Europeans) with "black"?
3. Why does the poet ask the Lord to admit spectators? Would black people be appropriate spectators? Do African Negroes, or Negroes in general, need to be spectators at such a spectacle? Why should whites be invited as spectators?
4. Is this poem primarily *assertion* or *protest*? Why?

One Wife for One Man

1. Interestingly related to the subject of this poem are some other works in African literature. One might read the following: T. M. Aluko, *One Man, One Wife* (Lagos: Nigerian Printing and Publishing Company, 1959); Mongo Beti, *Le Roi Miraculé* (Paris: Editions Buchet-Chastel-Corrêa, 1958), translated as *King Lazarus* (London: F. Muller, Ltd., 1960).
2. What is implicit in the concept of "new culture" (line 2)? Is change good in itself, or must it be evaluated according to criteria outside itself? Why?
3. In Stanza two the poet refers to tradition to support his opposition

to monogyny. To what extent is his argument valid? Was there no interest in equality of men and women before the Europeans went to Africa? How might the authors of "Anticipation" and "New Life at Kyerefaso" interpret this argument?

4. In Stanza three the author suggests that marriage exists primarily for the legalization of offspring, that a wife must bear children to be a proper wife. Why do people get married in your native culture? To legalize any children they might have? To give life to heirs who will revere the ancestors? To legalize the heirs who will revere ancestors? To please God? To have free sexual access with one another? Because it is "customary"? Does Imoukhuede's suggestion about the purpose of marriage resemble that in which your people believe? How is it similar and how is it different?

Defiance Against Force

1. Does this poem seem to be addressed chiefly to Africans, Negro-Americans, colonialized people in general, or what? Why? How do you support your answer?
2. How would you classify the substance of this poem—as advice, as protest veiled and made to appear as advice, as assertion? Why?
3. According to Diop, what are the losses Africa has suffered because of the white man? What can the African do to alter the situation?
4. Does Diop's tone most approximate that of Tshakatumba, Dadié, Senghor, or someone else? How? Why?

The Limits of Submission

1. What is the poet speaking about in this work? Were his actions really "kindness" or were they performance of duty? Does a relationship exist between kindness and duty? How are the acts separated from one another?
2. Can one more easily resent unsuccessful attempts to please another person because of one's duty or because of one's kind feelings toward the other? Why? Does duty "last" as a reason for action longer than kindness, or vice versa? Explain.
3. What precisely accounts for the great switch in behavior from the poet's performance of his dutiful (or kindly) acts toward the 'Iidegale Clan, and his desire to kill them, his act of revolt? Does this suggest a rigid friend-enemy distinction? What accounts for it?

4. This poem is a *geeraar*, a poem with lines of 6 to 8 syllables, normally unaccompanied, traditionally recited on horseback. War and conflict are the usual subjects for this form, which is commonly used to insult enemies. Does the poem have a tone which might suggest its use as an insult-vehicle?

The Death of Richard Corfield

1. This poem is a *gabay*, a verse of between 30 and 150 lines, with 14 to 18 syllables in each line and usually a caesura before the sixth syllable from the end of each line. Normally unaccompanied, the tempo of the *gabay* is slow and majestic, and the form is employed for very serious, sometimes even philosophical themes. Does the theme of this poem appear to suit the form? Why?

2. In 1899 Mahammad Hasan declared a *jihad* or holy war against the British and other enemies of the Ogaden Somali. It was in this protracted *jihad* that Corfield was killed. The poet says (lines 1–6) that Corfield is "Hell-destined," yet he will apparently see Heaven. How can you account for this? How does Corfield's being "Hell-destined" accord with his death and with his visit to Heaven?

3. What seems to be the function of the lengthy descriptions of Corfield's wounds and fears? Compare these, for example, with similar descriptions in other heroic literature, especially Homer's *Iliad*. The *Iliad* was a long epic told and retold to descendants (real and supposed) of the Achaeans; this poem was recited among the Somali who were fighting outsiders intent on stealing Somali lands. What appear to be some of the major differences of function of such descriptions, which otherwise resemble one another?

4. Relate Corfield's being "Hell-destined" to "schemes the djinns planted in me."

5. Hasan's poem has a defiant note, as distinct from the overtly more pessimistic shorter works, Nuur's "On the Partitioning . . ." and Gabiou's "Prophecy." Which of the three poets is most propagandistic? Why and how? How does Nuur's attitude toward the problem faced by Somalia differ from Hasan's? Is either poet wholly correct? How germane to the problem of Somali freedom and national independence is Gabiou's poem?

6. Works to consult:
   L. S. Silberman, "The 'Mad' Mullah: Hero of Somali Nationalism," *History Today*, X, No. 8 (August, 1960).
   A. S. Reyner, "Somalia: The Problems of Independence," *Middle East Journal*, XIV (July, 1960).

The Martyr

1. The Nigerian novelist Chinua Achebe said in "The Role of the Writer in a New Nation," *Nigeria Magazine*, No. 81 (June, 1964), pp. 157–160:

   ". . . how does a writer recreate the past? Quite clearly there is a strong temptation to idealize it—to extol its good points and pretend that the bad never existed. . . . We can either look for the accurate but maybe unexciting image or we can look for the glorious technicolour."

   Does Ngugi in "The Martyr" portray the situation of the Mau-Mau Emergency in Kenya in "technicolor" or faithfully? Consult, among other works, L. S. B. Leakey, *Mau Mau and the Kikuyu* (London: Methuen, 1952), and J. M. Kariuki, *Mau Mau Detainee* (London: Oxford University Press, 1963).

2. The Gikuyu have a proverb: *Komenya wero ne kootinda* ("To know a grassland you must live a day there," *or* "You do not know a person until you have lived with him."). Evaluate the situation of Njoroge and Mrs Hill in relation to this proverb. Did Njoroge know Mrs Hill? Did Mrs Hill know Njoroge? What were the blocks to mutual knowledge?

3. Is the author of this story dealing with character types rather than with individuals? Is there any validity to "type-casting" characters in such a story? Why or why not?

4. What is the European "civilising mission" which affected Mrs Smiles particularly? In what sense is Mrs Hill a white "liberal"? What does her use of the word "boy" indicate about her "liberalism"? How does this relate to the problem of her understanding of or failure to understand Njoroge and other Africans?

5. In what sense is Njoroge a "martyr"? Was he a sacrificial victim for a greater, spiritual good? What is that greater good, if such exists? Why does the author say that Mrs Hill felt remorse? Is this merely a sentimental tag at the end of the story, or does the author suggest its possibility earlier?

The Bench

1. A. Vilakazi in *Zulu Transformations* (Pietermaritzburg: University of Natal Press, 1962), p. 143, said that "in the political sphere in South Africa and in Natal where the Christians have had the

leadership of the African people, there has not developed the theory of 'négritude' or anything like it, such as has developed in French-speaking Africa, and which has been such an important ideology of nationalism there." Assess the probable validity of this statement in relation to "The Bench." What is Karlie seeking, and how does his goal differ from that of Senghor in "Prière aux masques" or Parkes in "African Heaven"?

2. Is Karlie's problem similar to that of Njoroge in "The Martyr"? What is the socio-political situation underlying each story? Do Karlie and Njoroge experience similar relationships with white people? Why or why not?

3. What stimulates Karlie to sit on the "white" bench? Does he have a reason for his action, or is he motivated by any force not of his own volition? Does he develop an attitude or determination in the course of the story's action? If so, what causes it?

4. What has Karlie accomplished by having sat on the bench? How does this accomplishment symbolize the broader struggles of South African Coloured and Bantu peoples against *apartheid* and racial discrimination?

5. Consult:

A. C. Jordan, "Six Portraits of Apartheid," *Africa South*, II, No. 4 (July-September, 1958), pp. 5–43.

Lewis Nkosi, "African Fiction, Part I—South Africa: Protest," *Africa Report*, VII, No. 9 (October, 1962), pp. 3–6.

Suggested Readings

I   Books—General Works.

P. Bohannon and G. Dalton (eds.), *Markets in Africa: Eight Subsistence Economies in Transition*. New York: Doubleday, 1965.

G. Carter (ed.), *Transition in Africa: Studies in Political Adaptation*. Boston: Boston University Press, 1958.

P. Fordham, *Geography of African Affairs*. Harmondsworth: Penguin, 1965.

M. Fortes and G. Dieterlen (eds.), *African Systems of Thought*. London: International African Institute, 1965.

M. Fortes and E. E. Evans-Pritchard (eds.), *African Political Systems*. London: International African Institute, 1940.

M. Fortes, J. R. Goody, and E. R. Leach (eds.), *Marriage in Tribal Societies*. Cambridge: Cambridge University Press Papers on Social Anthropology, No. 3, 1962.

J. L. Gibb (ed.), *Peoples of Africa*. New York: Holt, Rinehart, and Winston, 1965.

W. J. Hanna (ed.), *Independent Black Africa*. Chicago: Rand-McNally, 1964.

G. H. Kimble, *Tropical Africa*. 2 volumes. New York: Twentieth Century Fund, 1960.

H. Kohn and W. Sokolsky, *African Nationalism in the Twentieth Century*. Princeton: Van Nostrand, 1965.

P. J. McEwan and R. Sutcliffe (eds.), *Modern Africa*. New York: T. Crowell, 1965.

D. Paulme (ed.), *Women of Tropical Africa*. London: Routledge and K. Paul, 1963.

A. W. Southall (ed.), *Social Change in Modern Africa*. London: International African Institute, 1961.
P. Van den Berghe (ed.), *Africa: Social Problems of Change and Conflict*. San Francisco: Chandler, 1965.

II Periodicals.

Africa. Published quarterly by International African Institute, St. Dunstan's Chambers, 10–11 Fetter Lane, London E.C.4.
African Abstracts. Published quarterly by International African Institute, London.
African Forum. 401 Broadway, New York, N.Y. 10013.
Africa Report. 505 Dupont Circle Building, Washington, D.C., 20036.
Afrique. 21 rue Barbet-de-Juoy, 75. Paris VIIᵉ, France.
Afrique Nouvelle. B.P. 283. Dakar, Senegal.
Black Orpheus. Longmans of Nigeria, Ltd., W.R. Industrial Estate, Lagos, Nigeria.
Drum. 15 Troye St., Johannesburg, Republic of South Africa.
East Africa Journal. P.O. Box 30492, Nairobi, Kenya.
Ethiopia Observer. P.O. Box 1896, Addis Ababa, Ethiopia.
Jeune Afrique. Jeune Afrique Bureau, Room 491, United Nations, N.Y.
Journal of Modern African Studies. Bentley House, 200 Euston Road, London, N.W. 1.
Nigeria Magazine. The Marina, Lagos, Nigeria.
Notes Africaines d'IFAN. Institut Africain d'Afrique Noire, University of Dakar, Dakar-Fann, Senegal.
Okyeame. Institute of African Studies, Legon: P.O. Box M15, Accra, Ghana.
Présence Africaine. 42 rue Descartes, Paris Vᵉ, France.
Transition. Box 20026, Kampala, Uganda.

III Critical Writings: Books.

W. E. Abraham, *The Mind of Africa*. London: Weidenfeld and Nicolson, 1962.
M. Amosu, *A Preliminary Bibliography of Creative African Writing in the European Languages*. Ibadan: Ibadan University Press, Supplement to *African Notes*, 1965.
R. Colin, *Les contes noirs de l'ouest africain*. Paris: Editions Présence Africaine, 1962.

R. Colin, *Littérature africaine d'hier et de demain.* Paris: A.D.E.C. 1965.

M. Cook, *Five French Negro Authors.* Washington: Associated Publishers, 1943.

First International Conference of Negro Writers and Artists. Paris: Editions Présence Africaine, 1956.

J. Gleason, *This Africa: Novels by West Africans in English and French.* Evanston: Northwestern University Press, 1965.

L. Kesteloot, *Les écrivains noirs de langue français: naissance d'une littérature.* Brussels: Institut de Sociologie, 1962.

T. Meloné, *De la Négritude dans la littérature négro-africaine.* Paris: Editions Présence Africaine, 1962.

A. P. Merriam, *A Prologue to the Study of African Arts.* Yellow Springs: Antioch Press, 1962.

G. Moore, (ed.), *African Literature and the Universities.* Ibadan: Ibadan University Press, 1965.

—— *Seven African Writers.* London: Oxford University Press, 1962.

D. Nicol, *Africa: A Subjective View.* Accra: Ghana Universities Press, 1964.

Second Congress of Negro Writers and Artists: The Unity of Negro African Cultures. Paris: Editions Présence Africaine, 1959.

Three Essays on African Art and Literature. Tri-Quarterly (Spring, 1966). Evanston: Northwestern University Press.

B. Traoré, *Le théâtre négro-africain et ses fonctions sociales.* Paris: Editions Présence Africaine, 1962.

G. E. Von Grunebaum, *French African Literature / Some Cultural Implications.* The Hague: Mouton and Co., 1964.

C. Wauthier, *The Literature and Thought of Modern Africa / A Survey.* London: Pall Mall Press, 1966.

IV Critical Writings: Articles.

M. Aig-Imoukhuede, "On Being a West African Writer," *Ibadan,* No. 12 (June, 1961), pp. 11–12.

J. Allary, "Littérateurs et poètes noirs: aperçu bibliographique," *Documents pour l'Action,* III, No. 13 (1963), 38–49.

A. Babalola, "Yoruba Oral Poetry," *West African Review,* XXII, No. 281 (February, 1951), 130–131.

M. Banham, "The Beginnings of a Nigerian Literature in English," *Review of English Literature,* III, No. 2 (1962), 88–99.

R. Bastide, "Variations on Négritude," *Présence Africaine*, VIII, No. 36 (1961), 83–92.

U. Beier, "The Conflict of Cultures in West African Poetry," *Black Orpheus*, No. 1 (1957), 17–26.

———— "The Theme of the Ancestors in Senghor's Poetry," *Black Orpheus*, No. 5 (1959), 15–17.

J. P. Clark, "Themes of African Poetry of English Expression," *Présence Africaine*, XXVI, No. 54 (July, 1965), 70–89.

———— "Another Kind of Poetry," *Transition*, V, No. 25 (1966), 17–22.

C. M. Doke, "The Basis of Bantu Literature," *Africa*, XVIII, No. 4 (October, 1948), 284–301.

A. Drayton, "The Return to the Past in the Nigerian Novel," *Ibadan*, No. 10 (1960), 27–30.

H. Duncan, "Sociology of Art, Literature, and Music: Social Contexts of Symbolic Experience," in H. Becker and A. Boscoff (eds.), *Modern Sociological Theory in Continuity and Change* (New York: Dryden Press, 1957), 482–497.

R. East, "A First Essay in Imaginative African Literature," *Africa*, IX, No. 3 (July, 1936), 350–358.

B. Fonlon, "Culture Africaine et langues de diffusion, à propos de la Conférence de Kampala," *Présence Africaine*, XLV (1963), 182–196.

A. Gérard, "Elégies nigériennes," *Revue Générale Belge* (June, 1963), 39–49.

L. Harries, "Popular Verse of the Swahili Tradition," *Africa*, XXII, No. 2 (March, 1952), 158–164.

———— "Swahili Epic Literature," *Africa*, XX, No. 1 (January, 1950), 55–59.

N. S. Hopkins, "The Modern Theater in Mali," *Présence Africaine*, XXV, No. 53 (March, 1965), 159–191.

E. Hussey, "The Languages of Literature in Africa," *Africa*, V, No. 2 (April, 1932), 169–175.

A. Irele, "Négritude: Literature and Ideology," *Journal of Modern African Studies*, III, No. 4 (December, 1965), 499–526.

P. Joachim, "African Literature: French-Speaking Africa," *Africa Report*, VIII, No. 3 (March, 1963), 11–12.

K. Jones-Quartey, "Our Language and Literature Problem," *Africana*, I, No. 3 (Summer, 1949), 23–24.

A. C. Jordan and Others, "Towards an African Literature," *Africa South*, I, No. 4 (July, 1957); II, Nos. 1, 2, and 3 (1957–1958); III, No. 4 (July, 1959).

L. Longmore, "The Future of the Bantu Languages," *African Affairs*, LXI, No. 243 (April, 1962), 158–162.

C. Meillassoux, "The 'Koteba' of Bamako" (drama), *Présence Africaine*, XXIV, No. 52 (October, 1964), 28–62.

N. Mitchison, "An African Historical Novel?" *Transition*, No. 9 (1963), 30–31.

G. Moore, "Time and Experience in African Poetry," *Transition*, No. 26 (1966), 18–22.

———— "Towards Realism in French African Writing," *Journal of Modern African Studies*, I, No. 1 (1963), 61–73

F. Morisseau-Leroy, "Theatre in the African Revolution," *Présence Africaine*, XXIV, No. 52 (October, 1964), 63–70.

G. Moser, "African Literature in the Portuguese Language," *Journal of General Education*, XIII, No. 4 (January, 1962), 270–304.

E. Mphahlele, "The Language of African Literature," *Harvard Educational Review*, XXXIV, No. 2 (March, 1964), 298–305.

L. Nkosi, "African Literature: English-Speaking West Africa," *Africa Report*, VII, No. 11 (December, 1962), 15–17, 31.

J. Ramsaran, "African Twilight: Folktale and Myth in Nigerian Literature," *Ibadan*, No. 15 (1963), 17–19.

J. Reed, "Between Two Worlds: Some Notes on the Presentation by African Novelists of the Individual in Modern African Society," *Makerere Journal* (Kampala, Uganda), No. 7 (1963), 1–14.

———— "James Ngugi and the African Novel," *Journal of Commonwealth Literature*, I (September, 1965), 117–121.

N. Schmidt, "Nigeria: Fiction for the Average Man," *Africa Report*, X, No. 8 (August, 1965), 39–41.

L. S. Senghor, "Le poésie négro-africaine," *Problèmes d'Afrique Centrale*, IV, No. 12 (1951), 107–114.

———— "On Negrohood: Psychology of the African Negro," *Diogenes*, XXXVII (1962), 1–15.

A. J. Shelton, "Some Problems of Inter-Communication," *Journal of Modern African Studies*, II, No. 3 (1964), 395–403.

M. El Shoush, "Some Background Notes on Modern Sudanese Poetry," *Sudan Notes*, XLIV (1963), 21–42.

L. Silberman, "The 'Mad' Mullah: Hero of Somali Nationalism," *History Today*, X, No. 8 (August, 1960).

W. Whiteley, "The Concept of an African Prose Literature," *Diogenes*, XXXVII (1962), 28–49.

Okogbule Wonodi (G. O. Nwanodi), "The Role of Folk Tales in African Society," *Africa Report*, X, No. 11 (December, 1965), 17–18.

Notes

Introduction

1. Ezekiel Mphahlele, "African Literature," paper presented at First International Congress of Africanists, Accra, Ghana, December, 1962. See also Obi Wali, "The Dead End of African Literature," *Transition*, III, No. 10 (September, 1963), pp. 13–15.

2. Mphahlele, *ibid*. See also J. Jahn, *Bibliography of Neo-African Literature from Africa, America, and the Caribbean* (New York: F. Praeger, 1965).

3. Cyprian Ekwensi, "African Literature," *Nigeria Magazine*, No. 83 (December, 1964), p. 295.

4. Cyprian Ekwensi, "Problems of Nigerian Writers," *Nigeria Magazine*, No. 78 (September, 1963), p. 218.

5. Ekwensi, "African Literature," p. 299. See also J. Ki-Zerbo, "The Negro-African Personality," *Présence Africaine*, XIII, No. 41 (1962), p. 144; D. Rubadiri, "Why *African* Literature," *Transition*, IV, No. 15 (1964), pp. 39–42; Chinua Achebe, "A Look at West African Writing," *Spear* (June, 1963), p. 26, and "Where Angels Fear to Tread," *Nigeria Magazine*, No. 75 (December, 1962), pp. 61–62.

6. See A. J. Shelton, "The Cyclic Principle of African Personality," *Présence Africaine*, XLV, No. 1 (March, 1963), pp. 98–104; "Rebushing or Ontological Recession: Jagua's Return to the Village," *Présence Africaine*, XLVI, No. 2 (July, 1963), pp. 64–77; "The Presence of the 'Withdrawn' High God in North Ibo Religious Belief and Worship," *Man*, LXV, No. 4 (January, 1965), pp. 15–18.

7. One of the best short surveys of the subject is Paul Bohannon's *Africa and Africans* (Garden City, N.Y.: Natural History Press, 1964).

8. Abi Ojeikere, "The Effects of European Education on Nigerians," *The Beacon* (Ibadan, Western Nigeria), I, No. 7 (1961), pp. 5–6.

9. Kwame Nkrumah, *Ghana* (New York: T. Nelson, 1957), p. 47.

10. "Constructive Elements of a Civilization of African Negro Inspiration," in *Second Congress of Negro Writers and Artists: The Unity of Negro African Cultures* (Paris: Editions Présence Africaine, 1959), pp. 262–294.

11. "Race and Society," in *The Race Question in Modern Science* (Paris: UNESCO, 1956), p. 173.

12. W. B. Baikie, *Narrative of an Exploring Voyage up the Rivers Kwora and Binue in 1854* (London: J. Murray, 1856).

13. T. Hodgkin (ed.), *Nigerian Perspectives, An Historical Anthology* (London: Oxford University Press, 1960), p. 181.

14. *La Guinée et l'émancipation africaine* (Paris: Editions Présence Africaine, 1959), pp. 163–164.

15. S. C. Easton, *The Twilight of European Colonialism, A Political Analysis* (London: Methuen & Co., 1960), p. 315.

16. See Juan Comas, "Racial Myths," in *The Race Question in Modern Science* (Paris: UNESCO, 1956), p. 25. Consult also Otonti Nduka, *Western Education and the Nigerian Cultural Background* (Ibadan: Oxford University Press, 1964), pp. 10–20.

17. P. Marris, *Family and Social Change in an African City, A Study of Rehousing in Lagos* (London: Routledge and Kegan Paul, 1961), p. 141.

18. Compare A. J. Shelton, "Behaviour and Cultural Value in West African Stories," *Africa*, XXXIV, No. 4 (October, 1964), pp. 353–359.

19. M. J. Herskovits and W. R. Bascom (eds.), *Continuity and Change in African Cultures* (Chicago: University of Chicago Press, 1959), p. 6.

One: Traditions

1. L. Sainville, *Romanciers et conteurs négro-africains: anthologie I* (Paris: Editions Présence Africaine, 1963), p. 28.

2. A. H. J. Prins, *The Coastal Tribes of the North-eastern Bantu—Pokomo, Nyika, Teita* (London: International African Institute, 1952), p. 10.

3. Lyndon Harries (ed.), *Swahili Poetry* (Oxford: Clarendon Press, 1962), p. 51. See also A. H. J. Prins, *The Swahili-Speaking Peoples of*

Zanzibar and the East African Coast—Arabs, Shirazi, and Swahili (London: International African Institute, 1961).

4. Harries, p. 24.

5. See Chief Olunlade, the Otun Seriki of Ede, *Ede, A Short History* (Ibadan: Ministry of Education, 1961); translated by Timi Laoye. Compare D. Forde, *The Yoruba-Speaking Peoples of South-western Nigeria* (London: International African Institute, 1951).

6. O. Johnson (ed.), *The History of the Yorubas by Rev. S. Johnson* (Lagos: Church Missionary Society, 1921), p. viii.

7. See Lamine Diakhate, "The Myth in Senegalese Folk Poetry," *Présence Africaine*, XI, No. 39 (1961), pp. 13–31.

8. See Harries, pp. 48–70; Edward Steere (ed.), *Swahili Tales as Told by Natives of Zanzibar* (London: Bell & Daldy, 1870), pp. 439–453: *Hadithi ya Liongo*, and pp. 456–471; *Mashairi ya Liongo* ("Poem of Liongo"); A. Werner (ed.), *Myths and Legends of the Bantu* (London: Harrap, 1933), pp. 145–154: "The Story of Liongo Fumo."

9. Harries' text, *Sulutani Pate bwana*.

10. Some of this material has been drawn from "The Song of Shagga," a section of long-measure verse inscribed by the copyist Rashidi bin Abdallah and included in Harries, pp. 175–177.

11. See A. H. J. Prins, "The Didemic Diarchic Boni," *J. R. Anthrop. Inst.*, XCIII, Part II (1963), pp. 174–185.

12. In Steere, pp. 450–451.

13. From Harries, pp. 146–147, a copy by Muhammad Kijuma and the blind poet Mzee bin Bisharo al-Ausiy.

14. Note in Harries, p. 70: "The poem ends with a description of Liyongo's son ostracized and full of remorse, and he flees to the Galla country, his mother's original home."

15. From Steere, pp. 456–471: *Mashairi ya Liongo*, "The Poem of Liongo"; and Harries, pp. 188–193. *Mashairi* are song-poems which L. Harries in "Swahili Epic Literature," *Africa*, XX, (1950), p. 55, said are "usually attributed to Liongo Fumo, Prince of Ozi, c. A.D. 1150–1200."

16. Translated by Timi Laoye. See U. Beier, "Talking Drums of the Yoruba," *African Music*, I, No. 1 (1954).

17. In *Chief Olunlade*, p. 50.

18. From *Le pagne noir, contes africaines* (Paris: Editions Présence Africaine, 1955), pp. 19–24, my translation. *Le pagne noir* means "The Black Cloth" or, more specifically, "The Black Loincloth."

19. Originally published in *Atlantic Monthly*, April, 1959, this is the version revised by Achebe in November, 1966, and sent to the

editor. M. J. C. Echeruo in his Introduction to Achebe, *The Sacrificial Egg and Other Short Stories* (Onitsha: Etudo, 1962), p. 6.
20. See M. M. Green, *Igbo Village Affairs*, 2nd ed. (London: F. Cass, 1964), p. 37n.
21. See V. Uchendu, *The Igbo of Southeast Nigeria* (New York: Holt, Rinehart and Winston, 1965), p. 28.

Two: Images of Africa

1. The number of autobiographies by Africans, most of them revealing such problems, is rapidly increasing. One might consult, among many, the following: Camara Laye, *L'enfant noir* (Paris: Librairie Plon, 1954); Ezekiel Mphahlele, *Down Second Avenue* (London: Faber & Faber, 1959); R. Mugo Gatheru, *Child of Two Worlds, A Kikuyu's Story* (New York: F. Praeger, 1964); and Dilim Okafor-Omali, *A Nigerian Villager in Two Worlds* (London: Faber & Faber, 1965).
2. Louis-Vincent Thomas, "Time, Myth, and History in West Africa," *Présence Africaine*, XI, No. 39 (Winter, 1961), pp. 50–92.
3. From O. Bassir (ed.), *An Anthology of West African Verse* (Ibadan: Ibadan University Press, 1957), pp. 63–66.
4. From *Afrique, Supplément Trimestriel (Haute Volta)*, No. 2 (April, 1966), p. 52.
5. From *Presque-Songes*, traduits du Hova par l'auteur. Présentation de Robert Boudry (Tananarive: Chez Henri Vidalie, 1934). This copy from L. S. Senghor (ed.), *Anthologie de la nouvelle poésie nègre et malgache* (Paris: Presses Universitaires de France, 1948), pp. 187–188.
6. *Présence Africaine*, VIII, No. 36, pp. 120–126.
7. From *Traduit de la nuit* (Tunis: Editions de Mirages, 1935). This copy from Senghor, pp. 181–182.
8. From L. S. Senghor, *Chants d'ombre* (Paris: Editions du Seuil, 1945). This copy from Senghor, *Anthologie de la nouvelle poésie nègre et malgache*, pp. 149–150.
9. See D. P. Gamble, *The Wolof of Senegambia* (London: International African Institute, 1957).
10. From Senghor, *Chants d'ombre*.
11. From *Poésie Vivante*, No. 14 (September–October, 1965), p. 14.
12. From David Diop, *Coups de pilon, poèmes* (Paris: Editions Presence Africaine, 1961), p. 27.
13. Diop, Introduction, p. 8.

14. From Diop, p. 18.

15. E. Mveng, "Fundamental Structures of Negro-African Art," *Présence Africaine*, XXI, No. 49 (1964), p. 120.

16. See L.-V. Thomas, "A General Outline of the Schedule of Theoretical Studies," *Présence Africaine*, IX, No. 37 (1961), p. 138; and M. Griaule, *Conversations with Ogotemmeli* (London: International African Institute, 1965).

17. From *Poesie Vivante*, No. 14 (September–October, 1965), p. 9.

18. From *Nigeria Magazine*, XXX, No. 74 (September, 1962), pp. 87–88.

19. "Fundamental Structures of Negro-African Art," *Présence Africaine*, p. 120.

20. From *Présence Africaine*, XXIV, No. 52 (1964). p. 167.

21. From "Tshakatumba, poète congolais aux dimensions de l'Afrique," *Afrique*, No. 46 (May, 1965), p. 62.

22. From *Ethiopia Observer*, IX, No. 1 (1965), pp. 57–58.

23. See A. J. Davis, "The Church-State Ideal in Ethiopia," *Ibadan*, XXI (October, 1965), pp. 47–52.

24. From *Ethiopia Observer*, IX, No. 1 (1965), p. 54.

25. From Flavien Ranaivo, *L'ombre et le vent* (1947). This copy from Senghor, *Anthologie de la nouvelle poésie nègre et malgache*, pp. 209–210.

26. From L. Hughes (ed.), *An African Treasury* (New York: Crown Publishers, 1960), pp. 163–167.

27. See M. Manoukian, *Akan and Ga-adangme Peoples* (London: International Institute, 1950), pp. 30–32.

28. Under the pseudonym "Marjorie Mensah," the author wrote a regular column during the 1930's in the *West African Times*, including this appropriate passage on "Romance": ". . . what a prosy being a man becomes when he enters into possession. His tender words become curt, raucous yaps which leave us a little bored; . . . and we yawn our way into Prosy Street and forget romance. Men kill romance; they chase phantoms and pursue shadows, whilst romance sits unseen besides their very selves. . . ." Quoted from K. A. B. Jones-Quartey, "Sierra Leone's Rôle in the Development of Ghana, 1820–1930," *Sierra Leone Studies*, N. S., No. 10 (June, 1958), pp. 73–84.

Three: Middle Passage

1. Ezekiel Mphahlele, *The African Image* (London: Faber & Faber, 1962), p. 66.
2. From *Odù*, No. 3 (1957), p. 35. (This magazine is published in Ibadan, Western Nigeria.)
3. From D. Cook (ed.), *Origin East Africa, A Makerere Anthology* (London: Heinemann African Writers Series No. 15, 1965), pp. 78–80, a revised copy of the version in P. Rutherfoord (ed.), *African Voices* (New York: Grosset & Dunlap, 1958), pp. 90–91. See D. Stanley (ed.), *The Autobiography of H. M. Stanley* (Cambridge, Mass.: Houghton Mifflin, 1909), pp. 295–315.
4. Stanley, p. 295.
5. Stanley, pp. 309–311.
6. From *Transition*, III, No. 13 (March, 1964), p. 32.
7. From *Black Orpheus*, No. 14 (February, 1964), p. 20.
8. From *Black Orpheus*, No. 11 (October, 1962), p. 64.
9. From *Présence Africaine*, XXIV, No. 52 (1964), p. 171.
10. From *Okyeame*, I (Accra: Ghana Society of Writers, 1961).
11. From *Black Orpheus*, No. 6 (November, 1959), p. 33.
12. From Christopher Okigbo, *Heavensgate* (Ibadan: Mbari Publications, 1962), pp. 30–32. See S. O. Anozie, "Okigbo's *Heavensgate:* A Study of Art as Ritual," *Ibadan*, No. 15 (March, 1963), pp. 11–13.
13. Anozie, p. 13.
14. From H. Swanzy (ed.), *Voices of Ghana* (Accra: Ghana Broadcasting Corp., 1958).
15. Consult M. Manoukian, *Akan and Ga-adangme Peoples* (London: International African Institute, 1950).
16. See Manoukian, p. 52, on the *bara* rites.
17. From *Blackwood's Magazine* (Edinburgh, 1953). Revised and enlarged in *Two African Tales* (Cambridge: Cambridge University Press, 1965), pp. 35–76.
18. See M. McCulloch, *The Peoples of the Sierra Leone Protectorate* (London: International African Institute, 1950).
19. In McCulloch, p. 42.
20. From L. Hughes (ed.), *An African Treasury* (New York: Crown Publishers, 1960), pp. 134–143.
21. See E. D. Jones, "The Potentialities of Krio as a Literary Language," *Sierra Leone Studies*, N.S., No. 9 (1957), pp. 40–48.
22. From Cook, pp. 45–50.

Four: Reactions

1. L.-V. Thomas, "Senghor and Négritude," *Présence Africaine,* XXVI, No. 54 (1965), pp. 102–133. See also L. S. Senghor, "How We Became What We Are," *Afrique Action* (Tunis: January 31, 1961), and *Liberté I: Négritude et humanisme* (Paris: Editions de Seuil, 1964); A. J. Shelton, "The Black Mystique: Reactionary Extremes in Négritude," *African Affairs,* LXIII, No. 251 (1964), pp. 115–128; and the following in *Présence Africaine,* XI, No. 39 (1961): W. A. Jeanpierre, "Négritude, Its Development and Significance," pp. 32–49, and L. Lagneau, "The Négritude of L. S. Senghor," pp. 124–139. The authoritative work on this subject is Thomas Meloné, *De la négritude* (Paris: Editions Présence Africaine, 1962).

2. "The African Poet as Bard of His People," *Présence Africaine,* XXVI, No. 54 (1965), pp. 141–145.

3. Georges Balandier, *Sociologie actuelle de l'Afrique noire, dynamique sociale en Afrique centrale* (Paris: Presses Universitaires de France, 1963), p. 16.

4. Colin Legum, "Somali Liberation Songs," *Journal of Modern African Studies,* I, No. 4 (1963), p. 504. Compare B. W. Andrzejewski, "Poetry in Somali Society," *New Society,* I, No. 25 (March 21, 1963), pp. 22–24.

5. "Literature and Nationalism in Angola, "*Présence Africaine,* XIII, No. 41 (1962), pp. 120–122. See also G. M. Moser, "African Literature in the Portuguese Language," *Journal of General Education,* XIII, No. 4 (1962), pp. 270–304; A. Margarido, "Incidences socio-économiques sur la poésie noire d'expression portugaise," *Diogène,* XXXVII (1962), pp. 53–80; and E. Mondlane, "The Movement for Freedom in Moçambique," *Présence Africaine,* XXV, No. 53 (1965), pp. 8–37.

6. Meloné, pp. 17, 128.

7. "The Novelist as Teacher," in J. Press (ed.), *Commonwealth Literature, Unity and Diversity in a Common Culture* (London: Heinemann, 1965), pp. 201–205.

8. From *Afrique,* No. 46 (May, 1965), p. 60.

9. From *Epitomé* (Société Nationale d'Edition et de Diffusion, 1962). This copy from C. Wake (ed.), *An Anthology of African and Malagasy Poetry in French* (London: Oxford University Press, 1965), pp. 149–150.

10. Aímé Césaire, *Cahier d'un retour au pays natal* (Paris: Editions

268 The African Assertion

Présence Africaine, 1960), pp. 70–71.

11. *African Forum*, I, No. 4 (1966), p. 69.

12. From *Afrique debout* (Paris: Editions Seghers, 1950). This copy from *Poésie Vivante* (special number: Poésie de la Côte d'Ivoire), No. 14 (September, 1965), p. 12.

13. From *Présence Africaine*, XVIII, No. 47 (1963), p. 147. See also *Rediscovery* (Ibadan: Mbari, 1964).

14. From *Voltaique, Nouvelles* (Paris: Editions Présence Africaine, 1962), pp. 175–177, following and supplementing a short story titled "La Noire de . . ."

15. From *Présence Africaine*, XXIII, No. 51 (1964), pp. 90–91.

16. From *Présence Africaine*, XIII, No. 41 (1962), pp. 74–75.

17. From *Chants d'ombre* (Paris: Editions du Seuil, 1945). This copy from Wake. pp. 45–46.

18. From *Ethiopia Observer*, IX, No. 1 (1965), p. 54.

19. From H. Swanzy (ed.), *Voices of Ghana* (Accra: Ghana Broadcasting Corp., 1958).

20. See A. Kup, "Beads and Trade in Lower Guinea in the Sixteenth and Seventeenth Centuries," *Journal of African History*, 1962, p. 345, and M. D. W. Jeffreys, "Aggrey Beads," *African Studies*, XX (1961), No. 2.

21. From *Ibadan Magazine*, No. 8 (March, 1960), p. 11.

22. From L. S. Senghor (ed.), *Anthologie de la nouvelle poésie nègre et malgache* (Paris: Presses Universitaires de France, 1948). This copy from Wake, p. 140.

23. From B. W. Andrzejewski and I. M. Lewis (eds.), *Somali Poetry* (Oxford: Clarendon Press, 1964), pp. 134–137. The quotation is from page 134.

24. See I. M. Lewis, *Peoples of the Horn of Africa, Somali, Afar, and Saho* (London: International African Institute, 1955).

25. From Andrzejewski and Lewis, pp. 56–57.

26. Cited by J. Contini, "Somali Republic: A Nation of Poets in Search of an Alphabet," *Africa Report*, VIII, No. 11 (December, 1963), pp. 15–18.

27. From Andrzejewski and Lewis, pp. 70–74.

28. See also R. L. Huss, "The 'Mad Mullah' and Northern Somalia," *Journal of African History*, V, No. 3 (1964), pp. 415–433.

29. From Legum, p. 517.

30. From *The New African* (Capetown), I, No. 6 (June, 1962), and No. 7 (July, 1962). See J. M. Kariuki, *Mau Mau Detainee* (London: Oxford University Press, 1963), Chaps. I–III; and J. Kenyatta, *Facing*

Mount Kenya (London: Secker & Warburg, 1938), pp. 20–52: "The Gikuyu System of Land Tenure."

31. See R. Mugo Gatheru, *Child of Two Worlds, A Kikuyu's Story* (New York: F. Praeger, 1964), pp. 9–26, on the squatter system.

32. See Gatheru, p. 3.

33. See Gatheru, p. 170: "Mau Mau: The Nature of the Kikuyu Oath."

34. See F. D. Corfield, *Historical Survey of the Origins and Growth of Mau Mau* (London: H.M.S.O., 1960), 10–23. See also Kenyatta, pp. 42 ff.

35. From P. Rutherfoord (ed.), *African Voices* (New York: Grosset & Dunlap, 1958), pp. 58–63.

INDEX OF AUTHORS

Achebe, Chinua, 44
Adiko, Assoi, 82
Aig-Imoukhuede, Frank, 204
Awoonor-Williams, George, 182
Brew, Kwesi, 118
Casely-Hayford, Adelaide, 153
Chacha, Tom, 163
Clark, J. P., 84
Dadié, Bernard, 40, 74, 180
Diop, David, 76, 206
Dipoko, Mbelle Sonne, 113
Dove-Danquah, Mabel, 106
Gabiou, Scek Ahmad, 209
Gureh, Ali Abdullah, 211
Hasan, Mahammad 'Abdille, 209
Kéré, Abdoul Kader, 60
Medhen, Tsegaye Gabre, 90, 198
Neto, Agostinho, 192

Ngugi, James T., 213
Nicol, Abioseh, 55, 131
Nuur, Faarah, 207
Okara, Gabriel, 119
Okigbo, Christopher, 120
Ologoudou, Émile, 116
Ousmane, Sembène, 184
Parkes, Francis E. K., 200
Peters, Lenrie, 113
Rabéarivelo, Jean-Joseph, 62
Ranaivo, Flavien, 96
Rive, Richard, 223
Rubadiri, David, 107
Senghor, Léopold Sédar, 68, 196
Sutherland, Efua, 123
Tam'si, Tchicaya U, 178
Tshakatumba, 88, 174
Yambo, Ouologuem, 188

INDEX OF TITLES

Africa (To My Mother), 76
African Heaven, 200
Anticipation, 100
Aspiration, 192
Bad Days, 94
Bench, The, 223
Black Loincloth, The, 40
Blaze, The, 116
Continent That Lies Within Us, The, 55
Dancer, The, 82
Death of Richard Corfield, The, 209
Defiance Against Force, 206
Devil at Yolahun Bridge, The 131
Flute Players, 62
Girl Bathing, 87
Home-Coming Son, 198
Martyr, The, 213
Men of All Continents, 74
Homecoming, 115
Limits of Submission, The, 207
Lustra, Part IV of Heavensgate, 120
Message to Mputu Antoinette, Girl of the Bush, Friend of My Childhood, 89
Mista Courifer, 153
Native Land, 60

New Life at Kyerefaso, 123
Night of Sinê, 68
Night Rain, 84
1901, 188
Nostalgia, 184
On the Partitioning of Somalia by the Europeans, 208
One Wife for One Man, 204
Oriki (Praise Names) for Lagunji of Ede, 36
Ours, 90
Parachute, 113
Plea for Mercy, A, 118
Prayer to the Masks, 196
Prayer Without Echo, 174
Prophecy, 209
Road to Mara, 163
Sacrificial Egg, The, 44
Song of a Young Woman, 96
To a Black Dancer, 78
To Arms! 211
To Pre-Colonial Africa, 113
Totem, The, 72
To the Poets, 180
Translation No. 3: Sacrifice and Rebirth, 66
Utendi Wa Liyongo Fumo: The Epic of Liyongo, the Spear-Lord, 22
Years Behind, The, 182